ACT ON
THE FACTS

Information to steer by

Compiled by
Peter Brierley

All royalties from this book will go
towards the cost of further research for the church

MARC Europe
London
1992

British Library Cataloguing in Publication Data

Act on the Facts: Information to steer by
  I. Brierley, Peter
  200

ISBN 0 947697 99 3

Published by MARC Europe
Vision Building, 4 Footscray Road
Eltham, London SE9 2TZ
081-294 1989

Photoset and printed in the United Kingdom
by Stanley L Hunt (Printers) Ltd
Midland Road, Rushden, Northants NN10 9UA

To Cherry, who has patiently borne
all the traumas of being married to a statistician

and to Susan Leverton and Philippa King,
the editors for the first five years of
LandMARC and *Lausanne Link*.

ACKNOWLEDGEMENTS

Many have helped prepare this book. I am grateful to Carolyn Armitage for so graciously allowing MARC Europe to publish it when she thought she might do so, to Dee Franklin for hours of dedicated typing at a skill level almost unique, to Val Hiscock and Lindsey Mansfield (the present editor of LandMARC) for checking and updating numerous pieces of information, David Longley for helping to guide LandMARC since its inception, as well as Tony Collins for encouragement, the typesetter for careful typesetting, the illustrator and many others. Thanks are due also to Joy Horton and Ruth Murdoch who have spent hours soliciting advertisements for LandMARC without which it could not have been published.

SOURCES

LM 86/4	LandMARC Autumn 1986
LM 87/1	LandMARC New Year 1987
LM 87/2	LandMARC Easter 1987
LM 87/3	LandMARC High Summer 1987
LM 87/4	LandMARC Autumn 1987
LM 88/1	LandMARC New Year 1988
LM 88/2	LandMARC Easter 1988
LM 88/3	LandMARC High Summer 1988
LM 88/4	LandMARC Autumn 1988
LM 89/1	LandMARC New Year 1989
LM 89/2	LandMARC Easter 1989
LM 89/3	LandMARC High Summer 1989
LM 89/4	LandMARC Autumn 1989
LM 90/1	LandMARC New Year 1990
LM 90/2	LandMARC Easter 1990
LM 90/3	LandMARC High Summer 1990
LM 90/4	LandMARC Autumn 1990
LM 91/1	LandMARC New Year 1991
LM 91/2	LandMARC Easter 1991
LM 91/3	LandMARC High Summer 1991
LL	*Lausanne Link,* November 1989 to September 1991
ECC	English Church Census 1989, the results of which are published in *'Christian' England* and *Prospects for the Nineties,* both MARC Europe, 1991
NOP	National Opinion Polls, *Political, Social and Economic Review*
OPCS	Office of Population Censuses and Surveys, *Population Trends*
UKCH	*UK Christian Handbook,* MARC Europe, various editions

INTRODUCTION

The first issue of LandMARC appeared in the autumn of 1986, and its purpose was simple — to provide Christian leaders with pieces of information, gathered from a wide variety of sources, to help them in their work. Now, six years later, our aim is no different. Facts are pointers to help set our course in the turbulent waters of today. Hence the subtitle of LandMARC — 'Information To Steer By'.

Since it was launched, LandMARC has proved to be extremely popular.

> 'LandMARC is one of the best things I receive through the post. It's so full of practical and useful ideas and topical information.' (Methodist Church minister)
> 'The last two issues of LandMARC have been informative and very useful. Congratulations on "filling the gaps so well".' (Director of Ordinands)
> 'I appreciate the Bulletin. I often quote snippets in our church notices bulletin, and so keep the facts before our people.' (Baptist Church minister)
> 'It is simply crammed with fascinating information and up-to-date statistics on the world front. When I receive it, I read and digest the whole.' (Rector of large London church)
> 'Our readers in the library appreciate your journal very much.' (Basel Mission Library, Switzerland)
> 'I have found this a valuable source of information and guidance.' (Chairman)
> 'It is always good to get as much facts and figures as we can to help us reach more people.' (Aberdeen lady)

We are naturally delighted so many have found it useful. To make its contents even more widely available, this book has been compiled.

Act on the Facts contains all the main numerical items in the first five years of LandMARC. In addition, items have been added of more localised interest, stemming in part from the findings of the English Church Census, which was published towards the end of this five-year period in March 1991. We cannot include every item we would wish in LandMARC for lack of space; some of those items thus excluded are included here. In November 1989 we launched *Lausanne Link,* a paper of similar purpose to LandMARC, but covering items outside Europe, and often at greater length. Only seven issues were produced, for financial reasons, but all the articles in them are included in this volume also.

Although this volume bears my name as compiler, I should point out that I do not write LandMARC. Of the initial 20 issues of LandMARC, the first eight were edited by Susan Leverton, and the remainder up to the High Summer 1991 edition by Philippa King, whose place as editor has now been taken by Lindsey Mansfield. Philippa also edited all seven issues of *Lausanne Link*. To these we owe a great debt — of hard work, imaginative thinking, an ability to sense which pieces of information are likely to be relevant to church leaders, and to consider what the implications from those facts might be.

Some of the statistics included in the earlier LandMARCs have been updated, but it is not always possible to do this. A survey undertaken in 1986, for example, cannot have later figures inserted unless that study has been repeated. Where specific sources are known, these are given, but otherwise reference is simply made to the relevant issue of LandMARC. In retrospect we should have noted more details in some instances.

At the end of the day, however, facts are for using, though preferably not as Mark Twain suggested, 'Get your facts first, and then you can distort them as much as you please.' Rather we would echo the comments of the American professor and author, Oliver Wendell Holmes Sr, who said, 'All fact-collectors, who have no aim beyond their facts, are one-storey men. Two-storey men compare, reason, generalise, using the labours of the fact-collectors as well as their own. Three-storey men idealise, imagine, predict; their best illumination comes from above, through the skylight.' Whilst Christians may not agree their best illumination comes through the skylight, they will agree it comes from above! May such illumination help you use these extracts to the best advantage in your ministry; a full index, averaging 16 words per page, is given to help you get most out of the information to steer by.

Peter Brierley
September 1992

A

Abortions

There were 174,000 legal abortions in England and Wales in 1990. Since the Act permitting abortion was passed in 1967 there have been over 2.7 million terminations to the end of 1990. This means that if all the children had lived, there could now be 13.7 million children instead of only 11 million. Or, to put it another way, for every four children in Sunday School there could now be five.

Abortion is most common among women aged 25-34, but as the figures show, the number of terminations given to girls under 16 is alarming.

Women aged	Abortions	Percentage of total
		%
Under 16	3,400	2
16-19	35,500	21
20-24	55,300	32
25-29	38,800	22
30-34	22,400	13
35-44	18,100	10
45 or over	400	0

Five abortions in every eight (62%) were carried out on unmarried mothers.

These figures come from the Office of Population Censuses and Surveys and show that 650 abortions take place every weekday, the equivalent of three every four working minutes. What are the reasons for having an abortion in the first place? The following list, based on the 1990 figures, points to the main causes.

Risk of injury to the physical or mental health of the mother (90%).

Risk of injury to the physical or mental health of existing children (9%).

Risk of the child being born seriously handicapped (1%).

Included in the risk to the mother are emergency procedures carried out to save the mother's life — a rate of one in every 20,000.

In a survey carried out in the USA, 76% of women who had an abortion chose to do so because having a baby 'would change their life', perhaps by interfering with their career or education. Just 1% of abortions were due to rape or incest.

How old is the foetus when the abortion is performed? The following 1990 figures show that the median age is between nine and 12 weeks, though a substantial number are performed when the child is less than nine weeks old. However, a few abortions are performed when the foetus was more than 25 weeks old.

Weeks	Percentage of abortions
Under 9	36
9-12	52
13-14	5
15-16	3
17-18	2
19-20	1.16
21-22	0.60
23-24	0.23
25 or over	0.01

With an increasing number of women having abortions, for whatever reason, it is likely that some of those in our churches, or perhaps their daughters, will have had an abortion. The physical effects may wear off with time, the emotional will take longer to heal. How do we help women who perhaps are feeling guilt and loss? Should we as Christians be helping to prevent unnecessary abortions taking place by providing rooms in our homes for pregnant girls and women who have nowhere else to go?

Source: CARE Trust News June-August 1987; UKCH 1992/93 and updated, LM86/4, 87/3 and 90/1; OPCS Monitor July 1991.

Abstinence

One British adult in six says 'no' to a drink, according to a report published by Ansvar Insurance Co in 1987. There were nearly 1.5 million more non-drinkers in 1987 than six years previously, a 24% increase and evidence of a significant social trend.

The shift away from alcohol accelerated between 1983 and 1986, the effect of the trend towards health and fitness and the enforcement of drink-driving laws. Growth in non-drinking in these years centred in the South, rising from 13% to 16% in the region. There was a slight increase in the North of England, and Scotland continued to have the highest proportion of abstainers.

Women, manual workers and higher age-groups are most likely not to drink, with 65% of non-drinkers being female and 64% over 50. However, the non-drinking increased to some degree across all ages, regions and social classes, and among both sexes especially in London and the South East where 12% of men never drink alcohol. Even middle-class men show marginally higher levels of abstinence, with businessmen reporting the need to cut out lunchtime drinking in order to concentrate on the afternoon's work.

If public opinion towards drinking alcohol is changing, its acceptability and the tolerance of its ill-effects is likely to diminish — as has happened very quickly with cigarettes. This will doubtless affect the attitudes and drinking habits of Christians also.

Trends in non-drinking, by region

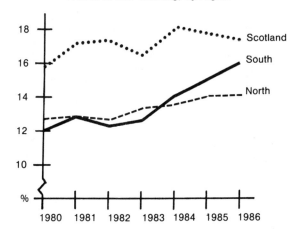

See also: Alcohol.
Source: Britain's New Abstinence, Ansvar Insurance Company 1987, quoted in LM 89/2.

Adoption

A million couples a year seek an adoptive child in the USA, almost exactly half the annual number of abortions, according to the country's *Citizen* magazine. However, the number of adoptions declined from 90,000 in 1970 to 25,000 in 1988, satisfying a mere one in 40.

Two factors have contributed to keeping the numbers low. Firstly, adoption is not seen or presented as a viable option for women with unwanted pregnancies, and secondly, most couples want to adopt blonde, blue-eyed, healthy babies.

In 1989 7,044 children were adopted in the United Kingdom, of whom three out of five were illegitimate. On the positive side more handicapped children were adopted and the number of parents wishing to adopt a child was as high as ever.

Two-fifths of all adoptions (2,990) were of children under five and 30% were between five and nine years old, so 28% are adopted when they are 10 or older.

For Christians the whole image of adoption has particular significance as God the Father has adopted us as His sons and daughters. It is a practical expression of that truth when a Christian family adopts a child.

Source: World Christian News, March 1990, quoted in LM 90/4, and OPCS Monitor August 1987 quoted in LM 88/1.

Age of churchgoers

There were 194,000 fewer children in church in 1989 than in 1979, largely due to a 4% decrease in the child population, but as a proportion of the under 15 population the percentage — 14% — was the same.

91% of older teenagers and 94% of people in their twenties do not go to church. These proportions both increased between 1979 and 1989. The following table gives the percentage of the population who do go to church.

Churchgoers as percentage of age-groups

| | 1979 | | | 1989 | | |
	Male	Female	Total	Male	Female	Total
	%	%	%	%	%	%
Under 15	13	15	14	13	15	14
15-19	11	14	13	8	10	9
20-29	8	10	9	5	8	6
30-44	8	11	10	7	10	9
45-64	9	10	10	8	12	10
65 plus	13	14	14	12	14	13
All ages	10	12	11	9	12	10

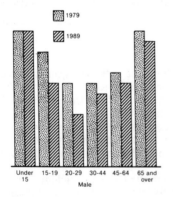
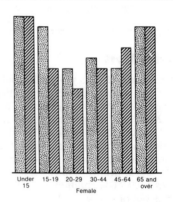

Source: ECC: LM 91/2 Easter 1991.

Alcohol

The UK as a nation spends as much on alcohol as on clothes, and one and a half times as much as on food. A total of £47 million each day is spent on alcoholic drink. About 1.5 million people are said to be drinking at harmful levels, with separated and divorced men drinking the most.

However, the average proportion of income spent on alcohol is getting smaller, while average spending on soft drinks is increasing rapidly — up by

82% overall between 1980 and 1988. And 21% of women and 12% of men were non-drinkers in 1988, a significant increase from 1971 figures of 16% and 8%.

Compared with the other countries of the European Community, alcohol consumption in Britain is low: the French drink almost twice as much. If price has a lot to do with this, the single market is likely to speed up the current trend towards drinking more wine in Britain.

But if crises such as family break-up are what makes people drink seriously rather than socially, price will make no difference. How the cause rather than the symptoms is to be addressed is the important question.

See also: Abstinence, Drinking.
Source: The Drink Pocket Book, NTC Publications Ltd and Social Trends 20, quoted in LM 90/2.

Astrology

A quarter of British adults dismiss astrology as 'complete nonsense', according to a 1990 survey. Only 11% say they believe in interpreting people and the future according to the star sign under which they were born.

Two-fifths of those surveyed thought it was a 'bit of fun, and something rings true', and one in five said, 'there might be something in it, although I don't altogether believe it'.

However, over half said they had looked at a horoscope in the past seven days, and 68% of the women had done so. Only one in six said they never looked at horoscopes, and two-thirds of these were far from those who regard it as 'complete nonsense'.

Attitudes to astrology
(Percentage of all responses)

	Men	Women	All
	%	%	%
'I believe in astrology'	7	14	11
'There's something in it, but I don't altogether believe in it'	15	25	20
'It's a bit of fun and sometimes rings true'	34	44	39
'It's complete nonsense'	37	14	25
'Don't know'	7	3	5

The French appear to take astrology rather more seriously, with 40,000 professional astrologers registered for income tax purposes, compared with 26,000 Roman Catholic priests. It is reported that the interest is among the well educated professional and business classes, with a number of major companies using astrology, tarot cards and pendulum-swinging in recruiting new employees.

How should Christians react to the horoscopes habit? If we don't think it's 'just a bit of fun', how do we communicate that?

Source: PAS survey reported in Daily Telegraph, December 1990, and Herald Tribune, October 1990, reported in World Christian News, quoted LM 91/3.

Australia

Churchgoing
If you could take a look at the churches in Australia on a Sunday morning, what would you see? First of all, there would be considerably more women than men in all the churches, and a distinct lack of under-thirties in all except the Pentecostal congregations.

Most people going to church on a Sunday are there because they want to experience 'communion with God' — and this is the same whatever their denomination. Many go to enjoy fellowship with other Christians, although this is less important for Pentecostals and Catholics, perhaps because their congregations tend to be larger. For Baptists and members of the Uniting Church, teaching is a high priority; Catholics expect to have their Christian values reinforced by Sunday worship, and Pentecostals want the opportunity to use their gifts.

Given their different expectations, people generally get what they want from their Sunday services. Opportunity for 'communion with God' is found by 71%, although this drops to 55% for members of Uniting Church congregations and is relatively low for the Baptists.

However, a significant number of people fear that church is largely irrelevant to life. A quarter of the members of the Catholic and Uniting Churches are concerned about this, and nearly 40% in each of these denominations don't consider they are getting much help in understanding the Christian faith. The Pentecostals are by far the most satisfied with their Sunday services, followed by the Baptists, and it is in these churches that you will find the highest proportions of committed weekly attenders.

Source: The Combined Churches Survey for Faith and Mission, Christian Research Association, 1987, quoted in LL February 1990.

Denomination changing
Up to 30% of churchgoers in some Australian denominations had moved recently from a church of a different denomination, the Joint Churches' Census discovered.

A report based on the Census data, called *Religious Musical Chairs,* looks at what makes people 'switch' churches. 'Switchers' are defined as people who had been going to their present church for less than five years, having previously attended a church of a different denomination.

Although, not surprisingly, people who had moved house in the previous five years were far more likely to have changed denomination than the average churchgoer, this was far from being the only reason. Half those who had switched denomination had done so while living in the same area.

Switching between Denominations – A Summary

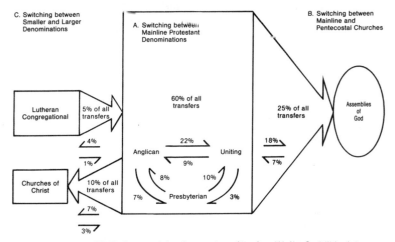

C. Switching between Smaller and Larger Denominations

A. Switching between Mainline Protestant Denominations

B. Switching between Mainline and Pentecostal Churches

Lutheran Congregational

5% of all transfers

60% of all transfers

25% of all transfers

Assemblies of God

4%

1%

22%

18%

Anglican

Uniting

9%

7%

Churches of Christ

10% of all transfers

8%

10%

7%

7%

Presbyterian

3%

3%

NB: The figures quoted are the percentages of transfers within New South Wales that occur along the paths in question.

A large proportion of switchers were in the 20 to 29 age group, generally more mobile and less rooted in a particular tradition. But in the Lutheran, Uniting, Anglican and Presbyterian Churches a similar proportion of 30 to 45 year olds had recently moved to these churches. In these denominations up to 60% of switchers are part of families with dependent children. This suggests that having a young family tends to change churchgoers' priorities about facilities offered, and sometimes a consequent switch of denomination.

The over 60's were much less likely to have changed churches recently, but nonetheless up to 20% of switchers in some denominations were over 60, perhaps explained by movement due to retirement. They were unlikely to have gone to Assemblies of God churches, which are characterised by large numbers of young people.

Major trends

The report tracks the major patterns of movement between denominations, and identifies a number of major trends. There is a high level of switching between the mainline Protestant denominations, the most common being from Anglican to Uniting Churches. Possible reasons for favouring the Uniting Church are that Church's more open stance to divorced people, or its greater openness, in general, to aspects of the charismatic movement.

The Uniting Church has the largest number of switchers but the smaller Assemblies of God make the greatest relative gains from transfer. There is a significant move to Pentecostalism, mainly from evangelical Anglican and Baptist churches, but also to an extent from Roman Catholic churches.

A third transfer path is between smaller denominations, such as Lutheran and Congregational Churches, and the larger ones. This is perhaps explained by their lack of churches in some areas, forcing attenders of these denominations who move house to look elsewhere.

This report presents a wealth of fascinating information for the different denominations to study, and raises many questions for them to answer. Perhaps the first study of its kind, it looks at a topic of increasing relevance in a society where even the Church is a victim of 'consumer culture'.

Source: Religious Musical Chairs, Report No 5 from 1986 Joint Churches Census, Peter Kaldor, Research Division, Uniting Church Board of Mission, quoted in LL September 1990.

Faith patterns

In any church of any denomination, people will not all have the same kind of faith. Labels such as 'fundamental' or 'charismatic', based on attitudes to perhaps only one issue are not much more useful in describing the differences than denominational affiliation.

The final report for the Combined Churches' Survey attempts to describe and understand from a sociological viewpoint the patterns of faith found in Australia's churchgoers. Four categories are used, based on the aspects of their faith, Church, and Christian life they consider most important.

Faith patterns by denomination

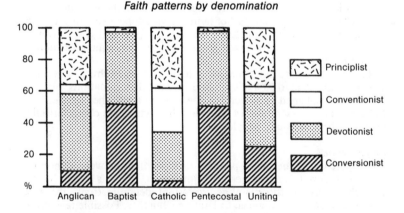

Conversionists: People with a strong sense of being 'saved' from the world, the most important aspect of their faith is their relationship with God. The Church is important, as the community of the redeemed, and its function is to spread the Gospel.

Devotionists: Similar in that the centre of their faith is a warm, personal relationship with God, they see the Church's role as providing opportunities to worship and place greater importance on attending worship services or mass.

Conventionalists: This group shared the emphasis on attending church services, but saw being a Christian primarily a matter of keeping the Ten Commandments. The Church's role is to promote Christian behaviour and values.

Principlists: Also seeing the Christian faith as primarily a way of life, this last group are guided by vague 'Christian principles', such as being caring and considerate to others. Believing the world is basically good, they feel the Church's role is to educate people.

The report shows how these patterns of faith are found to various extents in different denominations, and how they are related to the age, sex, environment, education and occupation of churchgoers. It looks at the different expectations people have from Church, and why some are always on the 'fringe' of church life.

Faith patterns by age

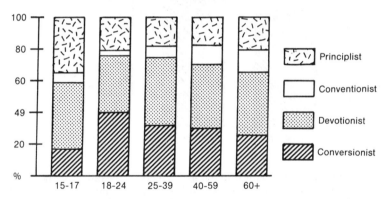

Without judging the worth of each kind of faith, this research describes their characteristics and discusses how the changes in society are reflected in the changing patterns of faith. It could be of immense use to ministers seeking to understand the people in their congregations — or outside them — and minister to them where they are.

Source: Patterns of Faith in Australian Churches, by Philip J Hughes and 'Tricia Blombery, Christian Research Association 1990, quoted in LL September 1990.

Clergy's religious values

Essential aspects of the christian life

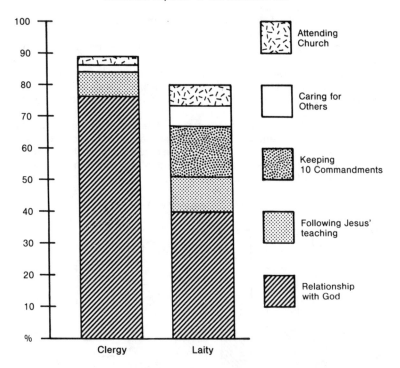

One of the most interesting findings in this report is the difference between the clergy and their congregations. Ministers of all denominations agreed that the most important aspect of the Christian faith was a relationship with God through Jesus Christ. Overall 77% agreed on this, with only 'following Jesus' teaching, which was considered more important by 14% of Uniting clergy, rated highly by a significant number.

Among their congregations, however, although 'having a relationship with God' was the most frequently chosen response, it accounted for only 43% of the responses. Significant numbers saw Christianity as being primarily a matter of 'keeping the Ten Commandments' — over 15% of the total sample and 27% of the Catholics. It was not affirmed by a single minister as either their first or second choice.

Source: The Australian Clergy, Philip Hughes, Christian Research Association, Australia 1989, quoted in LL February 1990.

Clergy's role

The role of clergy in Australia, as seen by churchgoers of different denominations, was one of the topics investigated by the Australian Combined Churches Survey. Ministers of different denominations saw their role as below.

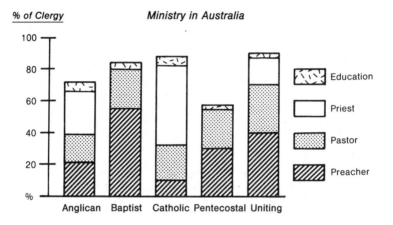

In Australia as in the UK, very few — only 4% — identified organisation and administration as one of the two primary roles. It was the area of work least enjoyed, and one in which many Uniting Church ministers felt least competent.

Source: The Australian Clergy, Philip Hughes, Christian Research Association, Australia 1990, quoted in LL February 1990.

Avon

Avon

Area (sq km)	Population 1989			Percentage change 1979-89	Percentage under 15	Non-churchgoers 1989
	Men	Women	Total			
1,346	462,100	490,700	952,900	+3.1%	18%	849,000

Churchgoers 1989			Percentage of population	Percentage change 1979-89	Percentage under 15	Number of churches	Percentage built	
Men	Women	Total					before 1500	since 1950
42,600	61,300	103,900	10.9%	−6.5%	24%	790	20%	16%

District	Area (sq km)	Population 1989	Percentage change 1979-89 %
Bristol	110	372,600	−8.8
Woodspring	375	189,700	+21.0
Northavon	462	133,700	+15.7
Kingswood	48	89,600	+7.4
Bath	29	84,700	+0.6
Wansdyke	323	82,500	+8.6

Source: Regional Trends 26, HMSO 1991 and English Church Census.

B

Bedfordshire

Area (sq km)	Population 1989			Percentage change 1979-89	Percentage under 15	Non-churchgoers 1989
	Men	Women	Total			
1,235	264,600	266,600	531,200	+5.2%	20%	474,000

Churchgoers 1989			Percentage of population	Percentage change 1979-89	Percentage under 15	Number of churches	Percentage built	
Men	Women	Total					before 1500	since 1950
24,000	33,200	57,200	10.8%	−13.0%	30%	432	32%	20%

District	Area (sq km)	Population 1989	Percentage change 1979-89
			%
Luton	43	169,900	+3.9
N Bedfordshire	476	137,300	+3.6
Mid Bedfordshire	504	114,400	+12.1
S Bedfordshire	212	109,500	+2.3

Source: Regional Trends 26, HMSO 1991 and English Church Census.

Berkshire

Area (sq km)	Population 1989			Percentage change 1979-89	Percentage under 15	Non-churchgoers 1989
	Men	Women	Total			
1,259	374,200	374,300	748,500	+10.0%	20%	686,200

Churchgoers 1989			Percentage of population	Percentage change 1979-89	Percentage under 15	Number of churches	Percentage built	
Men	Women	Total					before 1500	since 1950
27,400	34,900	62,300	8.3%	−11.9%	26%	471	22%	20%

District	Area (sq km)	Population 1989	Percentage change 1979-89
			%
Wokingham	179	148,500	+34.8
Newbury	705	139,100	+15.9
Reading	40	130,000	−6.7
Windsor and Maidenhead	198	125,200	−7.7
Bracknell	109	104,600	+30.3
Slough	28	101,000	+4.4

Source: Regional Trends 26, HMSO 1991 and English Church Census.

Bibles

Into how many languages has at least one book of the Bible been translated? By the end of 1991 the figure had reached 1,978. In 1400 it had been translated into only 12 languages, a figure which increased to 38 by 1500, to 51 by 1600, to 66 by 1700, to 73 by 1800, but with a huge jump to 621 by the year 1900. This figure doubled to 1,197 by the year 1950 and had more than tripled to 1,946 by the year 1990. The graph below shows this increase, which reflected the worldwide work of the United Bible Societies, Wycliffe Bible Translators and other such organisations.

Number of languages into which at least one book of the Bible has been translated 1800-1990

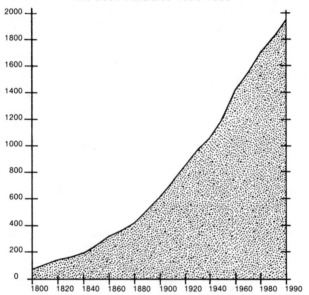

Source: UK Christian Handbook 1992/93 Edition and Bible Society.

Births

A new baby is a cause for rejoicing. How many new babies might your congregation expect to see next year? The percentage of live births in the population in your part of the country in 1989 is given below and as these rates do not change quickly, they are a reasonable guide for the 1990s. In calculating the number you might expect take your entire congregation (adults and children, single or married — the percentages are based on the total population for simplicity):

Live births by region 1989
(Percentage of population)

Region	%
North	1.27
Yorkshire & Humberside	1.35
North-West	1.40
East Midlands	1.34
West Midlands	1.41
East Anglia	1.27
South-East (North)	1.38
Greater London	1.52
South-East (South)	1.27
South-West	1.25
England	1.36
Wales	1.32
Scotland	1.25
N Ireland	1.65
United Kingdom	1.36

So if you live in the East Midlands, and your total Sunday congregation, including Sunday School children, but excluding any who attend twice, is say 80 people, you might expect next year $1.34 \div 100 \times 80 = 1$ (to the nearest whole number) new baby to attend your church. Prepare now!

In 1990 births outside marriage accounted for 28% of all live births in England and Wales, compared with 27% in 1989, 12% in 1980, and 9% in 1977. This meant 200,000 children were born outside wedlock in 1990, 8% more than 1989, whereas the number of children born inside marriage, 506,000, increased only 1%.

Unmarried teenage girls gave birth to 45,000 children in 1990. The abortion rate, 36% of all conceptions, remains unchanged — more pregnant women are deciding to give birth to more babies. The total number of births, 706,000 in 1990, rose from 688,000 in 1989, though the average number of births per woman at 1.84 is still below the 2.1 level needed for the long-term natural replacement of the population. The average age at which women have children was 27.5 in 1990, the highest since 1961.

Many women remain childless, however, and this trend is likely to continue. About one in six 35-year-old women had not had children in 1990.

Source: Regional Trends 26, HMSO 1991, Population Trends Autumn 1991.

Book buying

Should we buy Christian books at all? Smith Wigglesworth never read any book but the Bible after his conversion and his ministry was a catalogue of God working in a man's life through the marvellous and the miraculous.

With so many Christian books on the market are we in danger of being bogged down in a morass of Christian literature? With titles offering everything from the key to a successful marriage to growing a biblical garden, it is possible to get confused. The temptation to stop buying altogether must be overwhelming.

But is it? On average something like 500,000 customers visit the UK's Christian bookshops in the course of a year. The same number buy a religious book at a secular outlet, often as the result of a religious programme on the TV or radio.

Radio Four's *Priestland's Progress,* which explained religious belief and experience, attracted a huge audience, 24,000 letters and enough purchases to put the book of the series into the national bestsellers' list for several months.

What does this sort of success mean financially? Almost £30 million is spent on religious books from Christian bookshops every year and a further £15 million on religious books from secular outlets.

These rather impressive figures must be seen against the background of total UK publishing turnover, which, in 1991 was £2.4 billion. In the same year Christian booksales represented only 4% of the total, against 33% in the USA. Even taking into account that this latter figure includes the other products which come under the US publishing umbrella, and that the US Christian population is at least four times the size of the UK, it shows how much ground there is to be gained here.

So people do buy religious books. But who? And who reads them? In 1984 the Children's Book Action Group reported that while 30% of the UK population buy books 50% read them.

Religious books remain one of the largest categories of books published in the UK. Paul Johnson summed up the implications of this in the January 1986 issue of the *Spectator.* 'The size of this [religious books] figure indicates the existence of a huge sub-culture of belief in this country.' The number is undoubtedly increasing. [In 1985 one book in every 28 published was religious. In 1990 it was one in 27.]

Tastes in religious reading have also changed. Books on social issues and renewal movements, devotional and daily living, and comparative religion have all increased in the last half century.

Books on theology, local church activities, sermons, and the history or geography of the Church have barely held their own and the books on denominations and sects have declined considerably.

There remains a need for more Christian fiction and some call for books to be cheaper. Interestingly there is now a greater openness to books coming from the USA and these sales are increasing.

There is one Christian bookshop for every 10,000 churchgoers in the UK. But it is estimated that as many as four in ten churchgoers never enter a Christian bookshop, even once a year.

Hence there is an enormous wealth of books available for Christians who never read them. What an opportunity for the promotion of Christian teaching, devotion and living.

Source: LM 88/2.

Book power

America's National College of Education asked business and education leaders which book had affected their lives the most.

A quarter cited the Bible; Charles Dickens' *A Tale of Two Cities* was named by 4% and the *Book of Mormon* by 2%.

The heads of 1,000 major American companies and presidents of 1,200 US universities participated in the survey.

Source: The Church Around the World, September 1990, quoted in LM 91/3.

Book reading

Churchgoers in Britain read fewer than five Christian books a year on average, and four secular books — perhaps a surprise considering the wealth of material published in English.

Based on surveys of bookshop customers and church congregations throughout the country a 1987 report identified Christians' book-buying and reading habits, comparing them with those of the public in general.

A breakdown of the congregations by age, sex and occupation reveals groups that the Christian book trade fails to cater for. Teenagers, for example, read more secular books than any other age group, but find little to interest them in Christian publications.

Surveys show that someone walking into a Christian bookshop is likely to come out with twice the number of books they intended to buy! The report looks at the kind of books people buy — finding that mission, social issues and leadership are unpopular topics, with biographies and books on 'Christian lifestyle' at the top of the list.

Source: Bear, Book and Candle by Phil Back, MARC Europe Monograph No 23 and LL November 1989.

Broadcasting

When you hear people talking about 'the world today', the image conjured up in your mind won't just be affected by your own experience and education, but also by information gained through the media, particularly television.

Since 82% of Britons watch an average of four hours television a day, with teenagers in some areas spending as much time in front of the TV as at school, it is inevitable that the basically materialistic values that are so continually and persuasively presented will have some effect. Are we so used to this, and the sex, violence and bad language on our screens that as Christians we just accept it?

People make a fuss about political bias on television; they can see that the views held by the programmers can be conveyed not just in political documentaries but even in the news. The same applies to religious attitudes; so less and less 'real' Christianity is featured in the required hours of religious broadcasting and many feel the church is trivialised or ignored.

The 1990 Broadcasting Bill ended the BBC/IBA duopoly on broadcasting in Britain. The government's principles of freedom and competition have been applied to broadcasting, leading to more choice as licences are granted to new radio stations and satellite and cable TV channels.

62% of British adults see at least one religious TV programme a month; 65% are at least nominally Christians; 69% believe religion helps maintain the standards of society; and 73% are dissatisfied with the way moral standards have been changing.

Source: IBA and LM 90/1.

Brussels

A profile of Europe's capital city is provided by the co-ordinating committee of Project Bruxelles 91, a major evangelistic initiative on the part of many churches and missions. The statistics make clear the extent of the challenge.

Truly a cosmopolitan city, over a quarter of Brussel's population come from countries other than Belgium. International business people and Europeans working for the EC rub shoulders with 75,000 Moroccans and 20,000 Turks.

Moroccans living in Belgium by age-group

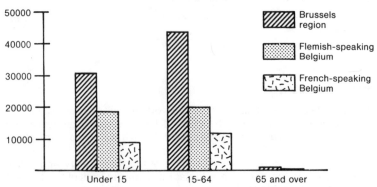

The report gives statistics for each area or 'commune' of Brussels, by nationality and age-group, and shows how this is changing. It highlights the main points of the statistics, and includes a list of evangelical churches in each commune — one for every 18,000 people in the population, on average, but none for 39,000 people in the commune of Jette, for example.

Source: Project Bruxelles 91, Statistiques sur les Communes et nationalites dans la region Bruxelloise. Research prepared for the Co-ordinating Committee by Bob Allen 1990, quoted in LL June 1991.

Buckinghamshire

Area (sq km)	Men	Population 1989 Women	Total	Percentage change 1979-89	Percentage under 15	Non-churchgoers 1989
1,883	314,100	320,000	634,300	+13.8%	20%	573,400

Men	Churchgoers 1989 Women	Total	Percentage of population	Percentage change 1979-89	Percentage under 15	Number of churches	Percentage built before 1500	since 1950
26,800	34,100	60,900	9.6%	−8.6%	24%	568	31%	16%

District	Area (sq km)	Population 1989	Percentage change 1979-89 %
Milton Keynes	310	182,400	+58.8
Wycombe	324	157,400	+0.3
Aylesbury Vale	904	147,300	+12.7
Chiltern	201	87,200	−7.7
S Buckinghamshire	144	60,300	−3.7

Source: Regional Trends 26, HMSO 1991 and English Church Census.

C

Cambridgeshire

Area (sq km)	Population 1989			Percentage change 1979-89	Percentage under 15	Non-churchgoers 1989
	Men	Women	Total			
3,409	322,800	332,200	655,000	+13.7%	20%	583,600

Churchgoers 1989			Percentage of population	Percentage change 1979-89	Percentage under 15	Number of churches	Percentage built	
Men	Women	Total					before 1500	since 1950
30,000	41,400	71,400	10.9%	+9.5%	24%	720	41%	14%

District	Area (sq km)	Population 1989	Percentage change 1979-89 %
Peterborough	334	153,800	+18.6
Huntingdon	924	149,100	+24.8
S Cambridgeshire	903	118,900	+10.7
Cambridge	41	99,000	−2.5
Fenland	552	74,000	+11.9
E Cambridgeshire	655	60,200	+14.7

Source: Regional Trends 26, HMSO 1991 and English Church Census.

Churchgoing is on the increase in Cambridgeshire. Against a nationwide pattern of decline, the number of adults attending church on a Sunday increased by 19% between 1979 and 1989, faster than the 13% population growth. That is nearly one extra person for every five in the pews ten years previously.

The English Church Census shows that 10% of Cambridgeshire adults went to church on Sunday 15 October 1989, the day of the Census count: 54,200 people. Of these 36% went to Anglican churches, 27% to Roman Catholic churches and 37% to the various Free Churches.

Anglican attendances increased by 3% from 1979 to 1989, attendance at Roman Catholic churches increased by a quarter and at the Free Churches by 39% overall.

Of the Free Churches, Methodists lost a fifth of their attenders during the 1980s, and groups such as the Salvation Army saw mixed growth and decline.

But the Baptists grew by 17% and the United Reformed Church had added by 1989 one to every two present in 1979 — one of only seven counties where they experienced growth.

Independent churches grew by 150% and are now the third largest group after Anglicans and Roman Catholics. The small group of Pentecostals trebled in size.

Young people and the church
Although more adults go to church, fewer children went to church or Sunday School in 1985 than five years previously. The number of children under 15 attending church fell 4% between 1985 and 1989, while the child population increased 4%.

However, children still make up 24% of churchgoers. The number of teenagers fell between 1979 and 1989, but the proportion of people in their 20s and 30s going to church increased, although still less than the proportion of those age groups in the population.

Where is churchgoing popular?
Over half Cambridgeshire churches are in rural areas, and these are growing overall; adult attenders increased by 14% in commuter dormitory areas and 4% in the more remote rural areas between 1985 and 1989.

Attendance also rose by 3% in the city centre where 16% of churches are situated, 2% in the suburbs, 9% in towns, 3% in inner-city areas and 50% in other built up areas. Only on council estates was there no change.

Churches growing
Overall 35% of churches attracted more people between 1985 and 1989, while 58% stayed about the same size and just 7% declined. Those with the most growing congregations were Independents, where 40% grew, and Anglicans, where 36% grew.

Which kinds of church are growing?
Different churches have different emphases, even within the same denomination, and it is often claimed that these contribute to their popularity. The Census shows that in Cambridgeshire churches of many different emphases attracted more people.

The most growth between 1985 and 1989 was in the charismatic churches, which grew by 22% compared with 7% nationally. Churches of 'catholic' churchmanship, usually but not necessarily the same as Roman Catholics, grew by 16%.

Also growing were 'liberal' churches (8%) and 'broad evangelicals' (7%), but 'anglo-catholic' churches declined 10%, 'broad' churches by 4% and 'low church' churches by 2%. Attendance at 'mainstream evangelical' churches was unchanged.

Why the growth?
The main reason for the growth in churchgoing in Cambridgeshire is the increasing population. People moving to the villages around Cambridge, often people in their 20s and 30s, appear to be going to church there, thus the growth the Census shows in these age groups and in the commuter dormitory environment. The same migration factor has generated growth

in other counties with good commuter links to London, especially Suffolk, Buckinghamshire, Hampshire and Kent.

Source: Regional Trends 26, HMSO 1991 and English Church Census and LM 91/2.

Canada

A recent study by Canadian evangelicals found that family and personal contacts are two of the most influential elements in bringing Canadians to Christ.

Before the 1980s the major influence was upbringing — whether or not a person was raised in a Christian home. In the 1980s personal witness — one to one relationships — became the main factor encouraging Canadians to commit their lives to Christ.

Of those who became a Christian as a result of personal witness, the majority said a friend was the main influence in their conversion; a third said it was the influence of their pastor; and only 1% were influenced by someone with whom they did not have a personal relationship.

This pattern supports the conclusion that we live in an increasingly relational world. Today people are more likely to embrace the Gospel because of the witness of friends than as a result of a large rally or an altar call at a church service.

Main influence in making personal commitment

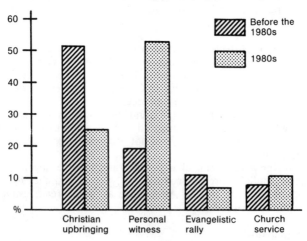

Source: Who Responds to the Gospel and Why? by Arnell Motz in Reclaiming a Nation, A Motz ed. Church Leadership Library 1990 and LL September 1991.

Capital punishment

In the wake of appalling crimes committed in the last decade or so, Parliament debated a bill in April 1987 to reintroduce the death penalty for certain crimes. The Bill was defeated but did this failure reflect the attitude of the British Public?

In September 1987 National Opinion Polls investigated public opinion on the death penalty. Over 1,000 people over 18 were surveyed.

Of those asked, 73% were for it, 23% against and 4% didn't know.

Excluding the don't knows, this means that three-quarters with a definite opinion wanted capital punishment brought back.

The percentage of those in favour increased the older they became:

Age group	In favour	Against
	%	%
18-34	68	32
35-54	76	24
55 and over	85	15
Overall	76	24

Source: LM 88/2.

Cars

UK car ownership 1981-88
(Percentage of households)

	With no car		With 1 car		With 2 or more cars	
	1981	1988	1981	1988	1981	1988
	%	%	%	%	%	%
North	48	46	41	41	11	13
Yorkshire & Humberside	46	43	42	41	12	16
North-West	45	39	42	42	13	19
East Midlands	37	31	47	46	15	22
West Midlands	38	35	46	43	16	22
East Anglia	31	27	51	48	18	25
South-East excluding Greater London	30	24	48	45	22	31
Greater London	45	40	42	43	14	17
South-West	31	25	51	49	18	26
England	39	34	45	44	16	22
Wales	38	32	47	50	15	18
Scotland	49	47	40	39	11	14
N Ireland	40	40	46	44	14	16
United Kingdom	39	35	45	44	16	21

The increase in the number of cars reflects the material prosperity of the country to some extent. In 1981 there were 28 cars for every hundred people in the land; by 1988 this had risen to 36. Personal transport being much more readily available means people don't have to go to their nearest church, but can have one which suits them. Likewise alternative pursuits become accessible and churches have to compete for attention. In 1990 the Bishop of Southwark said, 'We have moved from where Christianity is culture to where Christianity is choice.' How can we help people choose *our* church? How can we make it sufficiently attractive?

In 1989 there were 20.2 million cars on our roads, which were involved in 48,700 accidents. In 1981 there were 15.7 million vehicles about which were involved in 56,200 accidents. Had accidents continued at this rate we would have had 72,300 in 1989, 50% more than we did.

Source: Regional Trends 26, HMSO 1991.

Charity giving

Charitable giving is on the increase in the UK. During 1985, £5.90 was given away by every household each month. By 1987 this had risen to £6.20, and by 1991 to £6.90.

From this figure it can be estimated that in 1991 an average of £83 per British household was given away, compared with £75 in 1987.

The Royal National Institute for the Blind defines charitable giving as placatory or emphatic. Placatory giving is as simple as putting a few coins in a street collector's box during a Saturday shopping expedition.

Emphatic giving involves a more definite response, writing a cheque for a major charity, often through television and media appeals.

The Charities Aid Foundation discovered in a 1987 survey that 86% of British households give money to charities, representing 73% of people in the UK. Those who feel that religion is important to them gave £95 per annum in 1987 against the then national average of £75.

However, 1987 research for a major Christian charity showed that, even among committed Christians, there is a belief that a charity narrows its appeal (particularly among the young) if portrayed as religious. Yet, in spite of its clear religious base, the Salvation Army is extremely successful in its door-to-door collections.

Perhaps churches should attempt to overcome the public's bias towards religious giving and follow the Salvation Army's example. After all, in 1991 alone, £1.8 billion was given away to worthwhile causes.

Households contributions to charity

	1985/6	1987	1991
Total households	20.7 million	20.8 million	22.0 million
Total households giving	£1.46 billion	£1.55 billion	£1.82 billion
Average annual donation per household	£71	£75	£83
Average monthly donation	£5.90	£6.20	£6.90

Source: Charities Aid Foundation: A National Survey of Patterns and Attitudes to Charitable Giving by British Households.

Cheshire

Area (sq km)	Population 1989			Percentage change 1979-89	Percentage under 15	Non-churchgoers 1989
	Men	Women	Total			
2,238	470,100	488,500	958,600	+3.5%	20%	843,200

Churchgoers 1989			Percentage of population	Percentage change 1979-89	Percentage under 15	Number of churches	Percentage built	
Men	Women	Total					before 1500	since 1950
46,200	69,200	115,400	12.0%	−4.0%	19%	703	14%	13%

District	Area (sq km)	Population 1989	Percentage change 1979-89
			%
Warrington	176	187,900	+13.4
Macclesfield	523	151,700	+1.5
Halton	74	124,800	+1.6
Chester	448	114,200	−2.1
Vale Royal	384	114,000	+2.1
Crewe and Nantwich	431	100,100	+1.9
Congleton	211	86,500	+10.2
Ellesmere Port and Neston	82	79,300	−4.7

Source: Regional Trends 26, HMSO 1991 and English Church Census.

Children

Independence

The *Independent on Sunday* commissioned a broad research study on children in July 1991. Part of the survey asked parents at what age they would leave (or had left) their son or daughter either alone in the house for at least 30 minutes or to go on a journey outside their own road or street without supervision. The answers varied by parental status. For simplicity, those replying 'don't know' have been excluded.

It is interesting that parents were generally willing for their child(ren) to go on an unsupervised journey younger than they would let them be at home alone (or with no-one older present). Perhaps this was because the first is more likely to take place during the day and the latter at night. How do these figures reflect on your church youth work?

Age child first left alone in home for over 30 minutes

	Single parent	One natural parent	Two natural parents	All parents
	%	%	%	%
Under 6	3	1	1	1
6-7	1	0	1	1
8-9	4	4	4	4
10-11	20	18	27	26
12-13	44	45	43	44
14-15	20	26	19	19
16 plus	8	6	5	5
Average age	12	13	12	12

Age child first allowed on unsupervised journey out of own street

	Single parent	One natural parent	Two natural parents	All parents
	%	%	%	%
Under 6	3	1	2	1
6-7	4	3	7	6
8-9	17	20	19	19
10-11	33	33	43	41
12-13	29	37	23	25
14-15	13	6	5	6
16 plus	1	0	1	1
Average age	11	11	10	11

Source: NOP Political, Social and Economic Review No 86, July 1991.

Needs

In January 1988 an Evangelical Alliance conference called 'Reaching the Nation's Children' revealed the following horrifying facts about British society.

- 40% of 12-15 year-olds watch horror films at home
- 1 in 10 teenagers aged 15 was likely to be abused by age of 20
- 50,000 children are mentally or physically abused each year
- 52 children were battered to death in 1982
- 1 in 6 children needs some kind of special education
- 50% of girls lose their virginity by the age of 16 and only 8% of women are virgins on their wedding day
- 1 in 4 children are smoking by the age of 15
- The use of addictive drugs tripled between 1979 and 1988

Source: LM 88/2.

Churchgoing

Between 1992 and the end of the century the proportion of people in the United Kingdom aged 15 to 29 will drop, according to the Office of Population Censuses and Surveys. This is particularly important as many people get their church leadership experience during these years.

The report also forecasts a steep rise in the number of people over 45.

This has serious implications for the church. Increasingly, leaders working with young people will tend to be over 45 years old, clearly undesirable! For strategic planning in evangelism, these figures suggest that for the next few years, a local church should give priority to those now between 10 and 24 years old.

An increase in the number of children is predicted. The average number born per woman is likely to rise from 1.81 in 1989 to 1.99 in 2001. This is good news for churches, since many children do go to church; in 1989 some 25% of all churchgoers in England were under 15.

Source: LM 87/3.

Possessions

The *Independent on Sunday* commissioned research on children in July 1991. One of the findings related to their personal possessions, as shown in the following table.

	11-13	*14-16*	*11-16*
	%	%	%
Personal stereo	81	83	82
Bicycle	89	72	80
Camera	62	54	58
Television	50	59	55
Hi-fi system/music centre	46	61	53
Video recorder	5	8	6
Telephone	2	3	3
None	1	1	1

Source: NOP Political, Social and Economic Review No 86, July 1991.

Prayer

To what extent are prayer and worship natural responses of the child? How much are they shaped by social and environmental constraints? In a recent study Professors Leslie J Francis and Laurence Brown set out to explore the relative importance of social factors, such as church attendance and parental example, on prayer among 11-year-old children.

The majority of the children questioned agreed that praying is a good thing and that God listens to prayers. The proportion claiming personal benefit from prayer was considerably smaller — 35% of the boys and 46% of the girls agreed that prayer helps them a lot.

Several factors were found to influence a child's attitude towards prayer and practice of prayer:

- The expected sex difference emerged, with girls showing a higher frequency of private prayer than boys. Only 6% of the girls and 12% of the boys agreed with the statement 'I think people who pray are stupid.'
- Church attendance (of both children and parents) had a significant effect on a child's attitude towards prayer.
- Roman Catholic children were more likely to pray than children from other denominational backgrounds with similar levels of church attendance.

These data lend support to the theory that worship and prayer are clearly within the private domain of church and home, while schools are concerned with the public domain of education. The findings suggest that parents who would like their children to pray regularly and to have a positive attitude towards prayer, should begin by taking them to church. This will be more effective than sending them to church or campaigning for the local state maintained primary school to hold regular acts of Christian worship.

Source: The Predisposition to Pray by L J Francis and L B Brown, Journal of Empirical Theology, Volume 3 No 2 1990, and LL September 1991.

Church attendance

On an average Sunday 10% of England's adult population choose to go to church, and one in seven of those go to church twice on a Sunday.

The English Church Census of 1989 revealed that 3.7 million adults in England are churchgoers. And 1.2 million children under 15 attend church services or Sunday School, around 14% of the child population. This means over eight times as many people go to church each week as to Football League matches.

Described by Most Rev George Carey, Archbishop of Canterbury, as the 'most thorough and comprehensive survey ever done of English church-going', the English Church Census was carried out on 15 October 1989, a standard Sunday, avoiding festivals or holiday seasons which swell or reduce attendance.

Each minister in England was asked to complete a questionnaire, and the excellent 70% response rate gives the Census figures a high degree of reliability. By comparing the results with the last Census from 1979, a picture emerges of the trends in English church life.

Over the ten years from 1979 to 1989 there was an overall decline of 8% in the number of adults attending church. But it was in the first part of the decade that the churches fared worst, with attendance falling 7% between 1979 and 1985, and just 1% from 1985 to 1989.

Which denominations are growing?

Although the overall picture is of falling attendance, a quarter of churches grew significantly from 1985 to 1989, some from each denomination, while only 8% declined significantly. The majority, 67%, remained static. Pentecostals (35%), Baptist (33%) and Independents (33%) had the highest proportion of growing churches.

The decline was felt by most of the established denominations. *'Christian' England,* the report of the Census, highlights falling attendance from 1979 to 1989 at Roman Catholic (−14%), Anglican (−9%), Methodist (−11%) and United Reformed Churches (−18%). For all these churches except the Methodists, the rate of decline slowed in the late 1980s.

At the same time Independent churches grew by 42%, including a 144% increase in attendance at the so-called 'House Churches' and 46% at the Fellowship of Independent Evangelical Churches.

Afro-Caribbean churches grew by 4% over the 10 years, and the small number of Orthodox churches by 34%, while others' decline between 1979 and 1989 turned into growth after 1985. Pentecostals' 4% decline changed into 11% growth, Baptists moved from 3% decline to 2% growth and groups such as the Salvation Army, declining 17% before 1985, then grew by 2%.

Who goes to church?
Congregations are ageing, with higher proportions of older people, reflecting the country's demographic changes, and far fewer younger people.

Children under 15 attending church dropped by 14% from 1979 to 1989, compared with a 10% child population decline. Anglicans and Methodists between them lost 125,000 children.

There were also a serious drop in the number of older teenagers attending church. And only 6% of people in their 20s were churchgoers, although there was an increase in people of this age-group in the population as a whole.

Where is churchgoing popular?
Towns were the only environment where adult churchgoing increased overall between 1985 and 1989, by 2%. It declined fastest in city-centres (by 5%) and inner-city areas (by 3%). Yet churchgoing grew by 1% in inner London, and by 9% in the southeast London boroughs.

How does churchmanship affect growth?
Attendance at 'charismatic evangelical' churches rose 7% between 1985 and 1989, and at 'mainstream evangelical' churches by 2%. The greatest decline of 5% was in churches that described themselves as 'broad' or 'anglo-catholic'. 'Broad evangelicals' also declined by 3%, and there was 3% growth in the small number of churches of 'other' churchmanship.

'Growth and truth are not necessarily synonymous,' commented the Bishop of Southwark at the Census press conference. In *'Christian' England* it is suggested that 'it is unlikely that there is no connection between the charismatic emphasis of the Pentecostals and many Afro-Caribbean and Independent churches and their rapid growth'. However, it points out that the Census shows four-fifths of growing churches are not charismatic, and not all charismatic congregations are growing. With the Anglican church, for example, they declined by 6%.

What are we to make of statistics? Peter Brierley urges 'at the start of this Decade of Evangelism, I hope churches will not be daunted by the size of their task revealed by the Census, but will use the facts as a basis for planning and action'.

See also: Church attendance.
Source: ECC; LM 91/2.

Church Growth Associations in Europe

Austria
Institute for Evangelism and Church Development, Klaus Eickhoff, Wernhardstr 5, A-4522 Sierning. ☎010 43-7259-2872.

Finland
Church Growth, Esa Eravolo, Soukankuja 9.D.25, SF-02360 Espoo. ☎010 358-90-8023732.

Germany
Jörg Knoblauch, Postfach 1309, D-7928 Giengen. ☎010 49-7322-13650.

Norway
Anskar Institute for Mission and Church Growth, Hallvard Hagelia, Nedre Brattbakken 14, N-4635 Kristiansand. ☎010 47-42-43900.
Norwegian Church Growth Forum, Leif Nilsen, Salhusvegen, Stopp 4, N-5090 Nyborg. ☎010 47-2-601143.

Sweden
Institute of Church Growth, Professor Jörgen Ljung, c/o Linköping University, Department of Management and Economics, S-581 83 Linköping. ☎010 46-13-28 15 03.

Switzerland
National Swiss Church Growth Association, Walter Wieland, Pfarrhaus, CH-3452 Grunematt. ☎010 41-34-71 1426.

United Kingdom
British Church Growth Association, Mrs Monica Hill, 3A Newnham Street, Bedford MK40 2JR. ☎0234-327905.

Source: LL November 1989.

Church planting

New church planting rate 6,000 ÷ 93. That's the formula for determining the average number of SIM-related (Sudan Interior Mission) churches planted annually since the Mission began in 1893 (the ones we know about, that is: 6,000 is a round number). If you're not in the mood for arithmetic, don't fret: the answer is 64.5. It wasn't always so. The first 45 years produced only 150 churches. After that things really began to move.

	Churches started	Yearly average	Total
1893-38	150	3	150
1939-53	450	30	600
1954-63	600	60	1,200
1964-73	1,200	120	2,400
1974-83	2,400	240	4,800
1984-86	1,200	400	6,000

If growth continues at this rate, how many churches will there be by the end of the century?

Source: SIM Now, March 1987: LM 87/2.

Churchgoing

10% of English adults went to church on Sunday 15 October 1989, or 3.7 million people.

14% of children in England, 1.2 million in all went that day to church or Sunday School.

Roughly one-third of churchgoers are Anglicans, one-third Roman Catholics and one-third go to Free Churches.

There are 1.4 million adult catholics, not necessarily the same as Roman Catholics, one million evangelicals and 0.8 million who go to broad or liberal churches.

These proportions are smaller than in Wales and Scotland as the following table shows, where the total reflects the Scottish and Welsh figures extrapolated up to 1989:

Churchgoing in Britain

	Year of Census	Adults	Percentage of adult population	Children	Percentage of child population
England	1989	3,706,900	10%	1,221,500	14%
Scotland	1984	660,400	17%	203,300	19%
Wales	1982	280,000	13%	120,300	21%
Total	1989	4,914,300	11%	1,550,200	15%

Where do people go to church?
Church is most popular in Cumbria and Merseyside, where 14% of the population attend regularly.

Fewest people attend church in South Yorkshire, where only 6% of adults are churchgoers.

Overall, church attendance increased from 1985 to 1989 only in towns. It declined fastest in city centres and inner-city areas.

The regions with the highest percentage of growing churches were Greater London (29%) and the West Midlands (28%).

Methodist churches are most numerous in the North and South-West of England, Anglican churches in rural areas, Baptists North and West of London, and Independent churches along the South Coast.

Source: ECC, quoted in LM 91/2.

Cities

The world's ten largest cities with their population in 1990 and 1965 were (in millions):

		1965	*1990*	*Growth*
Tokyo-Yokohama	Asia	18.1	29.0	+60
Mexico City	Latin America	7.0	20.1	+187
São Paulo	Latin America	6.0	17.9	+198
New York	North America	16.5	17.5	+6
Osaka-Kobe-Kyoto	Asia	11.4	16.9	+48
Seoul	Asia	4.4	16.4	+273
Bombay	Asia	5.4	13.3	+146
Moscow	Europe	8.9	13.3	+49
Calcutta	Asia	8.1	13.0	+60
Buenos Aires – La Plata	Latin America	8.1	12.6	+56

See also: Megacities.
Source: Cities, Population Crisis Committee, New York 1990.

Cleveland

Area (sq km)	Population 1989			Percentage change 1979-89	Percentage under 15	Non-churchgoers 1989
	Men	Women	Total			
583	271,200	281,600	552,800	−3.9%	28%	495,100

Churchgoers 1989			Percentage of population	Percentage change 1979-89	Percentage under 15	Number of churches	Percentage built	
Men	Women	Total					before 1500	since 1950
23,100	34,600	57,700	10.4%	−17.3%	28%	291	9%	29%

District	Area (sq km)	Population 1989	Percentage change 1979-89 %
Stockton-on-Tees	195	176,900	+2.1
Langbaurgh	240	144,500	−5.2
Middlesbrough	54	142,700	−6.5
Hartlepool	94	88,700	−8.1

Source: Regional Trends 26, HMSO 1991 and English Church Census.

Cohabitation

More than half the brides and grooms in the UK now live together before tying the knot, according to the Office of Population Censuses and Surveys. They found in a recent survey that 58% of men and 53% of women shared a home with their partner before marrying them.

This is an option which has increased very rapidly in popularity — the number of single women under 50 living with a man trebled between 1979 and 1987. One in four single people under 20 now live with a partner, a total of 900,000 couples with 400,000 dependent children. So many children? Yes, because so many of these couples have a stable relationship but decide not to marry even when they have children. The proportion of all illegitimate children registered under two names was 73% in 1990.

It is likely that many cohabitating couples do not attend church, or at least they start living together before they do so. A Bradford church leader said that often one of the main ministries to new families joining the church was to regularise their marital relationship.

Source: Population Trends 58, Winter 1989, LM 90/2, 87/2.

Computers

We all know computers are here to stay. How many are there, though? The table below gives the figures.

Personal computer ownership in UK

	Companies	Home/education	Total
1981	110,000	170,000	280,000
1983	410,000	2,140,000	2,550,000
1985	900,000	4,600,000	5,500,000
1988	2,000,000	4,200,000	6,200,000
1990	3,100,000	2,900,000	6,000,000
1992	3,800,000	2,400,000	6,200,000
1994	4,400,000	2,500,000	6,900,000
1996	5,200,000	2,800,000	8,000,000

Source: IDC, 1992-96 projections quoted in Management October 1991.

Confidence in public institutions

How great is the British public's confidence in the national institutions? The results of a Gallup survey in 1986 show a wide variance, as follows:

	Much confidence %		Much confidence %
Armed forces	86	Parliament	48
Police	83	Civil service	44
Legal system	59	Education system	43
The church	56	The press	28
Major companies	53	Trade unions	25

Source: LM 88/1.

Consumer durables

What do people actually spend their money on? 13% of all expenditure is on household goods and services (see Expenditure). In recent years video machines, microwaves, and CD players have all made their appearance and all made rapid inroads. These are to the mid- and late 1980s what deep freezers and colour television were to the 1970s.

Household ownership of various commodities
(percentage of households)

	1979	1985	1990
	%	%	%
Television — colour	66	86	93
— black and white only	31	12	5
— Total	97	98	98
Telephone	67	81	88
Washing machine	74	81	87
Deep freezer (including fridge freezers)	40	66	81
Central heating	55	69	80
Video	n/a	31	74
Microwave oven	n/a	23*	50
Tumble dryer	19	33	46
CD Player	n/a	n/a	21
Home computer	n/a	13	20
Dishwasher	3	6	12

* Estimate
See also: Cars.
Sources: OPCS General Household Survey Monitor 1991.

Cornwall

Area (sq km)	Population 1989			Percentage change 1979-89	Percentage under 15	Non-churchgoers 1989
	Men	Women	Total			
3,564	221,800	242,300	464,100	+11.1%	18%	411,700

Churchgoers 1989			Percentage of population	Percentage change 1979-89	Percentage under 15	Number of churches	Percentage built	
Men	Women	Total					before 1500	since 1950
20,400	32,000	52,400	11.3%	−13.1%	26%	873	26%	7%

District	Area (sq km)	Population 1989	Percentage change 1979-89
			%
Kerrier	473	87,200	+5.4
Restormel	452	86,300	+12.5
Carrick	461	79,800	+6.8
Caradon	664	74,900	+13.4
N Cornwall	1,195	72,300	+14.7
Penwith	303	61,700	+17.8
Isles of Scilly	16	1,900	−5.2

Source: Regional Trends 26, HMSO 1991 and English Church Census.

Credit cards

There were 29 million cards in the UK in 1989, a doubling of the number since 1979, against 8 million in France and 2 million in Germany. The figures below plot both their growth and the colossal turnover they generate:

Credit card ownership and use

Access	Card holders	Annual turnover	Barclaycard	Card holders	Annual turnover
	Million	*£ million*		*Million*	*£ million*
			1966	1.0	4
1973	3.1	140	1973	2.4	170
1977	3.2	520	1977	3.8	590
1981	5.7	1,900	1981	6.1	1,700
1985	8.2	5,100	1985	8.0	4,400
1990	10.8	11,400	1990	8.6	10,300

See also: Debt.
Source: Management October 1991; Redemption magazine December 1989.

Crime

There is no doubt that, in many respects, we live in a more violent society than our predecessors of 90 years ago. Historical details of recorded crime show some interesting results.

Crime by category, England and Wales 1893-1989

	1893	1989
	%	%
Offences against the person	5	6
Burglary and robbery	9	21
Theft and handling stolen goods	82	52
Fraud and forgery	1	2
Criminal damage to property	1	17
Other criminal offences	2	1
Total offences (= 100%)	86,000	3,894,000

Although the proportion of crime against the person did not alter substantially, burglary and robbery increased, and with them the amount of violence involved. There is a corresponding relative decrease in non-violent theft. Perhaps not surprisingly, criminal damage to property has increased considerably.

Overall, the total number of recorded crimes increased 45 times in the period under consideration. Yet not all crimes are reported: the 1987 *British Crime Survey* indicated that only a quarter of all notifiable offences were actually recorded; the level of reporting in the 1890s is unknown.

The staggering crime levels in our society reflect the situation in Israel during the seventh and eighth centuries BC, when prophets such as Amos spoke so forcefully. During this period the moral and social breakdown in Jewish society had the inevitable dire consequences. Christians need to pray that the same may not be true of today's society.

How do we control crime? Is imprisonment an effective deterrent? If imprisonment does not function as a deterrent, is it an appropriate penalty?

The United States of America puts more people in prison as a percentage of the population than any other country except the USSR and South Africa. Yet the USA has the highest crime rate in the Western World. The FBI say that 74% of those released will be back in prison again within four years.

Source: Statistical News August 1987, and Justice, Scripture Press 1988, quoted in LM 88/1 and 89/2.

Cumbria

Area (sq km)	Population 1989			Percentage change 1979-89	Percentage under 15	Non-churchgoers 1989
	Men	Women	Total			
6,810	239,500	252,100	491,600	+2.8%	24%	419,900

Churchgoers 1989			Percentage of population	Percentage change 1979-89	Percentage under 15	Number of churches	Percentage built	
Men	Women	Total					before 1500	since 1950
28,700	43,000	71,700	14.6%	−9.5%	23%	763	22%	7%

District	Area (sq km)	Population 1989	Percentage change 1979-89
			%
Carlisle	1,030	103,100	+2.6
South Lakeland	1,551	101,200	+8.3
Allerdale	1,257	96,800	+1.5
Barrow-in-Furness	77	71,800	−2.7
Copeland	737	71,700	−2.0
Eden	2,158	47,000	+10.7

Source: Regional Trends 26, HMSO 1991 and English Church Census.

D

Dating

An off-beat indication that nominal or notional Christianity is still socially desirable in some circles comes from a computer dating agency.

Apparently, most 'lonely hearts' who join Dateline are looking for non-smokers, occasional drinkers, who live in London, have a degree, vote centre politics and believe in the Church of England.

Undesirables are those who smoke, drink, are poorly-educated, hold left-wing views and do not believe in God.

Source: Computer Weekly February 1991, and LM 91/3.

Death

By age

Cancer and heart disease claim significant proportions of the population aged 25 and above. These illnesses cause 70% of deaths within this group, more from cancer than heart disease.

Nearly 600,000 people died in England in 1990, an increase of over 1% on the 1989 figure.

The population divides into three main categories of causes depending upon age. The most common cause for those aged five to 24 is accident, for middle aged people cancer causes the most deaths, and for those over 65 years heart disease claims most victims.

Cause of death in England and Wales 1990

Age Group	Cancer %	Heart %	Other main causes	%
5-14	18	1	Accident	36
15-24	10	2	Accident	42
			Suicide	11
25-34	20	5	Accident	22
			Suicide	14
35-44	35	18	Accident	9
45-54	41	29	Stroke	5
55-64	40	33	Respiratory	7
65-74	33	34	Stroke	9
			Respiratory	10
75-84	22	32	Stroke	14
			Respiratory	12
85 and over	18	29	Stroke	16

How can Christian ministers and counsellors help those in churches face up to these facts? What message is given to those left behind after the sudden death of a relative? Or how to help people cope with a diagnosis for cancer or heart disease?

The question of suicide poses different problems, especially as the percentage in the 15-24 age range is increasing (it was 10% in 1985). How can the church contribute to making people feel wanted and needed in a disintegrating society?

See also: Heart Disease, Suicide.
Source: Office of Population Censuses and Surveys, September 1986.

By environment

How many people in an average church congregation are likely to die in the next year? It depends on many factors, but the most important is the age-structure of the congregation; where there are more older people the higher the numbers likely to pass away. Based on the figures given for life expectancy (qv) the percentage of adults likely to die every year (as measured in 1989) in a church is given below.

Annual adult death rate by environment

	%
City centre	1.18
Inner city	1.24
Suburban/Urban fringe	1.27
Commuter rural area	1.30
Other built-up area	1.36
Council estate	1.40
Town	1.43
Remoter rural area	1.64
All environments	1.30

This table reflects the younger average congregation in city centres church and the older congregations in remoter rural areas. In 1979 the all-environment figure was 1.22%, an indication of church congregations' ageing over 1980s. The 1989 population figure is 1.15%, reflecting the generally older population in church congregations.

Similar figures for the way a church is changing can also be given. The percentage of adults likely to die *per year* in a church which is:

> Growing is 1.22%
> Static   is 1.44%
> Declining is 1.52%

reflecting the lower age groups attracted to growing churches.

Source: ECC.

Debt

The average family in the United Kingdom owes a staggering £4,500 excluding mortgages, according to a 1989 survey by Familybase run by the Jubilee Centre.

According to the survey more than 500,000 debt cases reached the courts in 1986. Almost 5% of all personal lending is in arrears. Two million people are behind with their fuel bills and 300,000 home owners are three months or more behind with their mortgages, this shock report claims.

In August 1987 Research Surveys of Great Britain interviewed 1,815 adults about personal loans. One in five said that they were likely to borrow money over the next five years for purposes other than mortgages. Of those prepared to say how much they would be borrowing, 33% said less than £1,000, 37% between £1,000 and £3,000. The remaining 30% would be borrowing more than £3,000.

A majority (56%) required a loan to buy a car and 20% for home improvements. Men were more likely to borrow than women and teenagers aged 16 to 19 were twice as likely to borrow than any other age group.

There is no doubt that debt is a national crisis. A 1987 statement from Familybase highlighted the role of credit cards in the debt trap and claims that the 'scandal of high interest rates (is) pushing those in debt deeper into the red'.

Personal borrowing interest league 1987

	Pence per £ borrowed per month
Dixons	3.8
Halfords	3.7
Electricity Board (Eastern)	3.4
Habitat	3.2
Boots	3.2
Marks and Spencer	2.4
Harrods	2.3
Barclaycard	2.0
Access (Nat West)	2.0
TSB (Personal Loan)	1.7
John Lewis Partnership	1.7
Lloyds Bank (Personal Loan)	1.7

Source: LM 88/2.

Derbyshire

Area (sq km)	Population 1989			Percentage change 1979-89	Percentage under 15	Non-churchgoers 1989
	Men	Women	Total			
2,631	458,400	471,000	929,400	+2.1%	18%	843,100

Churchgoers 1989			Percentage of population	Percentage change 1979-89	Percentage under 15	Number of churches	Percentage built	
Men	Women	Total					before 1500	since 1950
35,400	50,900	86,300	9.3%	−6.2%	29%	869	18%	13%

District	Area (sq km)	Population 1989	Percentage change 1979-89 %
Derby	78	216,600	−0.5
Amber Valley	265	113,300	+4.0
Erewash	109	108,200	+6.2
Chesterfield	66	100,200	+4.6
N E Derbyshire	277	96,800	−0.9
High Peak	541	84,700	+3.5
S Derbyshire	339	72,200	+6.8
Bolsover	160	71,100	+0.1
Derbyshire Dales	795	66,400	−2.7

Source: Regional Trends 26, HMSO 1991 and English Church Census.

Devon

Area (sq km)	Population 1989			Percentage change 1979-89	Percentage under 15	Non-churchgoers 1989
	Men	Women	Total			
6,711	497,000	532,900	1,029,900	+8.4%	17%	903,600

Churchgoers 1989			Percentage of population	Percentage change 1979-89	Percentage under 15	Number of churches	Percentage built	
Men	Women	Total					before 1500	since 1950
51,800	74,500	126,300	12.3%	+1.6%	23%	1,403	31%	10%

District	Area (sq km)	Population 1989	Percentage change 1979-89
			%
Plymouth	79	255,000	+0.8
Torbay	63	120,100	+7.7
E Devon	817	118,600	+12.5
Teignbridge	675	110,500	+18.7
Exeter	44	102,300	+3.1
N Devon	1,085	85,700	+12.0
South Hams	877	77,500	+19.3
Mid Devon	916	64,100	+11.5
Torridge	985	51,800	+8.3
W Devon	1,160	44,400	+4.8

Source: Regional Trends 26, HMSO 1991 and English Church Census.

Dorset

Area (sq km)	Population 1989			Percentage change 1979-89	Percentage under 15	Non-churchgoers 1989
	Men	Women	Total			
2,654	313,400	343,400	656,800	+12.3%	17%	580,600

Churchgoers 1989			Percentage of population	Percentage change 1979-89	Percentage under 15	Number of churches	Percentage built	
Men	Women	Total					before 1500	since 1950
31,200	45,000	76,200	11.6%	−12.2%	25%	706	28%	12%

District	Area (sq km)	Population 1989	Percentage change 1979-89
			%
Bournemouth	46	154,300	+9.6
Poole	64	131,500	+11.8
W Dorset	1,083	85,600	+8.8
E Dorset	355	78,800	+17.9
Weymouth and Portland	42	64,700	+14.7
N Dorset	609	54,900	+15.2
Purbeck	405	47,100	+20.9
Christchurch	50	39,800	+5.0

Source: Regional Trends 26, HMSO 1991 and English Church Census.

Drinking in England and Wales

A 1986 survey for the Department of Health and Social Security in England and Wales asked more than 2,000 young people between 13 and 17 to complete a 'drinking diary' for one week. The United Kingdom Band of Hope also carried out extensive work on this subject. Some of the main findings highlight the gravity of the problem.

- In England and Wales 82% of boys and 77% of girls had their first alcoholic drink before the age of 13.
- Among 13 year olds, 2% of boys and 11% of girls said they drank at least weekly.
- Most 13 year olds did the majority of their drinking in the home. This decreased as they got older and began to frequent pubs, discos, parties and clubs.
- Half the boys aged 15 who drank consumed more than the equivalent of five pints of beer a week. One in six consumed about two pints a day.
- Of those aged 16, 40% drank illegally in pubs.
- Of 15-17 year olds, 52% of boys and 37% of girls said they drank weekly. For 17-18 year olds, 61% of boys and 54% of girls were drinking weekly.
- Only one in 10 of 17 year olds was teetotal.
- Boys and girls tend to favour cider and shandy initially. Boys later drink beer, girls a wider range of drinks.

Teenagers are the only age group in which drunkenness is increasing, and one in four people convicted for alcohol-related crimes will now be under the age of 21 compared with one in 30, 12 years ago.

In 1986 there were over 1,200 deaths from drunken driving; 95% caused by men. For every teenager in the United Kingdom who dies from abusing other drugs, 100 die for alcohol-related causes, mostly in driving accidents.

The report also states that these findings, shocking though they are, should be treated cautiously as it is difficult to obtain information about drinking from surveys since people frequently underestimate their drinking.

These sort of proportions show that almost certainly teenagers in the church fellowships, youth groups and other organisations will at least experiment with alcohol at some time. How best can we prepare young people for this? How do we warn them of the dangers? How do we help them cope with pressure from their friends at school and elsewhere? What sort of example do others in the Church set? Does your church have a policy towards alcohol, and do the young people know the reasons for it? How often is the subject debated at your young people's meetings?

See also: Alcohol, Students.
Source: LM 87/4.

Dull churches

Even regular churchgoers sometimes find services less than inspiring. In a survey conducted at the end of 1989, 42% owned up to falling asleep in church.

More than a third of those questioned look at their watch in church every Sunday, and a startling 10% owned up to having put their watch to their ear and shaking it, thinking it must finally have stopped.

While only 4% always wish they'd stayed in bed on a Sunday morning, 67% admitted they sometimes feel that way.

Source: 101 Things to do with a dull Church, Martin Lowe and Adrian Keith, Monarch 1989.

Durham

Area (sq km)	Population 1989			Percentage change 1979-89	Percentage under 15	Non-churchgoers 1989
	Men	Women	Total			
2,436	291,700	305,200	596,900	−3%	25%	527,100

Churchgoers 1989			Percentage of population	Percentage change 1979-89	Percentage under 15	Number of churches	Percentage built	
Men	Women	Total					before 1500	since 1950
27,800	42,000	69,800	11.7%	−9.5%	28%	513	14%	13%

District	Area (sq km)	Population 1989	Percentage change 1979-89
			%
Darlington	198	100,000	+1.8
Easington	143	95,200	−7.6
Sedgefield	220	88,300	−7.6
Durham	190	86,000	−3.5
Derwentside	271	85,200	−4.6
Wear Valley	505	64,400	+0.6
Chester-le-Street	66	53,100	+2.4
Teesdale	843	24,800	−0.1

Source: Regional Trends 26, HMSO 1991 and English Church Census.

E

East Sussex

Area (sq km)	Population 1989			Percentage change 1979-89	Percentage under 15	Non-churchgoers 1989
	Men	Women	Total			
1,795	332,700	379,100	711,800	+8.8%	16%	640,800

Churchgoers 1989			Percentage of population	Percentage change 1979-89	Percentage under 15	Number of churches	Percentage built	
Men	Women	Total					before 1500	since 1950
27,700	43,300	71,000	10.0%	−19.7%	22%	583	24%	17%

District	Area (sq km)	Population 1989	Percentage change 1979-89 %
Brighton	58	143,100	−5.3
Wealdon	837	135,800	+17.5
Lewes	292	91,300	+19.7
Hove	24	91,100	+4.6
Rother	510	85,200	+14.3
Eastbourne	44	82,800	+8.6
Hastings	30	82,700	+11.8

Source: Regional Trends 26, HMSO 1991 and English Church Census.

Education expenditure

How does the expenditure on your Sunday School compare with the local schools?

In 1965 the average expenditure per primary school pupil was £77, £148 for each secondary school pupil. These figures had risen to £969 and £1,653 respectively by 1988, increases of 1,160% and 1,020% against price increases of 720% in the same period. How much does your church spend per child in its Sunday School? Does it even have a budget for such expenditure?

Even if children are in Sunday School for only an hour a week compared with the hours spent in state schools, there is a case for spending around £10 per pupil based upon 1988 school expenditure. Should churches be spending money to provide more attractive and up-to-date books, visual aids and general equipment?

Source: Education Statistics for England and Wales, Department of Education and Science, and LM 87/2 updated.

Elderly

Projections from the Office of Population Censuses and Surveys show an increasing percentage of the population aged over 75.

The elderly in the UK population

	Total population	Population aged 75 or over	75+ as a percentage of total
			%
1989	57,236,000	3,932,000	6.9
1991	57,561,000	4,003,000	7.0
1996	58,413,000	4,179,000	7.2
2001	59,174,000	4,415,000	7.5
2006	59,681,000	4,513,000	7.6
2011	60,033,000	4,530,000	7.5
2016	60,379,000	4,902,000	8.1

Source: OPCS.

Employment

What do your church members do all day? Mostly they work! But what kinds of work do they do? That varies according to where your church is situated. How many working mothers do you have in your congregation?

UK employment 1989
(Percentage all employees)

	Male	Full-time female	Part-time female	Manu-facturing*	Construction, distribution, transport and com-munication	Other services
North	53	25	22	30	31	39
Yorkshire and Humberside	53	25	22	31	32	37
North-West	53	26	21	29	32	39
East Midlands	53	26	21	37	29	34
West Midlands	55	26	29	36	29	35
East Anglia	54	26	20	29	33	38
South-East (North)	53	26	21	25	33	42
Greater London	54	31	15	14	32	54
South-East (South)	51	26	23	22	34	44
South-West	52	25	23	25	34	41
England	53	27	20	26	32	42
Wales	53	26	21	30	30	40
Scotland	53	28	19	25	33	42
N Ireland	52	29	19	25	27	48
United Kingdom	53	27	20	26	32	42

* Includes agriculture, forestry, fishing, energy and water supply.

That varies too across the country. Knowing the type of work that is done, and the kinds of stresses and strains involved in that work enables the pastor to understand better the needs of his people and to make the sermons more relevant.

The figures in the previous table relate to 1989, but the percentages change slowly and will be much the same for the early 1990s.

Source: Regional Trends 26, HMSO 1991.

English Church Census

Every church in England was invited to take part in the second English Church Census on 15 October 1989, the most comprehensive survey of churchgoing in this country ever undertaken.

The results of the Census are of immense importance for the decision-makers and the media of our country, as well as for the churches. The results of the Census replaced the assumptions people hold about church life in England with the facts.

It provides an important tool for the Church, on both the national and local scale. At a national level the results of the Census help leaders to plan strategically for the 1990s 'Decade of Evangelism'. At the local level they allow individual churches and groups of churches to quantify the specific issues in their area, enabling them to develop their own strategies for evangelism and growth locally.

To say to a group of Christians, 'We've got to evangelise Blackburn!' doesn't motivate anyone. They don't know where to start. It gives some dimension to the task if we can say 'There are 80,000 people in Blackburn who are outside the churches. We need to reach these people.'

The information gathered
The Census focused on the number of people who attended Sunday church services, and the number of church members. Data was also collected on the age and sex of churchgoers, children's involvement, churchmanship and the nature of the community serviced by each church. From these, factors were identified which give rise to growth or decline.

Why was it necessary?
The last Census was carried out in 1979. Since then both society and the church in England have seen many changes. The *Faith in the City* report inspired many initiatives at both national and local level. Independent ethnic churches and the House Churches have continued to mushroom. Mission England and Mission to London achieved unprecedented levels of response, and Mission 89 has put Billy Graham — and Christianity — in the news, and evangelism on the agenda in thousands of churches. How have these factors affected the spiritual life of the country, and where has their impact been felt?

How was the Census conducted?

Dr Ajayi, the Census Administrator at MARC Europe, conducted two studies to refine both the methodology and the wording of the questionnaire.

Each church received an 11-question form, an explanatory letter and a reply envelope. The responses were analysed using specially designed software.

The analysis gave a detailed breakdown of church attendance in each local authority area. The results were fully published, and detailed results for each county, with a consideration of their implications, were made available to church leaders across the country at a series of local presentations in June 1991. Although the overall results were made public, information on individual churches was not divulged.

Backing of church leaders

The Census team were encouraged by the enthusiastic backing of church leaders from across the Christian scene. In particular, they appreciated the guidance and support of the Council of Reference, made up of leaders of different denominations and groups, plus respected people from other walks of life including academics, statisticians and representatives of the media.

'The Methodist Church has been keen to keep accurate statistics right from the time John Wesley kept a list of communicants on his journey to Georgia. We still see the great value of not missing anyone and of facing the facts about our growth or decline so that we may do something about it.'   *Rev Dr Donald English*

'Accurate information is rapidly becoming a new currency. Can we Christians afford to do without it?'   *Mr John Noble*

Most important findings

- 10% of English adults were in church on that day, 3.7 million people, a 1% drop since 1979 against an adult population increase of 4%. Cumbria and Merseyside had the highest percentage, 14%, and South Yorkshire the lowest, 6%.
- 14% of English children were in church that day also, 1.2 million children in all, the same percentage as in 1979, against a child population decrease of 4%. 82% of Free Church children were in Sunday School, 64% of Anglican.
- There were 513,000 fewer people in church in 1989 than in 1979. That represents a decline of 1,000 per week. 670 of that 1,000 were under 20, 370 were under 15 and 300 were 15 to 19.
- The adult decline was greatest in the Anglican (−9%), Methodist (−11%), Roman Catholic (−14%) and United Reformed Churches (−18%). The main growth was in the Afro-Caribbean (+4%), Pentecostal (+8%), Orthodox (+34%) and Independent Churches (+42%). The Independent Churches include the House Church Movement which grew by 144%, and the Fellowship of Independent Evangelical Churches which grew 46%.

- Of the 3.7 million adult churchgoers in 1989, 1.4 million were catholic in churchmanship, 1,000,000 evangelical, and 800,000 broad and liberal. Between 1985 and 1989 the catholics declined by 2%, the broad/liberal by 5% but evangelicals grew by 3%, due to the rapid growth of the charismatic evangelicals which number 400,000.
- 14% of adults who went to church in 1989 went twice each Sunday, an average of 28% Free Church, 10% Anglican and 4% Roman Catholic.
- Overall the adult church attendance grew only in the churches in separate towns, and declined most in city centre and inner-city areas. Greater London (29%) and the West Midlands (28%) had the highest percentage of growing churches.
- A quarter of all churches' adult congregations grew at least 5% between 1985 and 1989, an average of 39% rural churches and 14% non-rural. 8% of churches declined, 15% rural, 3% non-rural. 67% were static, 46% rural, 83% non-rural.
- Almost a quarter of all churches in England (53% of all Anglican) were built over 500 years ago. Five thousand still survive from 1100-1300, 500 from 450-850.
- If present trends continue churchgoing will drop a further 250,000 in the 1990s, mostly because of the deaths of elderly churchgoers. To prevent this happening the church needs quality leaders, pioneers and risk takers whose priorities and vision are crisp and clear — challenging churches to be active and attractive.

Source: LM 89/3, ECC.

Environment

There is no doubt that Europeans' awareness of 'green' issues and our willingness to act according to our concern about the environment has increased radically in a fairly short space of time.

In the UK 90% of consumers surveyed in 1989 claimed to consider pollution a serious issue, and around 78% were prepared to pay more for environment friendly goods. Only 13% said they would not contemplate paying more, mostly elderly people who showed the least awareness of the issues involved.

The under-25 age-group were by far the most concerned, and far more likely than average to object to slaughtering animals for food and testing cosmetics on animals. This attitude on the part of young people suggests that overall concern will rise in the future, and consumers' buying habits will change.

The authors of *The Green Consumer* predicted that manufacturers would make serious moves towards reducing energy consumption and pollution, and increasing recycling. The key pressure point would not, however, be consumer opinion, but the scientific data which is being steadily amassed, showing that we cannot survive if we continue increasing consumption at the current rate. For example, use of electrical energy alone escalated by 360% between 1957 and 1987.

Energy consumption per capita 1987

	KW per hour		KW per hour
USA	10,800	Spain	3,200
Finland	10,600	China	400
West Germany	6,700	Zaire	150
France	5,500	Uganda	40
USSR	5,400	Burkina Faso	17
UK	5,200	Chad	13
Italy	3,600		

However, the researchers state, 'The curbing of consumption is a task which runs counter not only to the instincts and desires of the human race, but also to the whole raison d'être of the world of commerce, which is geared to encourage rather than discourage consumption.' The heart of the green issue is that consumer society doesn't work and has to change — something Christians have been saying for a long time.

Therefore, our scruples about the hype, the New Age influence or the wrong emphases associated with green concerns shouldn't make us distance ourselves from them. The whole Gospel surely has something to say to young people seeking values and prepared for a radical change of priorities.

Source: Britannic World Data 1987, The Green Consumer 1989, Mintel Publications Ltd, and LM 90/4.

Essex

Area (sq km)	Population 1989 Men	Population 1989 Women	Population 1989 Total	Percentage change 1979-89	Percentage under 15	Non-churchgoers 1989
3,672	748,700	783,400	1,532,100	+4.1%	19%	1,406,200

Churchgoers 1989 Men	Churchgoers 1989 Women	Churchgoers 1989 Total	Percentage of population	Percentage change 1979-89	Percentage under 15	Number of churches	Percentage built before 1500	Percentage built since 1950
51,600	74,300	125,900	8.2%	−15.2%	27%	1,133	30%	17%

District	Area (sq km)	Population 1989	Percentage change 1979-89 %
Southend-on-Sea	42	166,000	+6.7
Basildon	111	157,000	+3.1
Colchester	334	151,900	+12.5
Chelmsford	342	151,300	+10.6
Tendring	335	132,200	+19.3
Thurrock	163	125,700	−1.7
Braintree	612	117,900	+5.8
Epping Forest	345	111,600	−5.7
Castle Point	44	83,900	−1.7
Rochford	169	73,900	+0.3
Harlow	26	71,300	−13.0
Brentwood	149	69,000	−5.7
Uttlesford	642	66,100	+6.8
Maldon	358	53,400	+13.5

Source: Regional Trends 26, HMSO 1991 and English Church Census.

Ethnic Churches

One person in 20 now living in the UK comes from an ethnic minority. If UK churches are to be proportionally representative, this means that 5% of congregations (or 200,000 people) should be from ethnic minorities.

Of course, many have established themselves into their own denominations, or have become absorbed into existing groups such as the Pentecostals and Seventh Day Adventists.

The so-called 'black' churches grew rapidly during the 1970s due to immigration, although the New Testament Church of God has several white ministers and members. It is therefore something of a misnomer to refer to solely 'black' churches existing in any great number anywhere in the UK.

These churches are filled with much younger people than the other denominations. Only 6% of the congregation is over 65, compared with 15% in the total population and 19% in other UK churches. These fellowships are usually to be found in the central parts of England and the London area. One church in 41 in the UK was a 'black' church in 1990; if present trends continue such churches will account for one in every 33 in the year 2000.

Source: LM 88/4 updated.

Europe

Europeans of the future will feel as much citizens of Europe as of their own countries, say observers of social trends. There is evidence of a new openness to the rest of the world along with a keen interest in the changes that the single European market will bring — although many consider the UK is behind other countries in this.

Already there are some who feel they have more in common with people in other countries who have the same interest or tastes than they do with fellow countrymen who don't. They are happy to belong to their own country and at the same time to Europe or to the world. They realise that, at least from an economic view, one country cannot develop independently from the rest.

As Christians, we should be the first to see ourselves as world citizens, part of a worldwide church. Why not let the influx of books, food, films and fashions from other countries enlarge our vision and encourage us to see the world as God sees it, not just our own locality or nation?

A proposal put to people from different European countries to compare attitudes to Europe was affirmed as follows:

'I feel close to other European people. I wish that my country and people were more open to the outside world.'

Italy	*Spain*	*France*	*UK*	*West Germany*
141	122	112	74	65
		100 = index for total Europe		

Source: Addison Consultancy Group report 1988, from an article by Dr Elizabeth H Nelson in Survey Spring 1990, LM 90/4.

European Community

How does the United Kingdom compare with the other eleven members of the EC? A number of features are given on the following page, all relating to the year 1988 unless otherwise indicated.

	Popula-tion (millions)	Persons per sq km	Percentage of population*		Gross domestic product*	Unemployment (Percentage working population)†
			under 15	65 plus		
			%	%	(EC=100)	%
Belgium	9.9	320	18	14	101	8
Denmark	5.1	120	18	15	109	8
France	55.9	100	21	13	108	9
West Germany	61.4	250	15	15	113	6
Greece	10.0	80	20	14	54	8
Irish Republic	3.5	50	29	11	65	17
Italy	57.5	190	18	13	104	11
Luxembourg	0.4	140	17	13	121	2
Netherlands	14.8	350	19	12	103	9
Portugal	10.3	110	23	12	54	5
Spain	38.8	80	22	12	75	17
United Kingdom	57.0	230	19	16	107	7
Total EC	324.6	140	19	14	100	9

* 1987   † 1989

Source: Regional Trends 26, HMSO 1991.

European family contact

Europeans keep in touch. The 1989 report in the British Social Attitudes series looked at how well adults keep in touch with members of their families they no longer live with. Focusing on children's contacts with their mother, they found marked differences between the seven countries surveyed, but some surprising similarities.

Italians, and to some extent Hungarians, tend to live close to their parents and are in touch with them very frequently, many seeing them every day. In other countries, particularly the USA and Australia, families tend to live farther apart and thus see each other less often. Obviously geography has a lot to do with this, plus factors such as the need to move

Percentage of adult children in daily contact with mother (excluding those who live with their mother)

	Phones/Visits	Sees/Visits
	%	%
Italy	29	27
Austria	21	13
Germany	18	14
USA	15	9
UK	7	9
Australia	7	4
Hungary	6	25

away to find housing or employment. But in these respects, Italy, West Germany and the UK are not so different from each other, so this cannot account entirely for the differences between them.

Source: British Social Attitudes, Special International Report 1989, edited by Roger Jowell, Sharon Witherspoon and Lindsay Brook, and LL February 1990.

European life

A Gallup survey of 22,000 adults in 17 countries in Western Europe found that Europeans generally consider themselves to be well-off and contented. Nearly three-quarters considered themselves 'very happy with life'.

This rises to 84% in Great Britain, where 75% consider themselves to be earning an adequate income — a higher proportion than Italians, Spaniards or Germans. Great Britain and Germany are the most urbanised countries, with 80% of the population living in towns and cities compared with 60% of Europeans overall. And the relative wealth of the continent is seen in the fact that 59% own their own homes (66% in the UK), and half of all homes have three bedrooms or more.

What do these comfortable people think of religion? Two-thirds think religion is a force in life, and half say they go to church at Christmas — 35% in Britain — indicating the remains of notional and nominal Christianity. But 43% of Europeans, 52% of Britons, say they have no confidence in the church.

Source: We Europeans, Reader's Digest February 1991, and LM 91/3.

Religious observance

The Christian church worldwide is growing faster than at any time in history — except in Europe. Across our continent various historical, cultural and economic factors have fostered contrasting beliefs and different church life from country to country, as the table on the following page demonstrates.

This shows weekly church attendance to be strongest in the countries with a Catholic tradition, though church affiliation is strong in the Protestant countries.

The highest proportion of people professing to hold traditional beliefs are to be found in Ireland, both Northern Ireland and the Irish Republic. Those who believe in no god at all are most numerous in the countries with lowest church attendance, Denmark and France. In fact these two countries are the only ones where secularisation is so entrenched that the number attending church each week is less than the number of self declared atheists. Belief in reincarnation is strongest in Britain, at 27% at the time of this survey and almost certainly higher in the early 1990s.

It is the huge church affiliation figures that scream from this table. How can 93% Danes belong to a church, while 21% do not believe in any kind of god? What this column highlights is the verse, 'they will hold to the outward form of our religion, but reject its real power'.

Religious activity and belief in Western Europe 1986
(percentage of population)

	Irish Republic	Italy	Denmark	Northern Ireland	Spain	Germany	Great Britain	Belgium	France	Netherlands	Average
Church affiliation	98	93	93	90	90	89	85	74	73	58	85
Weekly church attendance	82	36	3	52	41	21	14	30	12	27	32
Belief in											
God	95	63	29	91	58	72	76	44	62	65	75
Heaven	83	41	17	81	50	31	57	33	27	39	40
Hell	54	31	8	65	34	14	27	18	15	15	23
Reincarnation	26	21	11	18	25	19	27	13	22	10	21
Personal God	73	26	24	70	55	28	31	39	26	34	32
Life-force/spirit	16	50	24	18	23	40	39	24	26	29	36
Don't know	6	11	22	8	12	17	19	15	22	17	16
No god of any sort	2	6	21	1	6	13	9	8	19	12	11

See also: Religious beliefs.
Source: European Value Systems Study Group 1986, quoted in LM 89/3.

Evangelical Missionary Alliances in Europe

European Evangelical Missionary Alliance — *General Secretary:* Mr Torbjorn Lied, Norwegian Santal Mission, PO Box 9219, Waterland N-0134 Oslo 1, Norway. *Secretary:* Mr J Weber, Postfach, CH-3256 Dieterswil, Switzerland. *Chairman:* Mr Arthur Pont, INTERSERVE, 325 Kennington Road, London SE11 4QH, UK.

Denmark — Birger Schmidt, Missionsvennen, Kobenhavensvej 8, 3400 Hillerod.

Germany — Rev Ernst Vatter, Association of Evangelical Missions, Hindenburgstrasse 36, 715 Korntal, Munchingen 1.

Greece — Costas Macris, Hellenic Missionary Union, Lydias 12, 115 27 Athens.

The Netherlands — Hans Keijzer, SEZA, Mereveldlaan 89, 3454 CC De Meern.

Sweden — Mr B Svensson, Swedish Missionary Council, Gotgatan 3, 752 22 Uppsala.

Switzerland — Pierre Deriaz, Federation de Mission Evangeliques Francophones, Chemin de Rechoz, 1027 Lonay.

United Kingdom — Rev Stanley Davies, Evangelical Missionary Alliance, Whitefield House, 186 Kennington Park Road, London SE11 4BT. ☎071-735 0421.

Source: LL February 1990 and updated.

F

Family structure

One of the most notable trends in UK family life is the rising number of people living alone. From 12% in 1961, the proportion of households which consist of just one person has risen to a quarter (26% in 1990). This is caused not just by the growing numbers of old people, but because more young people choose to live by themselves.

At the same time the proportion of people living in 'traditional' families — a married couple with dependent children — dropped from 52% to 41%. Single parents bringing up children alone increased from 7% in 1971 to 19% in 1990.

The reason for the increase is a 77% rise in the number of single (never married) mothers, and an 80% increase in the number of divorced mothers between 1976 and 1987. Almost two-thirds of lone mothers are divorced or separated, and a third are single mothers (the remainder are widows).

There are now over a million single-parent families in the UK. One child in eight, or 1½ million children, come from lone parent homes.

A report by the Family Policies Study Centre shows that four out of 10 lone mothers work, seven out of 10 live in rented accommodation, and in 1986, 63% of one-parent families were either receiving supplementary benefit or earning less than the supplementary benefit level, compared with 10% of two-parent families.

Percentage change in the number of one-parent families 1976-1987

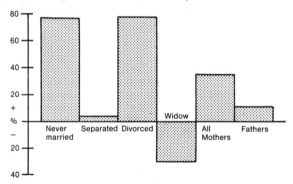

Another report shows that a family today is little more than a collection of individuals who happen to share the same address. Such are the findings from UK research by the National Family Trust.

Non-communication is the norm for about 90% of households, says the report. Even when members of the family share the same interests, they are increasingly likely to pursue them separately. So father and son might be watching the same television programme in different rooms, while mother and daughter will take separate cars to the same sports club.

Although most households try to get together for a meal once a week, notes left on the breakfast table are becoming more common than conversation as a means of communication. One American company has exploited this, apparently with some success, by marketing family cards with greetings such as 'Have a nice day, son' for those who have no time to scribble a note.

See also: Households, Lone Parents.
Source: Social Trends 21, Family Policy Studies Centre, Fact Sheet 3 and National Family Trust, LM 91/3 updated and LL February 1990 and OPCS Spring 1989.

Feminism

Is feminism dead? Sex equality is most evident in the fields of education and job opportunities in Britain. A Mintel survey in 1988 about youth lifestyles in the UK showed an 87% increase in the number of girls entering higher education between 1981 and 1986, compared with a 33% increase of boys, although more boys still go on to post-school education.

Entry to the professions is also becoming more equal, with law, medicine and accountancy reporting a balance of sexes at entry level.

Her job is the main source of satisfaction and fulfilment for 29% of married women. However, for 40% their partner is more important, according to a survey commissioned by the *Mail on Sunday* to try and identify the so-called New Woman.

A sample of women aged 18 to 34 in professional or managerial jobs was questioned, and nearly half reported that their career had a bad effect on their relationships.

Only 9% would describe themselves as feminist. Just over half the sample felt that feminism is still important, while 16% thought it irrelevant and 24% thought it was a bad thing because it is alienating.

Meanwhile, a report published in the USA shows that even in the best circumstances women have at most 87% of their husbands' and brothers' rights, and in the worst they have barely a fifth of the opportunities offered to their male counterparts.

'More than 60% of women and girls in the world live under conditions that threaten their health, deny them choice about childbearing, limit education attainment, restrict economic participation and fail to guarantee them equal rights and freedom with men,' the report claims.

So feminism may be dead for the small proportion of women in the world who consider they have all they want. But if the rights of women get less support from those in the West who consider equality to have gone far enough, should not the Church continue to speak up for the rights of those that society, in just about all of its various forms, treats as inferior?

Source: Mintel 1988 Youth Lifestyles, NOP and Population Crisis Committee report June 1988 Women — Poor, Powerless and Pregnant, LM 89/1.

Finland

What picture do you have of Scandinavians? An average British view might be of beautiful people living in snow-covered countryside or clean cities, with a high standard of living and a generally permissive standard of behaviour!

As well as being among the materially richest and most economically secure countries in the world, the Scandinavian countries are among the most secularised, on a level with Japan and certain of the socialist countries.

Research published in the *Finnish Christian Handbook* shows that participants in Christian activities have been decreasing steadily since 1956, and weekly church attendance stands at only 4% of the population, even though 89% are church members.

Although 70% of the population say they think the church is able to give answers to spiritual problems, the majority do not seem to think they need it.

Young people, men and residents of the Helsinki area were least likely to attend church, or accept its beliefs. In particular, twice as many men as women in their 30's and 40's were outside the church.

Just about everyone in Finland has some contact with the state church, the Evangelical Lutheran Church, through one of its many varied activities such as children's work and confirmation classes. The diversity of these is reflected in the fact that only one in 10 of the church's employees are parish pastors; far more are involved in children's or social work, and more than twice as many in the upkeep of cemeteries, a church responsibility. The state church is funded from a church tax and is responsible for the population register.

Although this means the church becomes an accepted part of most people's lives, a report points out the danger there can be in all these activities. Not only does the church itself risk losing sight of its purpose and its message, but people identify the church not as a community of Christians, but rather a provider of social and spiritual services. The proportion of the population who have baptisms and church funerals has been constantly higher than the national percentage of church members. Two-thirds of the population of Finland attends a church ceremony once a year.

This contact could be a stepping stone to reaching Finns with the gospel. On the other hand, nominalism can be an obstacle, when people think that they know what the church has to offer and consider it irrelevant.

There are, however, signs of a re-awakening of interest in religion. The media are paying increasing attention to religious matters and questions of ethics are seen to be more essential in future.

There is also a move towards emphasising feeling and experience. In Finland it is demonstrated in the context of the charismatic movement, the Pentecostal Church and in the number of new religious groups, which have grown greatly in recent years.

Now that people are beginning to feel dissatisfaction with their lives, in spite of their material wealth and sophistication, the church needs to respond to their spiritual search with the answer they are looking for. In Finland and in other parts of the prosperous West, the church should be offering a clear and positive alternative to the secular lifestyle.

However, religion is becoming increasingly privatised. Although 70% of people claim to believe in God, for many their form of belief differs from that of the church. This attitude is expressed by 30% of the younger generation and of residents of the Helsinki area. Rather less of both groups claim to believe in the God of the Christian faith.

Finns' belief in God

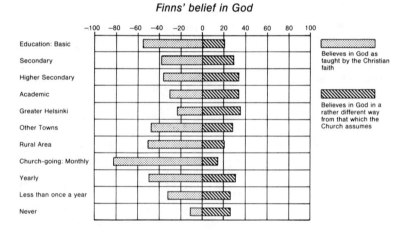

Percentage of population outside registered religious communities

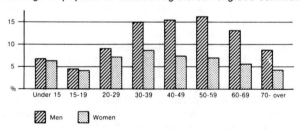

A report by the 'Church 2000' committee of the Evangelical Lutheran Church presents a summary of the changes in Finnish society and the Church's place in it. Looking to the future, it challenges the Church to reaffirm its identity and clarify its mission if it is to regain any of its lost authority in a secularised world — and provides guidelines for reviewing the different aspects of Church worship and life.

Source: Adapted with permission from Harri Heino's introduction to the Finnish Christian Handbook, published 1989 by MARC Europe and Suomen Kirkon Seurakuntatoiminnan Keskusliitto. Changes in Religiosity from the Finnish Viewpoint by Dr Harri Heino Publication No 37 of the Research Institute of the Lutheran Church in Finland, and Church in Finland, Documents of the Evangelical Lutheran Church of Finland No 1, published by the Church Council for Foreign Affairs Ecclesiastical Board, and LL November 1989, February 1990 LM 89/1.

Fifty something

The number and proportion of over-50s is increasing in most European countries, thanks to falling birthrates and longer life-expectancy.

The term 'Third Age' has been coined to describe the 50 to 70 age group, people who have probably finished bringing up a family and may have retired from work, but are still healthy and active. With more time, money and health than former generations, this growing segment of the population, currently about 25% in the UK, is not going to be written off as old. Rather their attitudes and preferences are likely to have increasing influence.

Market research suggests that people in this age-group:

● consider themselves morally superior to younger generations, are keen on fair play, and want to be seen as broad-minded — although they admit they are sometimes intolerant.

● feel satisfied with their situation, particularly compared with their parents' generation. Yet they feel a gap now that children have gone, and sometimes worry about losing their purpose in life.

● see themselves as being perceptive, liking simple and direct messages and not fooled by advertising.

● want to look and feel good. With money to spend, it is reckoned that consumers spend more on themselves between the ages of 50 and 75 than between 25 and 50.

● think it is important to be up-to-date with world news, and are avid consumers of news programmes, both local and national.

What of their religious attitudes? Currently older people are more religious than younger. But will unchurched middle-aged people become religious as they grow older, or will their material satisfaction and desire to enjoy life keep them away?

Source: Fiftysomething, article in Survey autumn 1990, and LM 91/1.

Flanders

The Flemish-speaking northern part of Belgium is considered to be the religious part of the country. Traditional Catholicism is stronger here than in the more secular French-speaking South, but the area is being rapidly secularised.

Whereas in 1968 just over half the population of Flanders were regular attenders of a Roman Catholic church, by 1985 this had fallen to around 27%, and continues to decrease at a rate of 1% each year. This contrasts with an attendance rate of 18% in the south and only 10% in Brussels. Throughout the country, it is estimated that only 45% of these regular attenders go to church every Sunday — so around 12% of the population of Flanders go to church each week.

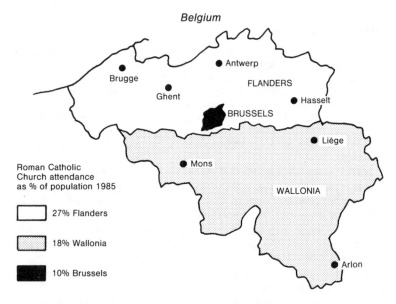

Belgium

Roman Catholic
Church attendance
as % of population 1985

27% Flanders

18% Wallonia

10% Brussels

Although many families still observe the 'rites of passage', even this is less popular among the younger generation. And while overall only 38% of the Flemish believe in a personal God, the proportion is even smaller, just 29%, in the 18 to 34 age-group.

Protestantism

Protestants number less than 100,000 in Belgium, under 1% of the population. With a history of severe persecution by Belgium's various rulers, they are still perceived, particularly in conservative rural areas, as a foreign sect. In such a society, how could a Protestant church begin to plant churches in areas where there are none?

This is the question Egbert Bos, a student at the Evangelical Theological Faculty in Leuven, Belgium, has addressed in his thesis *Church Planting in Flanders*. He surveys the background, the need, and in this context the demographic and social characteristics of Flanders, drawing out both obstacles and key points to focus on.

Among the keys for church-planters are the strategic value of the suburbs as a location for new churches, and the centrality of the family in Flemish life. The importance of making friends and becoming an accepted part of the community before attempting to share the Gospel is highlighted, and illustrated by several case studies.

Such a detailed study highlights the possibilities in a seemingly impossible situation, which should make it useful for all with an interest in this kind of work, whatever the location. It also shows the complexities of the task, and brings home the amount of time and commitment that is required to see the Gospel make an impression in this part of Europe.

Source: Church Planting in Flanders, Egbert Bos, MARC Monograph 32 1990, quoted in LL June 1990.

Food supply and distribution internationally

There is much confusion on global food and hunger problems. Although many factors can affect food production and distribution, the following information shows that there is enough food to go around. So why does the massive death-toll from starvation exist in this world?

Supply
- There is 10% more food in the world than is required to feed everyone.
- The world now produces 20% more food per person than 20 years ago.
- Future world food supply is predicted to be more than sufficient to feed the world population into the middle of the next century if food is distributed properly.

Hunger
- Nearly 25% of humanity is affected by chronic malnutrition.
- It is estimated that hunger and malnutrition kill nearly 50 million people every year. UNICEF claims that 15 million of these are young children.
- One in seven of the world's population (730 million people) receives insufficient calories to lead 'an active working life'.

Distribution
- 30% of the world's population consumes 75% of the world's food.
- The European Community considered destroying 20 million metric tons of 'surplus' beef, butter and grain. Total food surpluses are reported to cost £2,400 million a year to store, according to *Newsweek* (7/7/87).

- The estimated amount needed to give all the world adequate food, water, education and health would be £10,000 million a year. Remember that is approximately what the world spends on military arms every two weeks!

Source: Ted Vandeloo, GRID, World Vision Australia, 1987, LM 88/4.

France

About 13% of the French attend church at least once a month, of whom 95% are Roman Catholics.

It is estimated that by 1995 the Catholic churches will have lost around 100,000 people since 1975; although for a church of 6½ million this is hardly noticeable. Protestant church attendance, although tiny in comparison, will more than double over the same period. The total number of Protestants in 1990 was estimated at only 260,000.

The falling number of priests is the major crisis for the Catholic church in France, as in other parts of Europe. The decline has been severe in the past 40 years: in 1950 over 1,000 priests were ordained annually; in 1990 there were fewer than 100.

Population per Protestant congregation

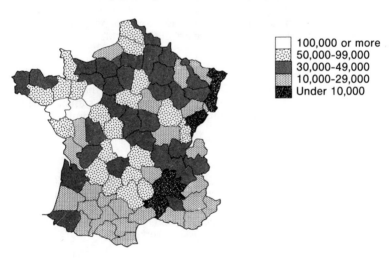

| 100,000 or more |
| 50,000-99,000 |
| 30,000-49,000 |
| 10,000-29,000 |
| Under 10,000 |

Leaders of the 2,500 or so Protestant churches are not without their problems. Small churches can get defeated by the size of the task before them, so there is a real need for pastors to support each other, seeking a vision for evangelism and working together.

The needs in France are immense; thousands of village communities are virtually unreached, as are the growing cities, three million Muslim immigrants, and over a million students. While the facts and figures in the *French Christian Handbook* show up the needs, they also show growth in many churches. God is at work in France and however unlikely it may seem at times, His purposes will be accomplished.

Attitudinal Study

In the summer of 1989 young people took the Gospel to the streets of Europe East and West as part of Operation Mobilisation's 'Love Europe' campaign.

In the town of Sète in the South of France a team of young people carried out a survey of attitudes to religion, sending the results − along with Biblical comments on the findings − to interested participants.

The 'OMers' interviewed 620 people, of whom 37% were tourists and 56% were men, either in their homes or on the streets of Sète. They found that 69% believed in God and 62%, even in this age of reason, disagreed with the statement that science had proved religion to be wrong.

However, church was less popular than God. Only 24% of those questioned were members of the Roman Catholic Church − although 73% described France as a Catholic country. Just over 6% of people interviewed were Muslims.

What did people think about Jesus? Rather more than believed in God were sure that Jesus had lived: 78%. Of these, 85% believed He was crucified, 71% that He rose again, and 50% that He is alive today.

Church membership and attendance in France

	Active members				Attendance				Attendance as % of membership	
	1980	1985	1990*	1995*	1980	1985	1990*	1995*	1980	1990
Baptist	5,251	7,078	8,770	9,910	7,619	9,860	12,450	14,500	145	142
Pentecostal	29,247	72,220	98,640	136,960	34,239	95,280	129,065	165,075	117	131
Traditional Protestant	24,208	26,656	30,345	33,650	16,662	19,401	23,180	26,400	69	76
Independent	23,103	28,538	34,725	40,610	31,995	37,485	45,170	52,090	138	130
Lutheran	51,798	50,562	49,305	48,030	25,765	25,180	24,625	24,060	50	50
Other Protestant	27,995	25,333	23,268	23,250	29,931	27,834	26,256	26,840	105	113
Total Protestant	161,612	210,387	245,053	292,410	146,171	215,040	260,556	308,965	90	106
Catholic	11,555,149* 11,507,772*		11,460,000* 11,410,000*		6,729,002 6,700,335		6,672,000 6,644,000		58	58
Orthodox	109,620	109,620	109,620	109,620	10,962	10,962	10,962	10,962	10	10
TOTAL ALL CHURCHES	11,826,381 11,827,779		11,814,673 11,812,030		6,886,135 6,926,337		6,944,058 6,963,927		58	59
% of Population	22	21	21	21	13	13	13	13		

* Estimate

Finally, not many people were sure about life after death. While 46% believed in heaven, and 39% in some kind of judgement, only 18% thought it was possible to be certain of going to heaven. Just 15% reckoned on going there themselves.

Designed by Mark Howe of Open Air Campaigners, with the assistance of David Buick of France Mission, this survey succeeded not only in finding some interesting facts, but in offering answers to those who admitted they didn't have any.

Source: La France Chrétienne/French Christian Handbook, MARC Europe 1989 and David Buick, France Mission, LM 90/1, LL November 1989 and December 1990.

Friendship

Young people in Britain put relationships top of their list of priorities. Going out or staying in with friends or partner is what 16 to 25 year olds most enjoy doing in their spare time, according to a National Opinion Poll survey.

What they like to do with their friends varies according to age and sex, from going to pubs or discos to playing cards and taking country walks. But one thing is certain: church is the last place they would choose to be.

Young men and the 18 to 20 age group are the least likely to go to church, although young women don't put it quite at the bottom of the list. Overall only 4% said going to church was one of the activities they enjoyed most.

What is it that puts them off? Surely the message of the church is about the greatest relationship of all, between man and God — something to which people should be attracted by the quality of the friendship we in church have for each other.

Answers to the question 'Thinking about how you spend your free time, could you tell me which of these you enjoy doing most?'

	All	Gender		Age		
		Male	Female	16/17	18-20	21-25
	%	%	%	%	%	%
Visiting friends or having friends round	55	45	63	63	46	55
Going out with groups of friends	50	51	49	53	54	47
Going out with partner	47	41	53	35	45	45
Going to the pub	37	44	31	26	47	37
Shopping	25	8	41	22	22	28
Going to sports events	14	23	6	17	15	12
Going to church	4	3	6	5	3	5

Source: NOP Political, Social & Economic Review 77 September 1989, and LM 90/1, LL November 1989.

G

German children

In West Germany in 1989 600,000 newborn babies competed with 3.6 million dogs for the attention of adults. Many West Germans treat dogs as equal members of the household, frequently as substitutes for children, and spend three times as much on pet foods as on baby food.

German sources commenting on the steady decline in the West German birth rate (1.02 million in 1967 going down to 600,000 in 1986 despite generous state subsidies) speak of a growing animosity to children. Compared to pets, they are too demanding and restrict the parents' self-development.

If people today can't cope with loving their own children, what does it say about our attitude to other people who make demands on us? And should people really be rated according to how much they contribute to our own lives?

Source: Puls Nachrichten quoted in World Christian News, LM 90/3.

Ghana

If you want to find a church in a Ghanaian town, the best thing to do is to walk around on a Sunday and listen for the singing. This is what researchers from the Ghana Evangelism Committee did, and as a result of their survey, some 600 churches were planted within six months of the project's completion.

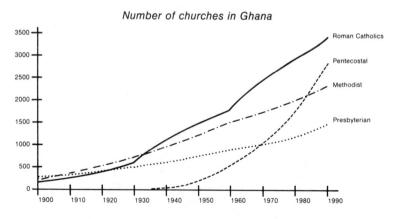

Number of churches in Ghana

The data was collected by visiting every village and community between 1986 and 1988. The researchers counted the churches and the number of people attending Sunday services, and compared these figures with national census data.

The south is the Christian part of the country, with 75% of the population professing faith. Yet the survey showed that only 15% went to church on a Sunday. Why was this so? One simple reason was that many people had no church to go to in their village, and the next one was too far away to walk to.

The results of the survey were presented to pastors and church leaders at regional conferences, and it was here that they caught a vision for the villages without churches. At first there was heated debate as to the cause of growth or lack of it in the different denominations, but as the conferences continued, focus shifted to the new opportunities revealed.

How to go about taking on the country-wide challenge? In Ghana many people equate 'evangelism' with crusade-style meetings requiring equipment beyond the means of most pastors. But teaching at the conferences introduced the use of small groups in church planting, enabling many to turn their vision into strategies. As a result the 600 new churches have been planted, and church growth has gone to the top of many denominational agendas.

Now the challenge is to provide pastoral care for so many new churches. And all the villages reached so far are in the south of Ghana. The cultural barrier has yet to be surmounted to see the Christians from the south taking the gospel to the largely unreached people of the north.

Church attendance by region

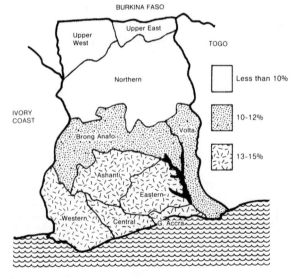

This strategy for church growth has aroused much interest in other African countries. And it encourages others to see how the findings of detailed research can lead to effective action. Altogether what's happening in Ghana is a practical example of an attempt to accomplish the Great Commission and to disciple a whole nation.

Source: Church Planting Ghana Style by Dr David Burnett published in Church Growth Digest spring 1988 and LM 89/3, LL November 1989.

Global data

	1980	1991	2000
	%	%	%
World Population			
Urban dwellers	41.0	43.0	47.0
Adult	62.0	61.0	61.0
Literate adults	66.0	68.0	71.0
By religion (%)			
Christians	32.8	33.3	34.1
Muslims	16.5	17.9	19.2
Hindus	13.3	13.4	13.7
Sikhs	0.3	0.3	0.4
Buddhists	6.3	6.1	5.7
Jews	0.4	0.3	0.3
Tribal religionists	2.1	1.9	1.6
New religionists	2.2	2.2	2.2
Other religionists	5.3	3.8	2.2
Atheists	4.5	4.4	4.2
Other non-religious	16.3	16.4	16.4
Total (million) (= 100%)	4,373.9	5,384.6	6,251.1
Christian Population			
Christian denomination (%)			
Roman Catholics	56.0	54.6	53.7
Other Catholics	0.2	0.2	0.2
Protestants	18.3	18.4	18.1
Anglicans	3.5	3.0	2.9
Orthodox	11.2	10.1	9.4
Non-white indigenous Christians	5.8	8.4	9.6
Marginal protestants*	1.0	1.1	1.1
Others	4.0	4.2	5.0
Total Christians (million) (= 100%)	1,432.7	1,795.9	2,130.0
of which Pentecostal/ Charismatic	11.0	21.8	26.4

* Jehovah's Witnesses, Mormons etc

(continued on page 76)

(continued from page 75)

	1980	1991	2000
	%	%	%
Christian Population			
Christians by major region			
Africa	12.4	14.6	16.6
East Asia	1.2	5.4	6.6
South Asia	8.1	8.9	9.5
Oceanic	1.2	1.1	1.1
Latin America	25.8	27.2	28.6
North America	13.5	11.5	10.3
Europe	30.5	24.7	21.2
USSR	7.3	6.6	6.1
Total Christians (million) (= 100%)	1,432.7	1,795.9	2,130.0
Christian finance			
Personal income per			
church member per year	£2,400	£3,100	£3,500
% given to Christian causes	1.7	1.7	1.7
of which % given to churches	64	52	45
of which % given to parachurch			
and institutions	36	48	55
Evangelisation			
Unevangelised			
(% of world population)	31.6	22.9	16.6

Source: International Bulletin of Missionary Research January 1991, David B Barrett, Annual Statistical Table on Global Mission 1991.

Global evangelism

Global statistics and how they can help us evangelise the world is the subject of a 1990 book in the AD2000 series, by Dr David Barrett and Todd Johnson, *Our Globe and How to Reach it.*

The global statistics, from the AD2000 Global Monitor database are presented in diagrams and listings, and cover nearly every dimension of life from missionaries (85,000), to pollutants in urban air (two million tons per year) or political executions (40,000 per year).

The authors hope the clear facts will aid realism and enable the church to make the best use of its resources in meeting world needs in the Decade of Evangelism. They point out that 'only 1% of Christian thinking, discussion and action concern mission in the un-evangelised world'.

The facts and figures also cover current Christian activity and almost 200 goals for the year 2000 that are being worked on. With this goes a plea for co-operation in the task.

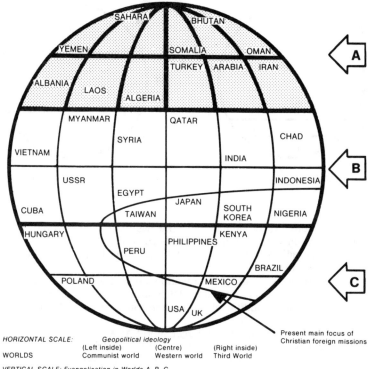

SAHARA
BHUTAN
YEMEN
SOMALIA
OMAN
TURKEY
ARABIA
IRAN
ALBANIA
LAOS
ALGERIA
MYANMAR
QATAR
SYRIA
CHAD
VIETNAM
INDIA
USSR
INDONESIA
EGYPT
JAPAN
CUBA
TAIWAN
SOUTH KOREA
NIGERIA
HUNGARY
KENYA
PHILIPPINES
PERU
BRAZIL
POLAND
MEXICO
USA
UK

A
B
C

Present main focus of
Christian foreign missions

HORIZONTAL SCALE:	Geopolitical ideology		
	(Left inside)	(Centre)	(Right inside)
WORLDS	Communist world	Western world	Third World

VERTICAL SCALE: Evangelisation in Worlds A, B, C

Source: *Our Globe and How to Reach it, Seeing the world evangelised by AD2000 and Beyond, by David B Barrett and Todd M Johnson, Foreign Mission Board of the Southern Baptist Convention 1990, and LL June 1991.*

Global mission

David Barrett divides the world into three groups:

World A = Non-Christians who have never come into contact with Christianity and have no knowledge of Christ and the Gospel.

World B = Non-Christians who are in contact with Christians and who have at least some knowledge of Christ and the Gospel.

World C = All those who individually call themselves Christian.

Until 500 years ago there was almost no contact between the three major races — Caucasoid, Mongoloid and Negroid. Some 93% of all Christians then were whites in Europe.

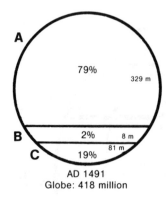

AD 1491
Globe: 418 million

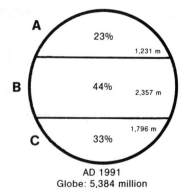

AD 1991
Globe: 5,384 million

Five hundred years later that picture has drastically changed. Mass communication, mass transport, mass migration and the resultant religious pluralism have put all the races in daily contact almost everywhere on earth.

But the trend is alarming. The world's population out of touch with Christians (World A) has risen from 330 million in 1491 to 1,230 million in 1991. Every year an additional 150 million souls are born, 45 million in World A.

Most mission agencies do not target World A: 90% of all evangelism is directed at Christians, not non-Christians; 91% of all foreign missionaries target World C; 95% of all Christian activity benefits World C; 99% of all the Christian world's income is spent on itself.

Source: International Bulletin of Missionary Research January 1991, David B Barrett, Annual Statistical Table on Global Mission 1991.

Global problems

Some development problems are not necessarily related to countries' geographical location or their level of development. According to an American, David C Korten, the needs that North and South, East and West increasingly have in common include:

- Restoring depleted soils
- Conserving and allocating scarce water resources
- Reducing air pollution
- Preserving and strengthening small farms
- Reducing chronic unemployment
- Ensuring human rights
- Financing micro-economic activities
- Arms reduction and demilitarisation

- Controlling global warming
- Providing housing
- Providing bilingual education
- Reducing hunger, illitercy and infant mortality
- Reducing teenage pregnancy
- Managing population growth and distribution
- Increasing citizens' awareness of global development issues
- Improving preparedness for natural disasters
- Reducing regional tensions based on racial, religious and ethnic differences
- Eliminating acid rain
- Treating AIDS victims and controlling spread of the disease
- Resettling refugees
- Controlling drug trafficking and abuse

An Australian, Peter Newman, looking at global environment issues lists them as:

- Rain forest deterioration
- Global population increase
- Land degradation
- Fish loss and pollution of water
- Chemical industry failure
- City growth and urban sprawl
- Greenhouse effect and ozone depletion
- Abject Third World poverty
- Environmental refugees
- Global military activity

Source: Getting to the 21st Century, David C Korten, Kumarian Press, 1990, Table 11-1, page 148, and Hope and Despair, The Human Condition in Environmental issues. Condition article by Peter Newman in Zadok papers Series 1, Paper 553 June 1991, pages 2 and 3.

Gloucestershire

Area (sq km)	Population 1989 Men	Women	Total	Percentage change 1979-89	Percentage under 15	Non-churchgoers 1989
2,643	255,700	273,800	529,500	+5.9%	18%	473,300

Churchgoers 1989 Men	Women	Total	Percentage of population	Percentage change 1979-89	Percentage under 15	Number of churches	Percentage built before 1500	since 1950
22,500	33,700	56,200	10.6%	−11.3%	23%	682	38%	8%

District	Area (sq km)	Population 1989	Percentage change 1979-89 %
Stroud	454	110,500	+10.2
Gloucester	33	90,500	−2.9
Tewkesbury	450	88,100	+9.7
Cheltenham	35	86,000	−0.1
Forest of Dean	528	78,500	+9.1
Cotswold	1,143	75,800	+11.0

Source: Regional Trends 26, HMSO 1991 and English Church Census.

God, ideas about

Young people in Finland and Latin America have different ideas about God. When school-leavers in Finland, Columbia and Ecuador were asked to write on the subject, 65% of the Latin Americans talked about their personal experience of God, while 59% of Finns had no distinct image of God at all.

Almost all the Latin Americans stressed the community dimension of their faith, and their essays contained reflection on the state of society. Those who did not write about their personal experience either expressed clear theories on what God was like, or wrote about the importance to them of religious ritual.

The Finnish essays were so different that the researchers found it impossible to use the same categories. In general, they were characterised by scientific or humanistic reflections and a negative attitude towards the church. Although 18% of the young Finns had never really thought about God, 60% saw the existence of God as a possibility, and 35% prayed each day. Half wrote about God as some kind of 'force'.

While 85% of the Latin Americans found their experience of God liberating, 9% of the Finns appeared to be experiencing pain, because they couldn't find what they were looking for.

This striking research highlights the difference between society and the church on different continents, and Europe's need of re-evangelisation. Perhaps young Latin Americans can come and help?

Religiosity of young Latin Americans and Finns

	Latin America	Finland
	%	%
Conceptual	19	4
Ritualistic	15	8
Personal	65	22
Indistinct	*	59

* Not included in Latin American classification.

Source: My idea of God – Mi Idea Sobre Dios by Leena Kurki, publication 39 of the Research Institute of the Lutheran Church in Finland, and LM 90/3.

Billy Graham

Mission England 1984

Thousands of people go forward at Billy Graham rallies, but hardly any of them join churches and stay with them! This is a common criticism of mass evangelism. Research for Mission England presents the facts, based on interviews with 300 of the participating churches 18 months to two years after Mission England in 1984.

● About 117 people from each participating church went to the mission. Of those, about a quarter were not linked to the church at that time.

● The average church had 22 people who had gone forward on the night referred to them, a substantial proportion of some congregations. About half these people were not known to the church, so a lot of work was needed for follow up — more than had been bargained for in some cases.

● Overall, about half these people referred to their local churches were still with that church 18 months to two years later, not allowing for those who may have transferred to a different church.

● A total of 9,400 people were involved in some official capacity in Mission England, about 20 for each of the 4,800 participating churches. The extent of this involvement may have contributed to the results.

Proportion of referrals staying with church

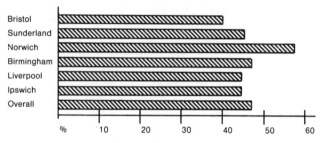

Mission 89

Almost 380,000 people went to hear Billy Graham at the Mission 89 meetings at three London venues in 1989, and 9% responded. Rather fewer went forward for acceptance or salvation than at previous missions, more for re-dedication or as enquirers. Compared with previous missions, a larger number of 36 to 60 year old people than usual were reached, perhaps because of the appeal of the advertising, perhaps because they knew and respected the reputation of Billy Graham.

Only 37% of those who went forward were men, which reflects the state of the church generally where only 42% of attenders are male.

Altogether 14,500 people in the London meetings indicted a decision to give their lives to Christ at Mission 89, 88% of them aged 12 or over. If all these joined a local church, as they were encouraged to do, the total churchgoing numbers in London will have increased by over 3%. Since the average size of a London congregation is 114, the increase in numbers would be equivalent to the formation of 112 new churches.

Source: Where Are They Now? Phil Back, MARC Europe, Monograph 21 1988, and LM 89/2 and What Happened at Mission 89? MARC Monograph 31, and LM 90/2.

Greater London

Area	Population 1989			Percentage change	Percentage under	Non- churchgoers
(sq km)	Men	Women	Total	1979-89	15	1989
1,579	3,273,800	3,482,600	6,756,400	−0.9%	19%	6,095,000

Churchgoers 1989			Percentage of	Percentage change	Percentage	Number of	Percentage built	
Men	Women	Total	population	1979-89	under 15	churches	before 1500	since 1950
277,800	383,600	661,400	9.8%	−5.5%	24%	3,549	6%	24%

Borough	Area (sq km)	Population 1989	Percentage change 1979-89	Total Church- goers 1989	Percentage of 1989 population
			%		%
Croydon	87	317,300	−1.5	45,000	14.2
Barnet	90	310,400	+6.4	15,700	5.1
Bromley	151	299,400	+0.4	31,700	10.6
Ealing	55	293,700	+5.2	21,400	7.3
Enfield	81	262,100	+0.5	32,900	12.6
Wandsworth	35	256,200	−2.7	27,500	10.7
Brent	44	254,700	+0.3	35,600	14.0
Lambeth	27	238,300	−7.2	21,900	9.2
Hillingdon	110	235,300	+1.0	20,000	8.5
Havering	118	232,600	−5.0	19,800	8.5
Redbridge	56	232,200	+1.6	23,400	10.1
Lewisham	35	226,700	−5.1	34,300	15.1
Bexley	61	220,000	+1.6	16,400	7.5
Southwark	29	219,800	+0.9	24,000	10.9
Greenwich	47	213,400	−1.2	17,700	8.3
Waltham Forest	40	211,700	−3.4	13,300	6.3
Newham	36	207,000	−3.4	9,600	4.6
Hounslow	59	195,900	−4.9	10,900	5.6
Harrow	51	193,800	−3.2	26,800	13.8
Hackney	19	191,800	+4.5	9,800	5.1
Haringey	30	190,000	−10.3	17,700	9.3
Camden	22	183,700	+3.3	15,900	8.7
City of Westminster	22	173,400	−9.7	32,100	18.5
Islington	15	169,500	+2.6	11,400	6.7
Sutton	43	168,900	−0.9	15,600	9.2
Merton	38	164,000	−2.6	15,100	9.2
Tower Hamlets	20	163,900	+16.2	10,900	6.7
Richmond-upon-Thames	55	163,700	+1.5	17,800	10.9
Hammersmith & Fulham	16	148,500	−2.2	11,400	7.7
Barking & Dagenham	34	147,500	−3.4	10,400	7.1
Kingston-upon-Thames	38	136,100	+1.8	16,200	11.9
Kensington & Chelsea	12	130,600	−8.4	23,900	18.3
City of London	3	4,300	−25.5	5,300	123.3!

Some of the Inner London boroughs reflect the drawing power of their large churches.

Source: Regional Trends 26, HMSO 1991, English Church Census, and London, Borough by Borough.

Greater Manchester

Area (sq km)	Population 1989			Percentage change 1979-89	Percentage under 15	Non-churchgoers 1989
	Men	Women	Total			
1,287	1,260,600	1,321,800	2,582,400	−1.7%	20%	2,293,000

Churchgoers 1989			Percentage of population	Percentage change 1979-89	Percentage under 15	Number of churches	Percentage built	
Men	Women	Total					before 1500	since 1950
118,700	170,700	289,400	11.2%	−14.5%	30%	1,444	3%	18%

District	Area (sq km)	Population 1989	Percentage change 1979-89 %
Manchester	116	443,600	−5.1
Wigan	199	309,600	−0.2
Stockport	126	291,300	+0.3
Bolton	140	265,000	+1.3
Salford	97	234,600	−6.2
Oldham	141	220,700	−0.4
Tameside	103	218,200	−0.1
Trafford	106	215,300	−3.6
Rochdale	160	207,600	−0.4
Bury	99	176,400	−0.1

Source: Regional Trends 26, HMSO 1991 and English Church Census.

Growth in church attendance

Adult church attendance by county 1985-89

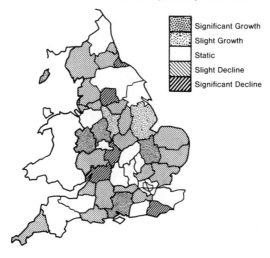

Significant Growth
Slight Growth
Static
Slight Decline
Significant Decline

What kind of churches are growing?

Adult church attendance overall as a percentage of the adult population declined by 1% from 1979 to 1989.

Anglican, Roman Catholic, Methodist and United Reformed Churches' adult attendance declined. And Baptist churches decline changed to growth after 1985.

The main growth was in Pentecostal, Afro-Caribbean, Orthodox and Independent churches. Independent churches include the House Churches, which grew 144%.

Evangelicals grew by 3% from 1985 to 1989, mainly due to the 7% growth of the charismatic evangelicals which number 400,000. Churches of catholic churchmanship declined by 2% and broad/liberal churchmanship by 5%.

Major groups of adult churchgoers 1975-2000

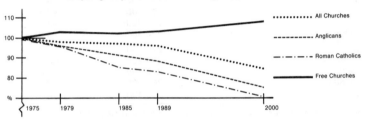

Free Church adult churchgoers 1975-2000

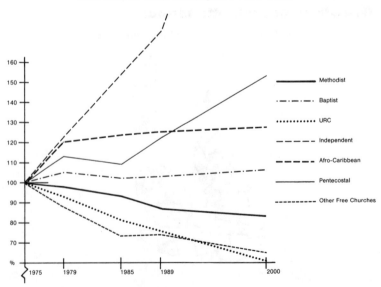

H

Hairs (of your head)

Jesus once said, 'The very hairs of your head are all numbered' (Luke 12:7). How many hairs does a person have on their head? On average, a

Dark haired person has 140,000   Less dark person has 120,000
Blonde person has 80,000

What use are such figures in a church setting? One Sunday an Anglican church in Southeast London was especially full because it was Harvest Festival. The preacher said, '30,000,000 Africans may die this year because of the famine. It is hard to imagine what 30 million is like'. 30,000,000 was the approximate number of hairs on the heads of that nearly 300 strong congregation that morning.

Source: Mike Lyth, International Finance Director OM, preaching at Christ Church, Bromley October 1991.

Hampshire

Area (sq km)	Population 1989			Percentage change 1979-89	Percentage under 15	Non-churchgoers 1989
	Men	Women	Total			
3,777	762,300	783,700	1,546,000	+4.9%	19%	1,400,200

Churchgoers 1989			Percentage of population	Percentage change 1979-89	Percentage under 15	Number of churches	Percentage built	
Men	Women	Total					before 1500	since 1950
59,800	86,000	145,800	9.4%	−1.5%	24%	1,047	27%	18%

District	Area (sq km)	Population 1989	Percentage change 1979-89
			%
Southampton	49	197,600	−7.2
Portsmouth	37	184,000	−4.9
New Forest	753	163,200	+15.5
Basingstoke and Deane	637	141,400	+10.1
Havant	56	116,300	+0.6
Test Valley	637	102,600	+12.0
East Hampshire	515	102,400	+14.8
Eastleigh	80	102,200	+12.7
Fareham	74	101,400	+17.8
Winchester	660	95,800	+3.9
Hart	218	86,000	+16.2
Rushmoor	36	76,600	−6.2
Gosport	25	76,500	−2.2

Source: Regional Trends 26, HMSO 1991 and English Church Census.

Happiest years

When asked which years of their lives British people felt to be the best so far, those surveyed responded:

	%
Childhood	8
Teens	24
Twenties	29
Thirties	16
Forties	8
Fifties	3
Over 60	2
No particular years	3
All the years good	7

Not surprisingly the 20s score the highest. This is the very age-group least represented in our churches. Is this because the church cannot compete or because our programmes for people in this age-group are so unattractive?

Source: Gallup Survey of Britain, LM 88/1.

Health

Doctors and dentists have experienced a decline in the numbers of patients over the 20 years between 1965 and 1985.

In 1965 a GP had an average of 2,400 patients. By 1985 this number had decreased by 400. A dentist in 1965 had 4,600 patients, only 3,300 20 years on.

The number of hospital patients in the same period increased by 39% from 5.6 million to 7.8 million. Out patient appointments experienced a similar increase, 35 million in 1965, 45 million by 1985.

So, how do people relax? In 1983, the latest year for which figures are available by gender, show walking and swimming the most popular:

	Men	*Women*
	%	%
Walking	20	18
Football (11-a-side)	6	—
Golf	4	1
Fishing	4	—
Swimming	10	10
Athletics (including jogging)	3	1
Cycling	2	2
Cricket	1	—
Snooker	15	2
Keep Fit/Aerobics	—	5
Squash	4	1
Badminton	2	2

How large a part is the church taking in helping people to remain healthy? How much is this thought through in the average church programme? One of the ways to reduce stress is to relax more, but how much teaching is given to relaxation or general fitness? Jesus knew the value of relaxation, Paul was concerned that his body should be fit for the task which the Lord had given him; how much do we encourage others to be like minded?

Source: UK in Figures 1987, Government Statistical Service, Social Trends and LM 87/2.

Heaven

There have been 73 million deaths in England and Wales since the official registration began in 1837.

By estimating that the world was populated by human beings in 40,000 BC, a meeting of the British Association for the Advancement of Science concluded that, up to 1980, there has been nearly 60,000 million deaths in the world.

Taking their estimates from 8,000 BC onwards together with those in David Barrett's *World Christian Encyclopaedia* showing the percentage of the world's population who have been Christian, it is possible to suggest the population of Heaven.

	World population (million)	Assumed annual death rate (per 1,000)	Total deaths between this date and next (million)	Percentage who are Christian	Total Christian deaths between this date and next (million)
8000 BC	6	50	3,450	—	—
5000	40	50	10,710	—	—
1200	100	40	3,696	—	—
400	162	40	3,268	—	—
1 AD	255	35	4,121	7	273
500	206	35	3,821	22	856
1000	254	35	6,910	19	731
1500	460	35	11,227	19	2,133
1900	1,633	25	3,159	34	1,211
1970	3,678	12	797	33	269
1986	5,000	11	227	34	77
1990	5,300	11	—	—	—
Totals			51,386		5,550

However, there are many assumptions built into these figures and they are intended to be taken with a very large pinch of salt!

With the current occupancy of Heaven estimated at 5,550 million let's hope there is room for a few more!

Source: LM 88/2.

Heart disease

Heart disease can be avoided more effectively than any other illness, according to three-quarters of English people in a 1986 survey by the Department of Health and Social Security.

While 93% of those asked were aware of the condition and had heard the term coronary, only 44% were prepared to take precautions. Only a third claimed to take any positive steps to avoid a heart attack, usually as part of a routine medical examination.

With 32% of adult male deaths in the UK being due to heart disease what could this mean for your church, your minister and the other men in the fellowship? When did the minister last have a medical examination? Was it at the church's expense? Should it be?

See also: Death.
Source: LM 88/2.

Hereford and Worcester

Area (sq km)	Population 1989			Percentage change 1979-89	Percentage under 15	Non-churchgoers 1989
	Men	Women	Total			
3,927	332,000	343,200	675,200	+7.7%	19%	608,000

Churchgoers 1989			Percentage of population	Percentage change 1979-89	Percentage under 15	Number of churches	Percentage built	
Men	Women	Total					before 1500	since 1950
27,600	39,600	67,200	10.0%	−5.5%	25%	823	42%	10%

District	Area (sq km)	Population 1989	Percentage change 1979-89
			%
Wychavon	666	101,400	+7.9
Wyre Forest	196	95,700	+5.4
Bromsgrove	220	88,900	+1.1
Malvern Hills	902	88,300	+4.5
Worcester	32	82,100	+10.4
Redditch	54	78,100	+19.7
S Herefordshire	905	51,900	+13.9
Hereford	20	49,400	+3.6
Leominster	932	39,500	+6.2

Source: Regional Trends 26, HMSO 1991 and English Church Census.

Hertfordshire

Area (sq km)	Men	Population 1989 Women	Total	Percentage change 1979-89	Percentage under 15	Non-churchgoers 1989
1,634	486,300	501,100	987,400	+2.9%	19%	890,700

Churchgoers 1989 Men	Women	Total	Percentage of population	Percentage change 1979-89	Percentage under 15	Number of churches	Percentage built before 1500	since 1950
41,600	55,100	96,700	9.8%	+1.2%	29%	624	18%	21%

District	Area (sq km)	Population 1989	Percentage change 1979-89
			%
Dacorum	210	133,000	+2.1
St Albans	161	128,400	+3.0
E Hertfordshire	477	119,100	+11.1
N Hertfordshire	374	113,500	+6.4
Welwyn Hatfield	128	92,100	−2.7
Hertsmere	98	88,700	+0.1
Broxbourne	52	82,700	+4.5
Three Rivers	88	80,300	+1.4
Watford	21	75,700	+1.8
Stevenage	25	74,000	−1.1

Source: Regional Trends 26, HMSO 1991 and English Church Census.

Holidays

Have you ever participated in a church holiday? Has your church ever run one? What kind of holidays do people like?

A survey through Association of British Travel Agents travel agencies from 1986 to 1990 of the types of holidays booked, summer and winter provided these percentages:

	Summer 1986	1988	1990	Winter 1986	1988	1990
	%	%	%	%	%	%
Hotel by a beach	61	50	41	51	43	34
Self-catering by a beach	16	24	26	9	11	12
Skiing	−	−	−	15	15	17
European holiday − flight only	9	11	11	11	14	14
Non-European − Long-haul flight	3	6	10	6	9	12
City	4	4	5	6	7	9
Lakes and mountains	3	3	3	−	−	−
Other types	4	2	4	2	1	2

Beach holidays are taken all the year, though not all at the same beaches! But there is a considerable movement away from hotels to self-catering accommodation, though despite this, there still has been a reduction in this type of holiday. More people book only the air flight since they have/make their own accommodation arrangements, perhaps through a timeshare arrangement. The long-haul flights are anywhere outside Europe, with Florida (and Disney) the second most popular resort after Majorca for British holiday-makers. Skiing in the winter clearly is very popular too — why not have a church reunion on the slopes of Mount Blanc?

Source: Survey magazine autumn 1991.

Home time

People in Britain choose to spend an increasing amount of time at home. They also spend more time and money on their houses, with half the population spending £3,600 million on DIY in 1987.

About 60% of people spent more time in their own houses than five years previously, according to a survey carried out in 1987. This figure rose to 67% among 25 to 34 year-olds, most of whom say having children is the main reason.

Watching television, listening to music or reading a book is the way most people spend their evenings at home.

Taking foreign holidays is also a big growth area, increasing by 19% since 1982. So is eating out, which has increased by 25% in the same period.

This may be an indication of a trend for individuals and families to be increasingly insular, isolated from any kind of community life or identity.

This is something which has long been considered characteristic of other countries in Europe and something which is quite contrary to the spirit of the church. Something to be on our guard against, and to offer a positive alternative to?

Source: Colouring Our Lives, survey commissioned by Crown Berger International reported in Daily Telegraph 14 April 1988, LM 89/1.

House Churches

When church statistics paint a picture of general decline, a movement which grows at the rate of about two new congregations each week is a striking feature. Over 190,000 Christians are members of the 'House Churches' which have appeared since 1970. Where did they come from?

The reason why history has to keep repeating itself is because we never learn what it is trying to teach us. Church history is no exception. Just a cursory glance at the two thousand years of the church's existence reveals repeated attempts by various individuals or movements to call her back from a wayward path to what they regarded as true New Testament Christianity.

In the late 60s and early 70s a number of leaders from around Great Britain were drawn together with this desire. Church attendance was in decline. The Church of England and many of the older established denominations were struggling to maintain the size of their congregations. Could something be done to reverse the trend?

These leaders felt that something entirely new was needed. They wanted to get away from a Christianity that was centred around buildings and meetings and give time to developing relationships, creating an atmosphere in which all the members of the church felt able to contribute and bring their unique gifts and abilities to bear.

Thus were the House Churches born. The mould was broken, not without controversy, misunderstanding and opposition. Their meetings began literally in homes, but quickly outgrew front rooms so moved to larger venues. However big they grew, the name 'House Church' seemed to stick.

From 1970 to 1975 the movement grew one hundredfold. Strong, charismatic leaders gathered people around them without too much effort and thousands of church members, dissatisfied with the diet they were receiving in their church, moved over to the House Churches. This did not, of course, endear the fledgling movement to the established churches.

A unique feature of the House Church Movement has been its identity with 'national' leaders. Around each of these leaders or 'apostolic' teams you will usually find a strong, fairly large church plus a network of other churches which could be spread right across the country and even abroad.

The House Church Movement has spread to almost every part of the British Isles. Thriving congregations have begun to spring up in Scotland. In Northern Ireland, tired of sectarianism and religious prejudice, a number of Christians in Ulster have sought to establish churches that more closely reflect the heartcry of Jesus for love and unity among his followers. One of the larger fellowships in Belfast, mainly Protestant, has taken the radical step of uniting with a similar group which is predominantly Catholic.

It is very difficult to assess the exact numbers involved with the House Churches. New groups seem to be beginning almost every week, and statistics are further complicated by some denominational churches aligning themselves with the House Church Movement.

While it is true that a good proportion of members are middle class, a number of groups have deliberately formed in working class areas. Among people who have been traditionally quite resistant to the gospel, these churches are beginning to experience some degree of success.

Growth by transfer from other churches is largely a thing of the past and mission now figures high on the agenda of most House Churches. A prime example of this is the Ichthus Fellowship in South London, which grew from a handful to around 1,500 members in 10 years.

Church history shows the sad fact that all new, radical movements fail to maintain the impetus. Now more than ever the House Churches face that challenge. Having broken the mould, will they begin to suffer from the growth of the new 'mould' of church? Or will the movement finally prove that the shackles of history can be broken once and for all?

	1970	1975	1980	1983	1985	1987	1990	2000
Members	100	12,000	25,000	60,000	95,000	120,000	190,000	240,000
Ministers	0	10	200	450	745	1,150	2,000	2,300
Congregations	1	180	340	700	1,150	1,900	3,400	3,800

Estimated figures for House Church Movement and fellowships of the same type not covered by House Church Movement leaders (*UK Christian Handbook 1989/90* and *1992/93*).

See also: Independent Churches.
Source: Article by Rod Boreham, editor of Team Spirit magazine 'Tomorrow Today' and compiler of the 'Body Book' and LM 89/2.

Household tasks

Who does the various jobs in any household, the man or the woman? And in an ideal family, who should do what? These questions were asked of 1,120 married people in 1984 and the results published in the British Social Attitudes Survey Report. 283 people who had never been married (so excluding widowed, divorced or separated respondents) were also asked who should do various tasks ideally. The results are given below with those replying 'don't know' excluded.

	Allocation of household tasks								
	Married people						Never-married people		
	Actual			Ideal			Ideal		
	Mainly man	Mainly woman	Shared equally	Mainly man	Mainly woman	Shared equally	Mainly man	Mainly woman	Shared equally
	%	%	%	%	%	%	%	%	%
Washing and ironing	1	90	9	0	79	21	0	69	31
Preparing evening meal	5	79	16	1	63	36	1	50	49
Household cleaning	3	74	23	0	53	47	1	42	57
Looking after sick children	1	64	35	0	51	49	0	49	51
Household shopping	6	55	39	0	36	64	0	31	69
Washing up	18	39	43	12	22	66	13	15	72
Organising household money and bills	33	39	28	24	16	60	20	16	64
Teaching children discipline	10	12	78	12	5	83	16	4	80
Repairing household equipment	86	6	8	81	2	17	76	0	24

While 90% of British people in a later 1990 survey thought women had a right to work whatever their family situation, one could rightly assume that many of the men who answered would have added, 'so long as they do the housework too'.

The survey found that most married or cohabiting women had no help with washing, ironing, cooking and cleaning. Men fulfilled their traditional roles of doing repairs and getting spiders out of the bath. Not surprisingly, 77% of respondents believed equality had yet to be achieved.

It is reported that in central European countries, the same situation is normal — but here most women have no choice but to work. They also have rather less choice as to the size of the family since family planning is rare, and without such labour-saving devices as washing-machines and freezers, they spend over 30 hours a week on housework.

It seems that microwaves, supermarkets and the pill lighten the burden on women in more economically developed countries. But neither Communist nor Western ideals of equality will make men take a share of it.

This issue will be increasingly relevant for Western European countries in coming years. With the falling birthrate, employers will be trying to attract more married women back into the workforce. The Church needs to be sure the 'Christian' attitude to a woman's role is based on thought-out Biblical principles rather than convenient stereo-types.

See also: Women.
Source: BSA 1984 Report, Social and Community Planning Research, Gower 1985.
NOP Political, Social & Economic Review, Number 79 January 1990 and the
Independent 2 July 1990, LM 90/4.

Households

The diversity of family groups present in private households in 1990 in Great Britain was high. Just 25% of households consisted of a married or

Proportions of types of household and the persons they represent 1990

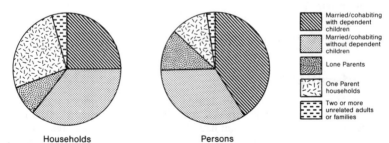

Households   Persons

Married/cohabiting with dependent children

Married/cohabiting without dependent children

Lone Parents

One Parent households

Two or more unrelated adults or families

cohabiting couple and dependent children (that is, those either aged under 16 or aged 16-18 and in full-time education), although such family units comprised 41% of all people. An additional 36% of households contained a married or cohabiting couple who had no dependent children, though 8% contained non-dependent children. These family units made up 34% of all people. A further 9% of households contained a lone parent with either dependent children (5%) or only non-dependent children (4%). One person households accounted for 26% of all households, but only 11% of individuals. The remaining 4% of households contained two or more unrelated adults or two or more families.

Source: OPCS General Household Survey Monitor 1991.

Domestic expenditure

What people spend their money on is shown in the following table:

Average UK household expenditure 1989	
	%
Food	19
Housing	17
Transport	15
Leisure	13
Household goods and services	13
Clothing and footwear	7
Alcohol and tobacco	7
Fuel, light and power	5
Other items	4
Total	100

Where should giving to the church and charity be put and how much should it be?

See also Families; Tenure.
Source: Regional Trends 26, HMSO 1991.

Huddersfield

Robin Hood is reputed to be buried in the ruined priory north of Huddersfield from which Kirklees, meaning 'church meadow' takes its name. The industrial revolution had important origins in the area, while north-eastern Kirklees has connections with the Brontës. The BBC television series *Last of the Summer Wine* is filmed in Holmfirth.

With a population of 376,000, Kirklees is one of the five district councils in West Yorkshire. Almost surrounded by the dramatic Pennine moorlands, it covers an area of 160 square miles extending from the high moorlands eastwards to the edge of Leeds and Wakefield. Textiles and engineering are the industrial mainstay of the area. The textile industry provides about 15% of jobs, with a further 11% in engineering. In all 43% of jobs are in some type of manufacturing.

In 1979 a sixth of the adult population was a church member. In the same year one in 12 people actually attended church. By 1986 one in six was still a church member. Of these, three-fifths were Roman Catholic, the rest belonging to one of the Protestant churches. On any Sunday in 1986 one in 10 of the adult population could be found in church. This increase came mostly from Pentecostals, Independent Christian fellowship and Afro/ West Indian churches. Roman Catholic church attendance remained relatively static during this period.

Teenagers have long been noted for their absence from church. In Huddersfield the proportion of teenagers attending is more or less what can be expected, about one in eleven of the total teenage population. Figures for child attendance, available only from Protestant churches, have fallen from 7.5% in 1982 for those under 15, to 7% of the total child population in the area. However, some of the smaller churches, particularly the Christian Fellowships and Afro-Caribbean churches are showing signs of increasing child and teenage attendance, but overall, the proportion of children who attend church in South Kirklees is substantially lower than the proportion of adults.

The Kirklees Church is not untypical in its age and sex structure. As far as children are concerned, there will be three girls for every two boys in Sunday School against an equal number of boys and girls in the population.

The real weakness of the Church in this area lies among people in their 20s. Again, only one in 11 of churchgoers are in this age-group, against one in seven of the total population. Men in particular are missing. The 30 to 44 year olds in the population, one in five, correspond quite closely to the one in six found in church. Again, the male presence leaves something to be desired. This inequality of male and female does not diminish throughout the different age groups, increasing considerably for those age 65 and over where females dominate because of their longevity — 16% of churchgoers are women in this age category, only 6% men.

These figures highlight a situation where two-thirds of those who attend church are female, in comparison with a local population where female predominance is by no means apparent. While this inequality of the sexes is not confined to Huddersfield, the area does show a greater weakness in the teens and 20s than the national figures.

In many ways the church in South Kirklees reflects the national situation; short of men and younger people, needing to encourage more outreach and evangelism. It is through surveying the numerical as well as spiritual state of the church that such weaknesses in the church population can be identified and strategies for improvement put into effect.

Source: Article adapted from Who Goes There? survey conducted into aspects of church life in South Kirklees, MARC Monograph 15 1989, LM 87/2.

Humberside

Area (sq km)	Population 1989			Percentage change 1979-89	Percentage under 15	Non-churchgoers 1989
	Men	Women	Total			
3,512	416,400	439,900	856,300	−0.2%	20%	793,300

Churchgoers 1989			Percentage of population	Percentage change 1979-89	Percentage under 15	Number of churches	Percentage built	
Men	Women	Total					before 1500	since 1950
24,600	38,400	63,000	7.4%	−11.1%	25%	693	26%	13%

District	Area (sq km)	Population 1989	Percentage change 1979-89
			%
Kingston-upon-Hull	71	245,100	−12.9
Beverley	404	115,200	+9.7
Great Grimsby	28	90,200	−3.2
East Yorkshire	1,044	87,800	+21.2
Glanford	580	73,100	+11.6
Cleethorpes	164	68,200	−0.9
Boothferry	647	65,600	+10.2
Scunthorpe	34	59,600	−12.6
Holderness	540	51,500	+13.8

Source: Regional Trends 26, HMSO 1991 and English Church Census.

Illegitimacy

More than one in four babies in Britain are now born outside of marriage, a trend which shows no sign of decreasing. Tom Griffin, the editor of *Social Trends,* the government's summary of British statistics, said 'If this trend continues, by the end of the century no baby will be born in wedlock'. And 14% of children lived in one-parent families in 1989, twice the proportion in 1971.

Live births outside marriage as percentage of all births

	1981	1989
	%	%
North	13	31
Yorkshire and Humberside	14	29
North-West	16	33
East Midlands	13	27
West Midlands	13	28
East Anglia	10	22
South-East (North)	9	20
Greater London	17	30
South-East (South)	10	23
South-West	10	23
England	13	27
Wales	11	28
Scotland	12	26
N Ireland	7	17
United Kingdom	13	27

The consequences of such figures are likely to be a continuing and even accelerating break-up of family structures. A survey in the USA showed teenage girls living in fatherless homes are 60% more likely to have experienced sex than those living with both parents.

Source: Social Trends 20, HMSO 1990, Regional Trends 26, HMSO 1991, LM 90/3.

Immigrants

The number of immigrants to the United Kingdom was 250,000 in 1989. This compares with 201,000 in 1984 and 197,000 in 1975. Offsetting this increase, 205,000 people emigrated in 1989, 164,000 in 1984 and 238,000 in 1975.

The majority of immigrants came from the Commonwealth countries;

others from America, South Africa, the Middle East and Pakistan. A small percentage came from other countries.

	1989 Immigrants	Percentage of total
		%
Commonwealth	96,000	38
Europe	69,000	28
USA	31,000	12
South Africa	12,000	5
Middle East	12,000	5
Pakistan	10,000	4
Other	20,000	8
Total	250,000	100

Overall, the number of immigrants is approximately one for every 230 (1989) of the present population. It is interesting that a predominant number are whites; more Australians (26,000) and New Zealanders (15,000) than Pakistanis.

What happens to these people once they arrive in the United Kingdom? Where do they settle? Over half settle in south-east England, more than one-third in the Greater London area.

Unless entrenched in their own religious culture, immigrants, like most newcomers, are open to new influences. Whilst it is not known how many are active Christians, many do come from 'Christian' countries, and may well have some form of church background they would like to pursue over here. It is an opportunity the church cannot afford to miss.

Source: Population Trends 63, OPCS, LM 87/4.

Income

Average annual gross salary of adult April 1990

	Men	Women
	%	%
North	13,800	9,400
Yorkshire and Humberside	13,900	9,400
North-West	14,300	9,700
East Midlands	14,000	9,400
West Midlands	14,000	9,400
East Anglia	14,600	9,700
South-East (North)	16,600	10,900
Greater London	19,900	13,500
South-East (South)	15,700	10,600
South-West	14,400	9,800
England	15,600	10,600
Wales	13,400	9,400
Scotland	14,400	9,700
N Ireland	13,200	9,400
United Kingdom	15,400	10,500

A key part of the church material resources is the money given to it. How much money is given varies in some measure with what people earn, which varies across the country as the table on the previous page shows.

It is easy to see the dominance of the higher salaries in the South-East and especially Greater London. Should churches in these areas 'twin' with churches in other parts of the country and share with them some of their financial resources?

There is also a huge disparity between what men and women earn. In Greater London, the average difference is over £6,000, but even in Northern Ireland where the difference is smaller it is still £3,800, equivalent to 29% of the male salary.

The UK figure is based on a male weekly income of £296 in 1990. This has increased over time as shown in the graph below, with the dotted line showing how the figure would have varied had it risen simply by the rate of inflation. Perhaps it is as well that it didn't!

Average weekly earnings for men 1970-1990

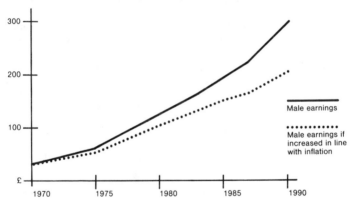

After tax, the average disposable household income in the United Kingdom in 1989 was £15,300. This is averaged over all households, whether they include children or retired people. 62% of this amount came through wages or salaries, 11% from Social Security payments, 10% from self-employment, 5% from investments, 5% from annuities and/or pensions and 7% from elsewhere. But the total per household varied greatly.

Disposable income	Percentage of households %
Under £4,200	16
£4,200 – 6,500	12
£6,501 – 9,100	10
£9,101 – 11,700	9
£11,701 – 16,900	18
£16,901 – 22,100	13
Over £22,100	22

If the average churchgoer's income was distributed in the same way, and they gave away 10% of their disposable income (though some teach we should tithe on money earned not money received) then £1,530 would be available. If half this were given to charity and half to the local church that would be the equivalent of nearly £15 per week per houshold to the church, or £6 per person. The reality is about £2 per person.

Source: Regional Trends 26, HMSO 1991, UKCH 1992/93.

Independent Churches

The explosive growth of the Independent churches was one of the most significant forces in English Church life in the 1980s, reveals the English Church Census.

Of the Independent churches 37% are so-called 'House Churches', 22% belong to the Fellowship of Independent Evangelical Churches, and others are Christian Brethren, chapels at Independent schools and other independent churches.

Independent churches attract many children, teenagers and people in their 20s and 30s, but lack older people, particularly over 65s. They are the only churches to have the same ratio of men and women as in the population, 49 to 51; churches overall have 42 men to 58 women.

Why are Independent churches popular? 'Because people want an experience of life on Sunday morning,' answered Clive Calver of the Evangelical Alliance. The Census did not explore reasons for the growth it charts, but two indicators did emerge.

Firstly, all the Churches which grew overall — Afro-Caribbean, Baptist, Independent and Pentecostal — are all characterised by the autonomy of local congregations. This may be linked to young people's distrust of institutions and dislike of denominational labels.

Adult churchgoers in the larger Independent groups 1979-1995

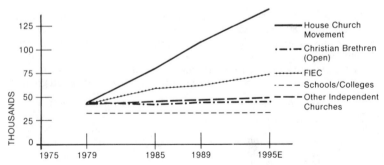

Secondly, growth in child attendance corresponded with growth in adult attendance — and the two fastest growing denominational groups are those where children are least likely to go to Sunday School. This suggests that services which involve the whole family attract whole families.

The commentary in *'Christian' England* adds that other research suggests 'visionary leaders' are an important factor in growth — the kind of leaders people want to follow. Other relevant factors seem to be that every member is valued and encouraged to be involved, and that a church is relevant, reaching out into its community.

Some would feel that House Churches tend to reflect these characteristics. One Bishop was reported as saying: 'I understand why people join House Churches. They feel they are joining something dynamic and useful, not just a holy club.'

See also: House Churches.
Source: LM 91/2.

Individualism

Western Europeans, for the most part, no longer worship God. What then determines their behaviour and their values? Here is a typical 'idol for today':

'Life is all about me. Not my community, not my family, but just me. I stand or fall alone. I am the master of my fate.' From a Christian viewpoint we disown such sentiments, but how do we reach those who espouse them? How do we help people to focus beyond their own well-being, or as Christians, to look beyond their own spiritual health?

Even trade unionists today talk less about collectivism and more about benefits to the individual, sounding much like the politicians. Joining clubs, societies, communities is less and less popular, and even the family unit is disintegrating. The church needs to find Christian answers, and we need to demonstrate the kind of love for one another that Jesus said would make us out as His.

Source: LM 91/1.

Inner cities

The number of people living in the inner city areas of Britain has been declining over the 20 years 1971-1991 and will continue to do so over the next two decades if current trends continue. Up to 6% fewer people will be living in metropolitan areas of England by 2001 than in 1983.

Population projections have dramatic implications for churches in these areas, as they plan ahead and seek to think through the implications of *Faith in the City,* the Archbishop's Commission Report published in 1985. If the population is slowly declining, should churches close and merge? Who will support the remaining church buildings? Can ministers be encouraged to care for churches as the surrounding population moves away?

However, the figures are good news for Sunday Schools. The number of children between 5 and 10 in inner London, for example, will rise 38% by the end of the century. What potential! But will there be enough teachers? While the population of inner city London may fall by 4% overall, there is expected to be a drop of 24% in pensioners — and in some inner city churches teachers come mainly from the retired members of the congregation.

The population of Birmingham will fall by a similar proportion to London's: 4%, but Sheffield and Manchester will drop 7%, Liverpool 13% and Newcastle an astonishing 15%. Against these declines the British population overall will increase by 3%.

So where are the people going? Buckinghamshire, Hampshire, Avon and East Anglia are among the most favoured areas. Is this following the motorway infrastructure? Or the microchip valleys? Should we expect to see rapid church building programmes in these areas? Or more House Churches? How will the church plan to reach these immigrants, for many people are open to a new approach on first moving? And what of the churches serving the inner city population left behind?

'Marriage breakdown, burglary, violence and vandalism are all higher in the inner city (in Britain) than elsewhere. There are more people living in bad housing, more single parent families, more old people living alone, more people without jobs. These are sort of things we mean by "poverty". Children who grow up under such pressures are at risk. They can find it hard to believe they matter — to God or anyone else.'

Source: New Society 4 July 1986 and LM 86. Outreach magazine, Scripture Union, October 1991.

Isle of Man

Estimated population 1989			Percentage change 1979-89	Percentage under 15	Non-churchgoers 1989
Men	Women	Total			
32,000	34,200	66,200	+8%	17%	57,400

Churchgoers 1989			Percentage of population	Percentage change 1979-89	Percentage under 15	Number of churches	Percentage built	
Men	Women	Total					before 1500	since 1950
3,500	5,300	8,800	13.3%	−22.1%	30%	108	12%	2%

Area of residence	Estimated population 1989	Percentage increase 1979-89
		%
Douglas	21,500	+0.9
Ramsey	6,200	+1.2
Peel	3,800	+0.5
Castletown	3,100	+0.4
All others	31,600	+0.8

Source: Isle of Man Census, ECC.

Isle of Wight

Area (sq km)	Population 1989			Percentage change 1979-89	Percentage under 15	Non-churchgoers 1989
	Men	Women	Total			
381	62,300	68,200	130,500	+13.3%	17%	118,000

Churchgoers 1989			Percentage of population	Percentage change 1979-89	Percentage under 15	Number of churches	Percentage built	
Men	Women	Total					before 1500	since 1950
5,000	7,500	12,500	9.6%	−10.6%	16%	161	23%	10%

District	Area (sq km)	Population 1989	Increase Percentage 1979-89
			%
Medina	117	73,000	+9.5
South Wight	264	57,500	+18.6

Source: Regional Trends 26, HMSO 1991 and English Church Census.

K

Kent

Area (sq km)	Population 1989			Percentage change 1979-89	Percentage under 15	Non-churchgoers 1989
	Men	Women	Total			
3,731	732,600	780,000	1,523,600	+3.3%	18%	1,386,600

Churchgoers 1989			Percentage of population	Percentage change 1979-89	Percentage under 15	Number of churches	Percentage built	
Men	Women	Total					before 1500	since 1950
57,500	79,500	137,000	9.0%	−9.0%	27%	1,177	32%	16%

District	Area (sq km)	Population 1989	Percentage change 1979-89 %
Rochester-upon-Medway	160	147,800	+3.5
Maidstone	394	137,400	+6.3
Canterbury	311	131,700	+9.8
Thanet	103	131,300	+9.8
Swale	369	116,800	+7.7
Dover	312	107,100	+4.4
Sevenoaks	371	105,800	−6.7
Tonbridge and Malling	240	100,400	+3.3
Tunbridge Wells	331	99,300	+1.1
Ashford	581	95,600	+12.7
Gillingham	32	94,600	−2.5
Shepway	357	88,800	+3.9
Faversham	100	88,700	−9.8
Dartford	70	78,400	+0.3

Source: Regional Trends 26, HMSO 1991 and English Church Census.

L

Lancashire

Area (sq km)	Population 1989			Percentage change 1979-89	Percentage under 15	Non-churchgoers 1989
	Men	Women	Total			
3,063	674,900	715,900	1,390,800	+0.5%	19%	1,199,200

Churchgoers 1989			Percentage of population	Percentage change 1979-89	Percentage under 15	Number of churches	Percentage built	
Men	Women	Total					before 1500	since 1950
78,600	113,000	191,600	13.8%	−14.0%	23%	1,034	8%	14%

District	Area (sq km)	Population 1989	Percentage change 1979-89
			%
Blackpool	35	143,100	−5.0
Blackburn	137	135,700	−6.0
Lancaster	577	130,800	+5.5
Preston	142	128,400	+2.0
W Lancashire	332	104,500	−3.4
Wyre	283	103,700	+5.5
South Riddle	111	101,600	+4.6
Chorley	205	96,700	+7.8
Burnley	118	90,900	−4.2
Pendle	168	85,100	−1.7
Hyndburn	73	79,200	−0.4
Fylde	165	73,200	+7.7
Rossendale	138	65,400	+0.9
Ribble Valley	579	52,400	−0.5

Source: Regional Trends 26, HMSO 1991 and English Church Census.

Leicestershire

Area (sq km)	Population 1989			Percentage change 1979-89	Percentage under 15	Non-churchgoers 1989
	Men	Women	Total			
2,553	440,900	451,000	891,900	+4.9%	20%	21,800

Churchgoers 1989			Percentage of population	Percentage change 1979-89	Percentage under 15	Number of churches	Percentage built	
Men	Women	Total					before 1500	since 1950
28,700	41,400	70,100	7.9%	−19.1%	25%	777	37%	12%

District	Area (sq km)	Population 1989	Percentage change 1979-89
			%
Leicester	73	279,700	−1.5
Charnwood	279	149,300	+8.2
Hinckley & Bosworth	298	97,600	+13.8
Blaby	130	84,300	+11.9
NW Leicestershire	280	80,400	+2.0
Harborough	593	68,100	+13.7
Oadby & Wigston	24	51,500	−3.6
Melton	482	44,100	+1.8
Rutland	394	36,800	+14.1

Source: Regional Trends 26, HMSO 1991 and English Church Census.

Life expectancy

England
How long can people alive in the 1990s expect to live? The table below, taken from the *English Life Tables* published by OPCS, gives the answer.

	Years of expected life								
Age	0	10	20	30	40	50	60	70	80
Men	70	62	53	43	33	24	16	10	6
Women	77	68	58	48	38	29	21	13	7

Currently, average life expectancy for men is 73, for women 78, though many live beyond this, particularly women.

This contrasts with the figures 70 years ago. Before the First World War men could expect to live only until their early 60s, often dying earlier still, depending on their trade or livelihood. Women in the same period lived until their late 60s or early 70s on average. With the increase in the standard of living, better health care and all that the late 20th century is able to provide there are more old people in society than ever before. What are the implications for the church?

What is the present age structure of your fellowship? How many will still be with you in 10 years' time? How many people do you need to join your church over the next 10 years just to maintain your present position?

The following table gives the percentage of adults likely to die in the next 10 years:

Current age	Men	Women
	%	%
15-19	0.9	0.3
20-29	0.9	0.5
30-44	2.2	1.5
45-64	15.0	8.7
65 plus	33.0	30.0

Without sufficient foresight and planning for evangelism the church could severely diminish in numbers as this century draws to its close.

The World

What of children who do survive in the harsh conditions in many parts of the world? What is their life expectancy? This table compares life expectancy at birth in 1950 and 1986.

	Life expectancy in years	
	1950	1986
Africa	38	51
South Asia	39	56
South East Asia	41	59
West Asia	45	63
Central and South America	50	65
China and East Asia	45	69
Industrialised countries	66	73
World	46	61

See also: Death, Seventh Day Adventists.
Source: LM 87/2 and 87/3.

Life satisfaction

What makes some people more satisfied with life than others? Some new research from an Australian survey yields some surprising answers.

The most important ingredient of a satisfying life is marriage. This is particularly striking because the quality of the marriage was not measured in any way.

The second most important source of a satisfying life was churchgoing. (Holding to Christian beliefs had no independent impact on life-satisfaction.) Those who attended church regularly reported significantly higher levels of life-satisfaction than those who said they had no religion. There was no difference between the major denominations.

Income was also found to be significant — people with higher incomes reported higher levels of satisfaction in life. It is encouraging to note that the old and the young lead equally satisfying lives, as do men and women.

Source: Jonathan Kelly and Mariah Evans, Ingredients of a Good Life, in National Social Science Survey Report, Australia, Vol 2, No 4, 1990 and LL September 1991.

Lincolnshire

Area (sq km)	Population 1989			Percentage change 1979-89	Percentage under 15	Non-churchgoers 1989
	Men	Women	Total			
5,915	288,200	298,700	586,900	+7.8%	18%	531,400

Churchgoers 1989			Percentage of population	Percentage change 1979-89	Percentage under 15	Number of churches	Percentage built	
Men	Women	Total					before 1500	since 1950
22,200	33,300	55,500	9.5%	−8.4%	26%	948	43%	7%

District	Area (sq km)	Population 1989	Percentage change 1979-89
			%
East Lindsay	1,762	119,200	+16.5
South Kesteven	943	105,800	+9.7
North Kesteven	923	85,000	+7.4
Lincoln	36	80,900	+7.3
West Lindsay	1,154	76,700	−1.4
South Holland	737	66,800	+9.2
Boston	360	52,400	−0.4

Source: Regional Trends 26, HMSO 1991 and English Church Census.

Listed buildings

When Jesus warned His followers to count the cost of following Him, He wasn't referring to the upkeep of historic listed buildings. And yet it would seem that a vast number of Christians in England today must include maintenance of ancient roofs and walls in the price of belonging to a congregation. That is, if they follow Christ the Anglican way.

In December 1985 there were 12,000 listed Anglican churches in England alone, and 1,200 Free churches, mostly Methodist. A quarter of English counties have 95% of their Anglican churches listed. Only in four northern counties — Durham, Greater Manchester, Merseyside and Humberside — does the figure drop to 30% or below. In all, 70% of Anglican churches are listed.

Norfolk is most burdened, the Norwich diocese having 711 churches in this category. Least burdened is Cleveland in the Durham diocese with only 27 listed buildings, or half its Anglican churches. Perhaps most typical is the situation in Kent, where 465 buildings are of listed status. So much for the figures, what of the costs?

The Church of England is reputed to be wealthy in land and historic buildings: United Kingdom churches of all denominations were valued at £11,000 million in 1985. But how much does this affluence signify when the cost of maintaining a single church can run into tens of thousands of pounds? Obviously all the fêtes, jumble sales and goodwill in the world can make little impact on a bill of such proportions.

And then there is the problem of major repair work. All Souls Church, Langham Place, in the heart of London's West End, spent £765,000 renovating the interior of its magnificent building in 1975/76. In 1986 it cost a further £700,000 to give the outside of the church a complete facelift.

Neither can the government offer a solution. The Historic Buildings Council, part of the government, gave £4.3 million in the period 1983/4, an average of a mere £360 per church. Just enough to pay one skilled workman for two weeks, but not enough to supply him with the necessary materials to do the job. Or, to put it another way, enough to renovate just six All Souls.

Counties where 80% or more of Anglican churches are listed buildings

Counties where 80% or more of Anglican churches are listed buildings

Of course, in practice many churches received more, finding in a few instances assistance from a wealthy diocese. The St Albans diocese in Bedfordshire came top of the list, its churches averaging £1,190 in diocesan grants apiece. The lowest grant was awarded to the Durham diocese of Tyne and Wear where churches were allocated just £10 each on average. Though having fewest listed buildings of any county, it would seem that the Anglicans in Durham do not have an easy time with their ecclesiastical inheritance.

Still more grim is the picture in South Yorkshire and the Isle of Wight, both of which received no diocesan grants.

The overall impression is a sad one. Many Anglican churches and cathedrals are renowned both locally and further afield for their architecture. It is easier, though by no means easy, to maintain your building as a Free church minister. In many cases these straightforward buildings can be adapted to the needs of the congregation. More and more congregations in Free churches are buying or building according to modern notions of comfort, warmth and adaptability.

The Anglican church faces quite a different picture. All too often the congregation has to adapt to the building; after all there is only so much time, energy and money to go around. Furthermore, if a local church has to maintain an expensive building, how much of a drain is it on the congregation's ministry and how long will it be before maintaining the building becomes the chief focus? What then? Is it a question of which comes first: your church or your people? Have missions and other initiatives shrivelled in the bud because of energies absorbed in the upkeep of the building? Is it time to abandon the old buildings and follow the example of the Free churches and the House Church Movement? Or do congregations, who give an estimated £50 million pounds a year towards church maintenance, see the upkeep of their beautiful buildings as a ministry in itself?

Source: Article by Anne Coomes, LM 86/4.

Literacy

A survey by the MORI organisation in 1990 showed that in a sample of young people aged 16 to 20, 25% felt their reading ability was inadequate, and 33% reported spelling problems. A new charity, 99 by 99, has subsequently been set up to enable 99% of children to leave school with 'adequate literacy for living and working' by 1999. How literate do we expect our young people to be?

Source: The Bookseller, Jennifer Taylor article, 30 August 1991, page 567.

London

See Greater London.

Lone parents

The number of families with dependent children headed by lone parents in Great Britain increased during both the 1970s and the 1980s, from 8% of households in 1971 to 13% in 1981 and to 19% in 1990. The proportion of such families headed by lone fathers is 1 or 2%; the majority has always been lone mothers. The average number of children in lone parent families has decreased slightly, from 1.8 in 1971 to 1.6 in 1981 and remained at 1.6 throughout most of the 1980s and in 1990. The following table gives details of *single parents with dependent children* (either under 16 or 16 to 18 in full-time education, in the family unit, and living in the household). The table excludes other types of household, such as single parents without dependent children.

	1971	1975	1981	1985	1988	1990
	%	%	%	%	%	%
Lone mothers	7	9	11	12	15	18
who are single	(1)	(2)	(2)	(3)	(5)	(6)
widowed	(2)	(2)	(2)	(1)	(1)	(1)
divorced	(2)	(3)	(4)	(5)	(6)	(7)
separated	(2)	(2)	(3)	(3)	(3)	(4)
Lone father	1	1	2	2	1	1
Married/cohabiting couple	92	90	87	86	84	81
Sample size (= 100%)	4,864	4,776	4,445	3,348	3,160	3,016

One-parent households are thus mostly mothers looking after one or more children. They are often lonely, economically disadvantaged, starved of friendship, rushed off their feet, but committed desperately to their children, working hard, making endless sacrifices for them. Such need all the help they can get from Christian people.

Depending on where you live in Britain the proportion of such households (out of all households) varied from 7% to 11% in 1990, with the country's average at 9%. This percentage has been rising though at about 1% per year.

How many people live in your area or parish? Divide that number by 2.5 if you live in England, 2.6 if in Wales, or Scotland, and 3.0 if you live in Northern Ireland to get the number of households. 9% of that figure is the number of single parents you have. What strategy are you adopting to reach them?

One London church had a parish of 10,000 population which meant 10,000 ÷ 2.5 = 4,000 households. In 1992 the percentage of one-parent households was 9% + 2% (1% for 1991 and 1992) = 11%. 11% of 4,000 is 440. 440 single parents on their doorstep! They asked for volunteers to visit them, gave them training, and made special arrangements to meet them, get to know them and help them. Several of those single mothers became Christians. Could your church do the same?

See also: Families, Households.
Source: OPCS General Household Survey Monitor 1991: Regional Trends 26, HMSO 1991.

Loneliness

A cross-section of people among the European populations were asked whether they would describe themselves as restless or lonely.

Nearly half the West Germans polled described themselves as restless, a third as lonely. Just over one-third of British people felt restless, but only one in seven lonely. The full figures are given below.

	Restless %	Lonely %
West Germany	45	33
United Kingdom	36	14
Netherlands	33	9
Spain	29	20
Italy	28	21
Belgium	27	15
Ireland	26	17
France	20	14
Denmark	19	8

It is interesting that more describe themselves as restless than lonely. Restlessness implies a desire for something better, something more. The result is a continual moving-on in the hope of attaining this. What should the Church be doing to combat such feelings among people? The Bible tells us that Christ can fulfil every need and set people free to be themselves. True satisfaction and security are to be found in God. Should churches be giving greater emphasis to this fact — that Christ is all in all?

In a recent survey 70% of dog-owners stated that their dog was their most loyal friend. And 84% of respondents said the greatest benefit of having a dog was the companionship provided.

Women more than men, older more than younger and blue-collar more than white-collar workers are likely to be lonely. People who are lonely are those who watch a lot of television, and, disconcertingly, they tend to be people who consider themselves very religious.

Familybase tell us that in a survey in a geriatric hospital, four out of five patients had a visitor less than once a week.

Source: LM 87/2, 89/3.

M

Manchester

See Greater Manchester.

Marriage

Only one in 100 marriages in the United Kingdom was a civil ceremony in 1838. By the turn of the century a third of marriages were solemnised outside the established Church. During the course of this century the proportion has increased; by 1990 almost half the weddings were civil ceremonies, as the table below shows, a slight fall on the 1980 figure.

Marriages in England and Wales

		Percentage civil ceremony
		%
1970	415,487	40
1975	380,620	48
1980	370,022	50
1985	346,389	49
1989	346,697	48

Many of the civil ceremonies were second marriages involving divorced people. Over 1,000 couples who divorced in 1979 were traced to see if either or both partners remarried quickly. 34% of men and 33% of women remarried during the first three months following their divorce.

The growing number of divorced people of both sexes and all ages provides an opportunity for witness and service to those who might never have any Christian contact otherwise.

A 1990 survey of engaged couples in the UK revealed that nearly 40% accepted that their marriage would not last. Indeed, 5% of brides and 4% of grooms admit to being unfaithful to their partner even before they reach the altar.

The couple are likely to have been engaged for around 18 months, having met at a party or disco. Only 5% of women and 4% of men will have had no previous partners but most of the fiancés are not bothered by this.

Although 91% of those surveyed will opt for a church wedding, it is more because it is traditional, or because they want a 'proper' wedding than for religious reasons. Nonetheless, it provides perhaps the first opportunity in a long time for serious thought about the Christian faith.

How old are people when they marry for the first time? 3% of men are under 20, 39% are aged 20 to 24, and 58% are 25 and over. But men tend to be older than women when they marry for the first time, for 10% of women are under 20, 51% aged 20 to 24, and only 39% are 25 and over.

Source: OPCS, Population Trends 48, Wedding and Home readers survey 1990, quoted in LM 87/3, 91/1.

Maternity care

In an examination of world childcare by UNICEF in 1986 it was found that in Africa only 59% of women have any infant care available and only 34% of all births are attended by qualified personnel, against 98% attended and 100% availability of infant care in the industrialised countries.

The situation is even worse in South Asia, where only 20% of births are attended by qualified staff. The following table shows the comparison around the world.

Estimated coverage of maternity care

1986 Percentage of births attended by qualified personnel	
	%
South Asia	20
Africa	34
Developing countries	48
South East Asia	53
West Asia	61
South America	64
East Asia	93
Industrialised countries	98
World	55

While 24% of the world's population live in industrialised countries, only 14% of all births occur there. The lack of maternity and infant care in the developing world is reflected in the number of children who survive. While there were 111 million births in developing countries in 1986, 14.1 million children up to the age of five died, as did 494,000 mothers. Contrast this with the 18 million births in industrialised countries, where, in comparison, 320,000 children under five and 6,000 mothers died.

But the situation is not just one of despondency, as all the figures of maternity care show an increase, if a slow one. The percentage of the world's children who survive past the first five years is increasing. The following figures highlight the change in various countries around the world.

Percentage who survive to reach the age of 5

	1960	1985
	%	%
Afghanistan	62	67
Ethiopia	71	74
Senegal	69	77
Yemen	62	79
Pakistan	72	83
India	72	84
South Africa	81	90
Iraq	78	90
Vietnam	77	90
USSR	95	97
Czechoslovakia	97	98
Israel	96	98
United Kingdom	97	99
USA	97	99
Australia	98	99
Japan	96	99
Sweden	98	99

Is such an imbalance throughout the world acceptable to 20th century Christians? The survival figures are disturbing and indicate the need for more responsible giving by Christians, specifically to funds used to benefit mothers and young children in real need.

Source: LM 87/3.

Media

How far the media truly effect opinions and attitudes awaits definitive research, but it is most unlikely that it has no effect at all. The average Briton watches 24 hours of television every week, rather less for children and rather more for older people. 90% of the population watch it once a day, and virtually everybody sometime during a week. Drama and light entertainment are the most popular, with audiences of 14 or even 20 million, but programmes such as *Songs of Praise* attract six million.

Radio is heard by half the population each day, with 8.15 am being the peak time with 10 million listeners. On average people listen to their Independent radio station for 13½ hours a week, Radio 1 for 11½ hours, Radio 4 10½, and their local BBC radio station eight hours a week.

In October 1989 the average daily sale of the 12 main daily newspapers was 15½ million, with a readership of some 40 million (a quarter choosing the *Sun*). The 10 Sunday newspapers sell over 18 million copies a week with a readership of over 42 million.

How good is this for Christianity? A morning religious programme on a local station will be listened to by about 60,000 people — equivalent to 15 years of preaching every week in the average sized church! What image do people have of the church? The key personalities are the Pope, Mother

Teresa, Billy Graham, Cliff Richard and the two Liverpool Bishops.

The media will always use good stories, raise religious issues in a graphic way, and can be encouraged to keep Christianity on the agenda — if we bother to use it!

See also: Radio broadcasting.
Source: Speakers at Tomorrow's Church Conference April 1991.

Megacity

Megacities are those with over one million inhabitants. There were 256 such cities worldwide in 1985, a figure destined to double to 511 by 2010 if present trends continue. Figures for the continents are given below:

Number of megacities by continent 1990-2020

	1990	2000	2010	2020	Percentage change 1990-2020	Percentage of total 1990	2020
					%	%	%
Africa	35	59	83	98	+180	12	17
Americas	75	95	113	127	+69	25	21
Asia	116	170	229	280	+141	39	47
Europe	43	47	48	49	+14	14	8
Old USSR	24	31	32	35	+46	8	6
Oceania	5	6	6	7	+40	2	1
World Total	298	408	511	596	+100	100	100

The proportions increase in Africa and Asia but decrease elsewhere. Urban evangelism will become more and more important in these two continents in the early 21st century. What steps do we take now to help meet those challenges?

Source: Together magazine Sept-Oct 1991, Page 15.

Men and Christ

Men Called by God is written by Jim Smith, an evangelist with Church Pastoral-Aid Society and author of three Christian books on men, and this article.

'But, vicar, why are there so few men in our church?' I've heard this comment at church meetings throughout England, and it expresses a serious situation in our fellowships. The population is 49% male, and yet most churches have nothing like this percentage in their congregation. On average, there are rather more women than men; in some fellowships there are two women to every man and the situation doesn't appear to be getting any better.

Yet men are not anti-Christianity. On a recent tour of this country, I spoke to 6,000 men over 20 nights. When asked, most had non-Christian male friends, and the majority of these were not anti-Christianity.

So where is the problem?

It is partly to do with male psychology. Men

- are easily embarrassed, and the church is seen as a place where doing the wrong thing is very easy
- feel that church is a woman's place
- don't see the need for God or Church
- are too honest — they know that there is much wrong in their lives, and feel that they cannot come into the presence of a holy God in this condition
- feel that the challenge of Christ is not put in a masculine way.

I am convinced that the starting point for dealing with the problem is to look at the lives of men who do believe in Christ. Many of us are not living the kind of life which shows our friends the difference that Christ makes. Our personal lives, our marriages, our home lives, our working or non-working lives, our social activities, should all be challenged by the presence of a vibrant and dynamic Christ living in and through us. If this isn't the case — and for many of us it isn't — then our friends won't see the difference and won't bother with Christ. In fact a lifeless faith may only confirm them in their unbelief.

Challenges

The real challenge is to those of us who do know God. Are we truly Christlike? Are we shaped and changed by Him? Have the men in your fellowship ever sat down together and, over a period of weeks or months, discussed what it means to be a Christian man and the differences and difficulties this raises? All over this country we need to do this, to lay the foundation for a genuine outreach to the non-Christian men of our land in the years to come. We cannot neglect the work at this stage, however painful it may be and however long it takes.

A beginning is being made. As groups of men take their position in Christ seriously, they are finding a concern and a basis for reaching their non-Christian friends. Men's mission suppers, breakfasts, study groups, working parties, prayer fellowships; all sorts of things are beginning to happen. For them to continue we must be prepared to allow Christ to change and fill us continually.

Not God's will

I do not believe that the situation in England is God's will. He has not ordained that the Church lacks men and I believe we can turn the tide if we are prepared for the effort. It has saddened me to discover how many churches and ministers have given up believing in God for an answer to the problem. Instead of condemning these men, often working under intense pressure, we should encourage them to believe that the situation is not hopeless.

I have four sons and I want them to grow into Christian men, men who serve God alongside other men in the Church. This is not detrimental to the women in our fellowships; without them many churches would not survive, but a male-female balance is necessary. Has God placed the future of men in the Church in the hands of present believers? I think He has. The question remains whether we are equal to the challenge.

Source: LM 87/4.

Men's lifestyle

Men are outnumbered in church congregations. English churches have 58 women to 42 men on average, with some denominations having over six women to four men. And over the 10 years 1979-1989, the proportion of men declined by 3%.

A major consumer research survey on the lifestyle of men in Britain has useful insights to those concerned about the church's failure to reach them. It shows some major shifts from traditional roles and stereotypes.

Image

British men are no longer trying to portray a 'macho' image. Being seen as sophisticated, successful or 'one of the lads', let alone chivalrous, are not self-images which received high ratings in the survey.

The modern man, or so he says, is far more interested in being perceived as understanding, sensitive, loyal and trustworthy. In a church situation, this might mean young men appreciate being given responsibilities with visible accountability.

Work

The survey points out drastic changes in the age-structure of the male population. In the year 2000, there will be one million fewer 20 to 29 year olds and half a million more 0 to 19 year olds.

The traditional dominance of men in the workforce will change, as employers encourage women to return to work. While numbers of working men are likely to remain static, it is predicted that 700,000 more women will be working by the year 2000. With more women professionals too, this also implies a rise in the number of wealthy households with two skilled workers.

Leisure and looks

While going to the pub and playing snooker are still top leisure activities for men, 30% of those surveyed said they last went to the pub more than a year ago. What activities for men does your local church provide?

As further evidence for the decline of the 'macho' image, the survey found that men are more domesticated than their forebears and are concerned about their appearance. Men are just as likely as women to be into healthy eating, and it is fashionable for men to buy special toiletries for their skin and hair. With regard to what they wear, 18% say they are actively interested in fashion, and 30% want their clothing to reflect their personality. What image do church leaders project by the way they dress?

Ambition

The researchers were surprised to find that although most men recognise a connection between status and earning power, few seemed to mind. Just 10% of men admitted to spending more than they can afford to keep up appearances.

And while men are no less ambitious, the survey concluded that the ambition to get rich and buy things has been superseded by the desire to spend money having a good time now. The researchers note 'a strong hedonistic streak in the ambitions of men, with a good life in terms of leisure taking its place alongside success at work'. Christian men need to know in their experience and demonstrate to their friends and colleagues that living for Christ is better than living for yourself or for work or anything else. How do we help them to do that?

Source: Mintel, British Lifestyle 1990, and LM 91/3.

Merseyside

Area (sq km)	Population 1989			Percentage change 1979-89	Percentage under 15	Non-churchgoers 1989
	Men	Women	Total			
652	697,200	750,800	1,448,000	−5.8%	20%	1,234,900

Churchgoers 1989			Percentage of population	Percentage change 1979-89	Percentage under 15	Number of churches	Percentage built	
Men	Women	Total					before 1500	since 1950
87,400	125,700	213,100	14.7%	−17.0%	26%	750	3%	24%

District	Area (sq km)	Population 1989	Percentage decrease 1979-89 %
Liverpool	113	465,900	−12.2
Wirral	158	336,200	−1.6
Sefton	151	299,600	−0.4
St Helens	133	188,800	−1.0
Knowsley	97	157,500	−11.7

Source: Regional Trends 26, HMSO 1991 and English Church Census.

Missionaries in Europe

Over 3,800 North American missionaries were working in Western Europe in 1988. France had the highest number, over 700, and West Germany over 660.

There's no doubt that Western Europe these days is a mission field, but many people question the need of American missionaries there. Many Americans have returned to the USA or Canada, disillusioned by the problems and hostility encountered in countries where they felt they were returning to their roots.

Based on extensive experience as well as research, the doctoral thesis written by Bill Wagner, of the Foreign Missions Board of the Southern Baptist Convention, gives not only an overview of the history, nature and motives of American missions in Europe, but a thorough critique of the problems encountered and the failure, as well as successes, experienced.

He looks at questions some American missionaries didn't expect to have to answer — of differences in theology and attitudes between American and European Protestant churches, of the rights and wrongs of planting new churches where old ones already exist, and of the extent to which the indigenous church or the mission should call the tune.

He recommends future actions to highlight areas where Americans could have a strategic role in Europe.

Source: North American Protestant Mission in Europe: A Critical Appraisal, by Dr William L Wagner 1988, quoted in LL June 1990.

Missionaries in the Third World

Almost 30% of the world's Protestant missionaries are from the 'two-thirds world' — Africa, Asia, Latin America, and Oceania. Although comparison is complicated by problems of definition, the growth-rate of 'emergent missions' has been calculated as five times that of missions from Western countries. If this is maintained, by the year 2000 more missionaries will come from countries we tend to think of as on the receiving end than come from the West.

This may challenge some of our assumptions about Christian work; might it also shake us out of our complacency?

Number of missionaries from the 'two-thirds world' working in Europe

Austria	5
Belgium	11
Cyprus	3
France	26
West Germany	144
Italy	8
Malta	3
Netherlands	15
Portugal	41
Spain	48
Switzerland	4
UK	75
Yugoslavia	1
Total	384

Source: From Every People, a handbook of two-thirds world missions by Larry Pate, MARC International 1989, LM 90/1.

Mosque attendance

In June 1985 Dr Jim Holway, Deputy Headmaster, Winton School, Croydon, carried out an inquiry into attendance at mosques in the United Kingdom. The questions he set himself were:

(a) How many Muslims are there in Great Britain?

(b) Can they be identified by country of origin?

(c) What is their geographical distribution?

(d) How many mosques are there in Great Britain?

(e) What is the extent and pattern of mosque attendance?

Methodology: For questions a, b and c, a variety of sources was employed. No question on religious affiliation has been asked in a census of population in the United Kingdom since 1851. Information was therefore gathered from:

i.   Census analysis of private households. This provides information on the birthplace of the head of the household, size of household, and the number of dependent children born within and outside of the United Kingdom.

ii. Census analysis of all persons by their country of birth.

iii. The proportion of Muslims in the population of the countries of origin as reported in the *World Christian Encyclopedia.*

For questions d and e reference was made to the Registrar-General's register of places of worship. The register is a public document, open to inspection by appointment, maintained under the Places of Worship Registration Act of 1855. From the 1985 list of 314 mosques a selection of 183 was made on a subjective basis, aimed at achieving a reasonable geographical spread and covering towns of different sizes. A questionnaire and explanatory letter were sent out, from which 60 usable replies were received during the ensuing two months. The replies were not all completed in respect of every question asked.

The size, countries of origin and distribution of the Muslim population

An appraisal of information gathered from the sources mentioned above produced the figures shown in Table a, giving the distribution of Muslims in Great Britain in 1985. The estimated total was 852,000 of whom one-half live in the South-East, including London, and a further one-quarter in the West Midlands, Yorkshire and Humberside regions.

The total figure represents 1.6% of the population of Great Britain. Within the regions the Muslim population is heavily concentrated in the metropolitan areas. On the other hand, most towns in Great Britain have at least one Muslim family resident.

Table a:
Distribution of Muslims in Great Britain by standard region, 1985

Standard region	Population (nearest 100)	Percentage
		%
North	15,500	1.8
Yorkshire and Humberside	95,000	11.1
North-West	91,000	10.7
East Midlands	44,300	5.2
West Midlands	117,400	13.8
East Anglia	12,900	1.5
South-East	408,800	48.0
South-West	25,600	3.0
England	810,500	95.1
Wales	14,100	1.7
Scotland	27,400	3.2
Great Britain	852,000	100.0

The countries of origin of the Muslim population are shown in Table b. These figures include young people born in this country whose parents came from elsewhere. Bearing in mind that many of the Muslims coming from East and Central Africa originated from India a generation or more earlier, it would be fair to say that approximately 70% would acknowledge the Indian subcontinent as their ancestral home, and approximately 15% hail from the Arab lands. These proportions were reflected in the answers to the questionnaire about the vernaculars which were used.

Table b: Estimated numbers of Muslims in Great Britain
by the country of origin of the family, 1985

Country of origin	Number*	Percentage
		%
Pakistan	357,000	42.0
India	84,000	10.0
Bangladesh	64,000	7.5
Kenya	52,000	6.1
Iran	50,000	5.9
Egypt	34,000	4.0
Nigeria	25,000	2.9
Turkey	21,000	2.5
Tanzania	20,000	2.3
Uganda	15,000	1.8
Malawi	12,000	1.4
Libya	11,000	1.3
Morocco	10,000	1.2
Other Middle East	66,000	7.8
Other countries	27,000	3.3
Total	841,000	100.0

* (Rounded to the nearest thousand. Only numbers exceeding 10,000 listed.)

The number of Mosques

Many secular rooms and buildings were adapted for use as mosques as successive waves of Muslim immigrants came to this country. Increasingly purpose-built mosques are being erected. Mosques of all descriptions should be registered with the Registrar-General under the Places of Worship Registration Act of 1855. Hitherto only a small number have been registered, but the proportion is increasing. Table c gives the totals at 30 June each year, as supplied by the Registrar-General's Office. These figures are not completely accurate. Of letters to 183 mosques on this register, three were returned, marked 'mosque demolished'. These data are also displayed graphically in Figures a and b.

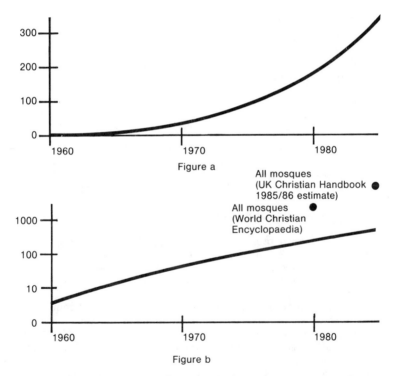

Figure a

All mosques
(UK Christian Handbook ●
1985/86 estimate)

All mosques ●
(World Christian
Encyclopaedia)

Figure b

From the questionnaire survey, information was supplied for about 134 mosques for approximately 137,000 Muslims, which is about one mosque for every one thousand Muslims and would gross up to 833 mosques for the whole country. The *UK Christian Handbook 1985/86* estimates 2,000 mosques in the country, but this includes a large number of temporary 'house mosques', roughly comparable to House Churches. The ratio of one mosque to one thousand Muslims is comparable to one church for every 790 Christians in the United Kingdom in 1980, given by the *World Christian Encyclopedia* (63,600 congregations for 50 million Christians) and one church for every 840 adult Christians in Great Britain in 1985-6, given by the *UK Christian Handbook 1985/86* (53,600 congregations for 45.2 million adult Christians).

Table c: Number of mosques registered as places of worship in England and Wales at 30 June annually, for various years

Year	Number of Mosques	Increase	Annual Percentage Increase
			%
1960	4	–	–
1965	8	4	15
1974	81	73	29
1979	169	88	16
1980	193	25	14
1981	223	30	16
1982	246	23	10
1983	268	22	8.9
1984	290	22	8.2
1985	314	24	8.3

After a rapid increase in registration in the 1970s, the present decade has seen a settling-down to a steady annual numerical increase. There has also been a steady increase in the number of mosques and of Muslim Appointed Persons registered for the celebration of marriages.

The pattern of mosque attendance

The questionnaire asked for estimates of the number of Muslims living in and around the town, or in the area. The population encompassed by the answers to these questions totalled 137,326, about one-sixth of the total Muslim community as shown in Table a. Respondents were asked to report on small towns — such as Aylesbury, Banbury and Bedford — or on localities in larger cities, such as Sparkhill (Birmingham), Croydon (London) and Rusholme (Manchester). The medium size of community reported was approximately 1,000. The numerical information received from respondents was analysed, and the results shown in Table d, sub-divided into 31 large communities (Group A) and 22 communities of 1,000 or less (Group B).

In Table d, item a is a calculation which assumes that the reporting mosques were of average size amongst the mosques in the neighbourhood. From it we see that approximately one-half of the Muslim community may be expected to attend a mosque during one of the main Muslim festivals. Among Muslims only men normally attend the mosque during the festivals. This would be particularly true of idul-Fitr, marking the end of Ramadan, the month of fasting. (The questionnaires were purposely sent out near this festival.)

Table d: Attendance at mosques

Item	Group A	Group B	Overall A + B
	%	%	%
a Festival attendance at the reporting mosque as proportion of the Muslim community in the area	41	63	51
b Friday attendance as proportion of Festival attendance	29	37	32
c Daily attendance as proportion of Festival attendance	6	12	8
d Attendance of children as proportion of Festival attendance			20
e Attendance of children as proportion of Friday attendance			65
f Women attending meetings at the mosque as proportion of Festival attendance			7
g Women attending meetings at the mosque as proportion of Friday attendance			21
h Attendance of children as proportion of attendance by women			309

Attendance at Friday prayers: Friday is the Muslim day of corporate prayer, corresponding to the Christian Sunday, although it is not necessarily a day of rest. The questionnaire asked for an estimate of the attendance at the mosque on Fridays, and Table d (b) indicates that approximately one-third of the adult male Muslim population attends the mid-day Juma prayers, despite the fact that Friday in the United Kingdom is a working day. Attendance is better in smaller communities.

Daily attendance at the mosque: Table d (c) shows that approximately one-tenth of the adult Muslim population attends a mosque daily. Muslims are required by their religion to say five ritual prayers daily but no restriction is placed on where these should be said. The fact that daily attendance is one-tenth of festival attendance suggests that the mosque is a centre of worship, and, particularly in small communities, it becomes a social centre for Muslim men, where the vernacular can be used. In this respect it resembles the place of the pub or club in English social life.

Classes for children: The questionnaire asked for the number of children attending a class at the mosque. Of the 55 mosques answering this question, seven reported a nil return. The attendance at the other 48 totalled 7,536 children, averaging 157 children per mosque. In relation to other figures calculated earlier, the ratio of 7,536 children to 38,226 attenders at these 48 mosques at festivals is shown in Table d (d) to be 20%, and in comparison with an attendance of 11,576 on Fridays at these same 48 mosques, the ratio was 65% — Table d (e). This suggests a rather low attendance of children. The *World Christian Encyclopedia* reported that in 1980 there were about 1,200 mosques and 5,000 Qur'an schools in the

United Kingdom, in other words, children receive their religious education from teachers at other places than mosques.

Classes for women: The questionnaire asked for the number of women attending a class at the mosque. There were 44 replies to this question, of which 20 said that no meeting was held. Of the 24 where a meeting was held, the attendance totalled 1,114, averaging 48 women at each mosque. For these 24 mosques the attendance figures were: Festivals 16,635, and Fridays 5,380. Table d (f) and (g) express women's attendance as percentages of these figures. Clearly, if women participated as much as men the percentages would each be 50%. Traditionally women do not worship at the mosque, and the 21% in Table d (g) compares very favourably with the mosque attendance of women in most of the countries of origin shown in Table b. It suggests an enhanced use in this country of the mosque as a focus of social life. For women it is a place where they can receive instruction in English, and in aspects of life in their new country, as well as religious instruction. It could also indicate a response on the part of both men and women to a more liberal attitude towards women than is found in some conservative Muslim societies.

Attendance of children: The questionnaire asked for the number of children attending the mosque. Twenty-one mosques indicated attendance of children and of women, and Table d (h) shows these figures as a ratio of 3:1, which seems a reasonable figure in relation to family size. If the *World Christian Encyclopedia* is correct in its estimate of 5,000 Qur'an schools, it follows that Muslim children are usually given religious instruction elsewhere than in the mosque.

Muslim denominations: Respondents were asked to comment on the attendance of members of the various sub-divisions of Islam. Of the 37 who mentioned the Sunni-Shia division, 21 mentioned Sunni only; one mentioned Shia only; and the remaining 15 reported a Sunni majority. Where a Sunni percentage was entered it ranged from 90 to 99%.

Some respondents claimed not to understand the phrase 'madhhab al-fiqh', which refers to the schools of Law found amongst both Sunnis and Shias. Amongst the Sunnis there were 15 replies. One stated that 'all madhhabs' were represented (unlikely). The others all reported that they followed the Hanafi madhhab, and one mentioned Shafii as well. The Shia respondent named the Jafferia madhhab. The predominance of Hanafi was a reflection of its majority position in India and Pakistan.

Five replies mentioned the presence of Sufi tariqs, the Naqshabandi and Allwijah being mentioned by name once each. At one mosque it was claimed that four tariqs were represented.

Vernaculars used besides English: Vernaculars were named 73 times. Their frequencies are shown in Table e. While these data are too few to draw any conclusions, they are not inconsistent with the percentages by country of origin tabulated in Table b.

Attitude of respondents: There was a response rate of about 35%. The format of the questionnaire and the wording of the letter were designed to allay the fears of a community who might fear racial harassment through

Table e: Use of vernaculars by mosque attenders

Vernacular	Number of times used	Percentage
		%
Arabic	8	11
Bengali	8	11
Gujarati	12	16
Malay	1	1
Persian	2	3
Punjabi	13	18
Urdu	29	40

the malicious manipulation of the information supplied. Where letters accompanied the replies, these were invariably courteous. There was no response from Ismaili sources. Two people wrote asking for further information regarding the purpose of the survey, but although a letter of explanation was sent, nothing further was heard from them.

Conclusion

The project showed the willingness of some Muslim leaders to divulge information about attendance at their mosques, and I am grateful for their co-operation.

Answers were obtained to the five originating questions, and are presented in the text of this report. The reliability of the numerical results has not been calculated with statistical rigour, and clearly it varies from item to item. I would suggest an accuracy of ± 1% for the data presented in Table c, ± 10% for Tables a and b, and no better than ± 20% for Tables d and e.

The general picture which emerges from this survey is of a religious community of close on one million people who have come from homelands in which an unchallenged Islam ruled their daily existence. Here in this country they have made the mosque a centre of religious and social life in which the old traditions can be perpetuated. Attendance by men at the major festivals is almost complete, and at other times it is as high as circumstances permit. As temporary mosques give way to permanent buildings the place of Muslims in society seems to be the better established.

But whether they wish it or not, Muslims are unlikely to remain unaffected by the values of the non-Muslims among whom they live. To give but one example revealed by this survey — for various reasons women frequent mosques to a greater degree in this country than they do in Muslim countries.

Europe's largest mosque

The largest mosque so far in Europe opened in Madrid in 1990. The white marble building has a 100 foot high minaret, and is a gift from King Fahd of Saudi Arabia to the 80,000 Muslims living in Spain.

Source: Article by Dr Jim Holway, in UK Christian Handbook 1987/88 edition. The Church Around the World, January 1990, and LM 90/3.

N

Nairobi

The population of Kenya is growing faster than any other country's and the cities are growing even more rapidly. There are about 500 new people every day in Nairobi, half coming from other parts of the country to find work.

The Summary of the Nairobi Church Survey, published by Daystar University College, shows that the Church has seen tremendous growth, multiplying five times in the last 25 years. But as a proportion of the population, it has remained roughly the same. Just to keep up with future population growth, each congregation will need to plant two new churches of the same size every year — three times the current rate — and more than this if the Church is to grow.

Population growth of Nairobi

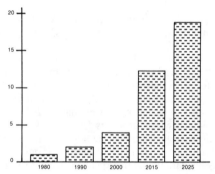

Nominalism

Researchers visited 600 congregations, questioned 1,500 churchgoers and interviewed 400 ministers to present this detailed survey of church life in Nairobi. Correcting the impression that Nairobi is teeming with lively Christians, the survey found that only 8% of people in the capital go to church every Sunday, 20% each month. Although 80% of the city's people claim to be Christians, 75% of these never go to church: nominalism is far from being only a European problem.

Unreached groups

There are 800 churches in Nairobi, one for every 2,000 people, but the average congregation is 200 strong, with over half having under 100. The churches are not evenly distributed, and the survey highlights the needs of the poorer parts of the city, which are the most densely populated, the Asian areas and some large housing estates with no churches.

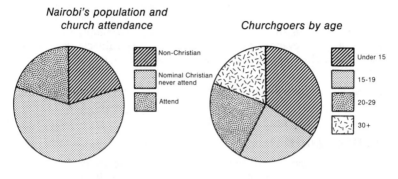

Nairobi's population and church attendance

Churchgoers by age

There are fewer men than women in most congregations, despite there being three men for every two women in the population as a whole. The age of churchgoers reflects the young population — over 70% are under 30, 30% under 14. Church people tend to be better educated and thus better off than average. Both the very poor and the very rich are groups which are largely unreached.

Churchgoers' educational level

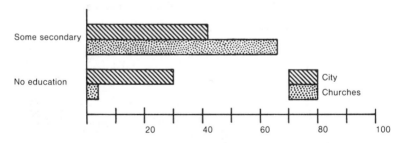

Commitment

The researchers found that for over two-thirds of those who do not go to church, going to the Sunday service was the extent of their involvement. Most ministers felt that their congregations were not interested in sharing their faith with others. Rather they see evangelism as the responsibility of the minister.

The leaders themselves saw their main problems as lack of time, money and training; half of them work in other paid jobs. The report suggests teaching ministers to equip lay people to take responsibility for pastoral work, especially evangelism. This will be essential if the churches are to take up the challenges so graphically highlighted by the results of this survey.

Source: Summary of the Nairobi Church Survey, Daystar University College, and LL June 1990.

Netherlands

It must be tempting to define the Dutch people as predominantly Protestant, but this would be an inaccuracy, according to the *Handboek van Christelijk Nederland* published in 1986. In 1985, throughout the Netherlands as a whole, 56% of Church members were Roman Catholic, 29% Dutch Reformed, 11% other Reformed and 4% other Protestant.

Church membership in the Netherlands is relatively static despite population increases. Membership stood at 61% of the population in 1975, but was only 57% in 1980.

Growth
Whilst overall membership may be static, growth is evident in particular groups. The Orthodox church and the Pentecostal Assemblies of God have been on the increase. The largest growth has taken place among the independent Evangelical and Pentecostal fellowships, from 195 churches in 1980 to 274 in 1985 — an average of 16 new churches every year.

Membership, ministers and churches changes 1975-1985

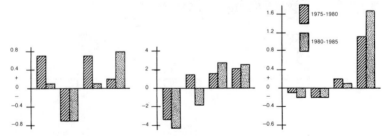

Participation
Where has this growth come from? It is the groups which emphasise participation and experience which seem to be on the increase. This is underlined by the growth of the Pentecostal churches. Interestingly, the smaller denominations are growing, and sometimes, as with the independent fellowships, so are smaller units. As evidenced by the House

Church movement in the United Kingdom, growth occurs especially where people can identify strongly with a group, where they can feel they belong and are cared for, and supported.

The situation is not so optimistic for the Roman Catholic church. Paradoxically, while churches and fellowships are on the increase, the number of priests is declining, which must have serious implications for the catholic community.

Mission

There are 217 Dutch missionary organisations with personnel serving outside the country. Of these 135, or nearly three-fifths, are Roman Catholic.

In 1985 6,500 Dutch missionaries served with these 217 organisations, the majority based abroad. 27% were serving in Asia, reflecting perhaps the past colonial accomplishments of the Dutch.

Commitment and dedication

It may be surprising that, of the 1,700 Christian organisations of all kinds based in the Netherlands, over half started in the 25 years 1960-1985 as the Church saw needs and endeavoured to meet them. Dutch Christian organisations employ over 71,000 people, 44,000 in the welfare services alone. The remaining 27,000 serve with 1,500 different societies, 27% of which do not have any full-time members of staff. The motto of Christian activity in the Netherlands must be commitment. Their dedication is such that many people give up much of their spare time to work in societies as different as the Vereniging Kinderzorg (Childcare Association) and the Internationale Christen Vredes Dienst (International Christian Peace Service). And they are not fighting alone. Welfare organisations in particular benefit from substantial government support, and so average nearly 300 staff members each.

So Christian life in the Netherlands is rich, alive and diverse. It is also visionary and imaginative. Dutch Christians work hard at seeking to spread the Christian message at home and abroad. The Netherlands reflects the tremendous diversity of interests and concerns, and shows how Christianity is embedded in Dutch national life today.

Source: LM 87/1.

New Age movement

You have almost certainly seen signs around you of an interest in things that are spiritual — but not Christian. From pagan symbols on the hooded T-shirts young people wear to some weird articles in the weekend newspapers, there are many signs of the popularity of the New Age movement.

It is not a movement as such. As John Stott points out: 'it has no structure, no membership, no headquarters or hierarchy and no statement of faith or religious ceremonial.'

It defines itself as 'a movement devoted to making the earth a happy and safe place to live in'. The different influences which have contributed to the New Age movement range from neutral things such as Jungian psychology, possibility thinking and the theory of relativity to Christian Science ('Sin is just imagination'), Theosophy ('Look for the truth within you'), pagan religions and ritual magic.

What are its beliefs?

The core of New Age thinking is that God is everything and everything is God. People just need to become conscious of the god within them and tap into their divine potential. New Agers talk about moving towards the 'higher self' in an 'age of enlightenment', and for many reincarnation is an important part of their beliefs. They talk of the power of Mother Earth, and of being in harmony with the cosmos. Techniques from meditation and chanting to 'channelling' spirits are used to reach the mystical realm or 'focus on the god within'.

One aspect of New Age thinking is a belief in a hierarchy of spirits, at the top of which is the Solar Logos. Under this come seven rays, then the Sanat Kumara, known as the Ancient of Days of the One Imitator. Below this are seven Masters, of which one is said to be Jesus.

The new age is the Age of Aquarius, which is believed to be dawning as different and higher energies flow into the earth from the cosmos, via ley lines. This is going to be an age of peace where 'yin' and 'yang' are in harmony, as opposed to the 'yang' dominated age of aggression and conflict we are leaving behind. This was the Age of Pisces, characterised by the dominance of Judeo-Christian beliefs.

Some New Agers look for one new universal religion, one world economy and one world government that will bring peace among the nations as we recognise our common humanity.

Why is it so popular?

Much of this appeals to people dissatisfied with today's materialism. It focuses on a desire for personal and social transformation, leading to a better and more peaceful society. At the same time it contains elements of the supernatural, which has always fascinated people.

In the climate of notional Christianity in Europe today, the beliefs of the New Age movement appeal to people's innate religiosity. While many say they believe in God, research shows that they are uncertain exactly what they believe, being prepared to accept such things as astrology, clair-voyance and fortune-telling.

It is easy to get into New Age thinking via the popular movements for peace and conservation or interests such as yoga, health food, animal rights and alternative medicine. Even techniques for meditation, possibility thinking or reducing stress are sometimes influenced by New Age thinking, although involvement in any of these things by no means equals involvement in the New Age movement.

What's wrong with it?

The movement makes such things as a desire for peace, wholeness and saving the planet into a religion in itself, which can be followed as an alternative to Christianity. However, it does not provide the means to achieve these desires.

Perhaps more dangerous is that people interested in raising their consciousness are opening their minds to the spirit world, but not to the Holy Spirit. Since the roots of the movement are in pagan religions, witchcraft and non-Christian sects, there is great potential for people getting involved in the occult.

Should we be doing anything?

All Christians need to be aware of the New Age movement, because they are sure to come across its influence, or meet people who are interested. A wealth of new books on the subject can help us be informed: try *What is the New Age?* published by Hodder & Stoughton.

Churches will be affected by the increase in occult activity; we need to be praying. We also need to be confident of the truth, living it whole-heartedly and prepared to share it with those who, in the 'post-Christian vacuum' of today's society will otherwise turn to the New Age movement to satisfy their spiritual hunger.

Source: LM 90/3.

New towns

Milton Keynes, Cumbernauld, Peterborough and Telford are typical New Towns. Their population and employment opportunities have grown rapidly over the years. Have the churches been able to grow as quickly?

Milton Keynes	Population	Employment
1967	40,000	18,350
1971	46,500	23,350*
1976	70,500	37,000
1981	95,800	46,060
1986	128,400	61,650
1991	148,800	84,100
* Estimate		
Cumbernauld	Population	Employment
1966	23,100	6,100
1972	34,300	9,500
1977	44,700	14,000
1982	48,450	13,000
1987	49,750	14,200
1991	50,900	17,600

(continued on page 134)

NEW TOWNS *(continued from page 133)*

Peterborough	Population	Employment
1967	81,000	45,500
1971	87,600	51,800
1976	98,000	58,900
1981	113,900	66,000
1986	128,100	71,620
1991	140,000	77,500

Telford	Population	Employment
1968	74,750	35,800
1971	80,800	36,200
1976	94,000	42,000
1981	105,400	39,400
1986	111,000	46,000
1990	119,000	61,000

Source: Relevant Development Corporations Agencies, quoted in Management October 1991, page 82.

Nominal Christianity

How 'Christian' is England? The number of people attending church is not the only measure of how Christian a country might be. In Great Britain, about 65% of the population say they believe in Christianity, a proportion which is changing slowly.

The English, Welsh and Scottish Church Censuses show that 18% of the population either go to or belong to a church, leaving 47% who can be called notional Christians. These are the people who would say they are Christian but are outside the churches, and this proportion has not changed in ten years.

However, the number of nominal Christians, people who belong to a church but don't go to it, decreased by 1% to 8% of the population, a drop of half a million people. But the number of Christians who both go to church and are church members increased 1% to 9%, suggesting greater cohesion and a greater emphasis on membership and its implications.

This leaves a 2% decline in people going to church who are not yet members. Given the apparent fluidity of opinions, the ease of transport and the desire for lack of specific commitment, particularly among the young, this is a surprise. It suggests people are not willing to 'go and see' what church is like: it is more for 'insiders'.

These trends imply that Christianity in Britain is becoming a more active faith, as nominal Christianity and perhaps churchgoing as a merely social activity decline.

The Census findings also suggest Christianity may become more 'closed', as the variety of viewpoints within the churches slowly decreases. In the Anglican church, which of all churches stands for so many things,

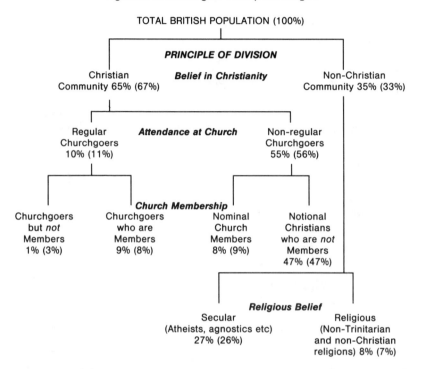

Religious structure of population in Great Britain 1990
Figure in brackets give 1980 percentages

TOTAL BRITISH POPULATION (100%)

PRINCIPLE OF DIVISION

Christian   ***Belief in Christianity***   Non-Christian
Community 65% (67%)   Community 35% (33%)

Regular   ***Attendance at Church***   Non-regular
Churchgoers   Churchgoers
10% (11%)   55% (56%)

Church Membership

| Churchgoers but *not* Members 1% (3%) | Churchgoers who are Members 9% (8%) | Nominal Church Members 8% (9%) | Notional Christians who are *not* Members 47% (47%) |

Religious Belief

Secular   Religious
(Atheists, agnostics etc)   (Non-Trinitarian
27% (26%)   and non-Christian
                     religions) 8% (7%)

only the mainstream evangelical and 'catholic' groups — both known for believing something — are growing.

The warning to be drawn from these figures is that Christianity needs to become more attractive. People are not always attracted to closed, active groups which can seem rather like pressure groups. Christians need to show love — not just for one another but for those outside the churches too, perhaps becoming more involved in the real world.

These figures do not suggest we are likely to lose much of our God consciousness. They show other religions and sects becoming more popular — they gained half a million people between 1980 and 1990 — and secularisation increasing only slowly. They do not suggest cataclysmic change but rather a continuing window of opportunity. How well will we take it?

Source: ECC and LM 91/2.

Norfolk

Area (sq km)	Population 1989			Percentage change 1979-89	Percentage under 15	Non-churchgoers 1989
	Men	Women	Total			
5,367	364,300	384,200	748,500	+9.0%	18%	670,600

Churchgoers 1989			Percentage of population	Percentage change 1979-89	Percentage under 15	Number of churches	Percentage built	
Men	Women	Total					before 1500	since 1950
31,900	46,000	77,900	10.4%	−13.9%	23%	1,154	51%	8%

District	Area (sq km)	Population 1989	Percentage change 1979-89
			%
W Norfolk	1,426	134,300	+13.9
Norwich	39	117,400	−8.5
Broadland	552	105,300	+9.3
Breckland	1,305	104,100	+9.6
S Norfolk	907	101,700	+8.6
N Norfolk	965	95,700	+19.0
Great Yarmouth	173	90,000	+13.4

Source: Regional Trends 26, HMSO 1991 and English Church Census.

North Yorkshire

Area (sq km)	Population 1989			Percentage change 1979-89	Percentage under 15	Non-churchgoers 1989
	Men	Women	Total			
8,309	351,900	370,400	722,300	+9.0%	17%	626,900

Churchgoers 1989			Percentage of population	Percentage change 1979-89	Percentage under 15	Number of churches	Percentage built	
Men	Women	Total					before 1500	since 1950
39,100	56,300	95,400	13.2%	−7.7%	24%	1,141	27%	8%

District	Area (sq km)	Population 1989	Percentage change 1979-89
			%
Harrogate	1,334	147,700	+6.4
Scarborough	817	106,200	+4.8
York	29	101,200	−1.1
Selby	725	93,600	+22.1
Ryedale	1,599	91,600	+9.0
Hambleton	1,312	78,900	+6.3
Richmondshire	1,317	52,200	+25.6
Craven	1,176	50,900	+8.3

Source: Regional Trends 26, HMSO 1991 and English Church Census.

Northamptonshire

Area (sq km)	Population 1989			Percentage change 1979-89	Percentage under 15	Non-churchgoers 1989
	Men	Women	Total			
2,367	283,400	292,700	576,100	+10.8%	20%	525,200

Churchgoers 1989			Percentage of population	Percentage change 1979-89	Percentage under 15	Number of churches	Percentage built	
Men	Women	Total					before 1500	since 1950
22,400	28,500	50,900	8.8%	−11.6%	25%	593	45%	13%

District	Area (sq km)	Population 1989	Percentage change 1979-89
			%
Northampton	81	184,000	+20.1
Kettering	234	75,100	+6.4
E Northamptonshire	510	67,500	+10.2
Wellingborough	163	66,900	+4.3
S Northamptonshire	634	66,700	+4.3
Daventry	665	64,400	+13.9
Corby	80	51,500	−2.4

Source: Regional Trends 26, HMSO 1991 and English Church Census.

Northumberland

Area (sq km)	Population 1989			Percentage change 1979-89	Percentage under 15	Non-churchgoers 1989
	Men	Women	Total			
5,032	148,300	155,300	303,600	+2.1%	25%	270,700

Churchgoers 1989			Percentage of population	Percentage change 1979-89	Percentage under 15	Number of churches	Percentage built	
Men	Women	Total					before 1500	since 1950
12,800	20,100	32,900	10.8%	−0.5%	16%	357	24%	7%

District	Area (sq km)	Population 1989	Percentage change 1979-89
			%
Blyth Valley	70	79,500	+2.8
Wansbeck	66	58,900	−7.3
Tynedale	2,222	57,500	+7.9
Castle Morpeth	619	50,400	+1.3
Alnwick	1,080	31,000	+9.3
Berwick-upon-Tweed	975	26,300	+0.9

Source: Regional Trends 26, HMSO 1991 and English Church Census.

Norway

According to popular belief, the first major breakthrough for Christianity in Norway was the killing of King Olav Haraldson at Stiklestad in AD 1030, as since that time the Church has played a major role in the life of the country. After the Reformation the Evangelical Lutheran Church was made the state church of Norway, and even today claims 92% of the 4.2 million population as members.

The Church holds an important place in Norwegian society, and is active worldwide through its 1,500 or more missionaries. Yet the wealth and freedom of the Scandinavian lifestyle have undermined the personal faith of many. Churchgoing is at an all time low, and the more exotic — and less demanding — spirituality of the New Age movement is attracting those who are beginning to question secular values. Popular magazines reflect the growing interest in horoscopes, divination and the occult. The Church in Norway today, as in the rest of Europe, has no room for complacency.

The state Lutheran Church in Norway has little competition from Free Churches. It has 60% of the church buildings, 47% of the ministers and 88% of active members. Its strength stems from the revivals in Norway in the 19th century. Although the established Church leaders at the time did not like the ordinary people meeting together to pray, Hans Nielsen Hague, the revivalist preacher, encouraged the newly-stirred lay people to remain in the Church as reform movements rather than break away. So the state Church benefited both from revival and from remaining united.

The lay organisations formed at that time became the equivalent of the para-church organisations found in other countries, with activities from children's choirs to social work. Large sections of the community are still involved with these branches of the Church.

Reaching the nominal

Most Norwegians have some contact with the Church, either through these groups or through attending occasional services. Nearly 90% of babies were baptised in the Church in 1988 — although the figure was 99% until 1969. About 90% of teenagers were confirmed, the same proportion as in 1959, although it has fluctuated over the years.

In recent years opposition within the Church has been growing to the state Church system which gives the government some authority in Church matters. In particular, tension over the issue of abortion on demand has convinced many that the Church will have to gain full independence as the Church of Jesus Christ, and not be a religious service structure within a secular government system.

The above may give the impression that Norway is a very Christian country, but in reality it has become increasingly secular. Opinion polls show that about 50% of the population say they believe the basic Christian doctrines, but only 15 to 20% would call themselves committed Christians or believers in a more personal, involved way.

The average attendance at Sunday morning services at Norway's 1,600 churches is relatively low, only 3% of the population. But national radio and TV services are widely listened to, particularly in rural areas where churches that have to share a pastor do not always hold services every Sunday.

Many believers meet mid-week at the 3,000 prayer houses, or Bedehus, owned by the different mission organisations.

These are the product of the 19th century revival in Norway, built by lay people who wanted to meet to pray together in spite of the opposition of the established church authorities.

Norwegian missions

The Church of Norway, like the state church in other Scandinavian countries, involves many people in its different activities. Missionary work from Norway is particularly strong. In 1987 there were 1,530 people working overseas, 15% more than in 1983. While 62% of these are women, the ratio of women to men is beginning to even out, particularly in the larger societies.

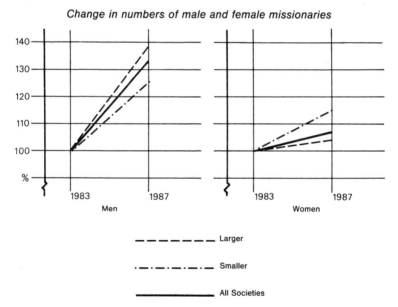

Change in numbers of male and female missionaries

Source: Norsk Handbok for Kirke og Misjon/Norwegian Handbook for Churches and Missions, MARC Europe 1990, and LM 90/2.

Nottinghamshire

Area (sq km)	Population 1989			Percentage change 1979-89	Percentage under 15	Non-churchgoers 1989
	Men	Women	Total			
2,164	499,700	515,100	1,014,800	+2.8%	19%	931,600

Churchgoers 1989			Percentage of population	Percentage change 1979-89	Percentage under 15	Number of churches	Percentage built	
Men	Women	Total					before 1500	since 1950
34,900	48,300	83,200	8.2%	-11.4%	26%	724	29%	15%

District	Area (sq km)	Population 1989	Percentage change 1979-89
			%
Nottingham	74	273,300	-2.1
Gedling	112	111,000	+7.9
Broxtowe	81	110,100	+6.8
Ashfield	110	109,400	+3.1
Bassetlaw	638	105,500	+3.1
Newark	662	103,600	-1.2
Rushcliffe	410	101,100	+10.9
Mansfield	77	100,800	+1.0

Source: Regional Trends 26, HMSO 1991 and English Church Census.

O

Ordinands

Leslie Francis looked at personality profiles of men and women training for ordained ministry in the Church of England, using the Eysenck Personality Questionnaire. The ordinands did not emerge as typical of either religious people in general or of adults in general.

Working relationships tend to be based on well-established gender differences in personality profiles. Men tend to be more extrovert — sociable, lively and dominant. Women on the other hand tend to be more neurotic, making them anxious and emotional, and less psychotic, which makes them less tough-minded, more unselfish and warm.

However, among the ordinands, the female clergy were found to be no less tough-minded and no less stable than the men. On the scales of both psychotic and neurotic their personalities were characteristically masculine. Female clergy were also found to be more extrovert than men in general, while the male ordinands were more introverted than women in general.

It is surprising that male clergy tend to be introverted, characterised by being shy in company, reticent on public occasions, unwilling to take risks and not self-assured. These seem to be the opposite of the qualities generally associated with the public and social profile of their occupation. This incompatibility between personal preferences and public role expectations may cause frustration and a sense of failure, says the researcher, or might lead to the shaping of an unhealthily detached public persona, in order to cope.

For female clergy, the low neurotic scores could mean difficulty in empathising with other women. And for both male and female clergy, the personality profiles which emerge suggest some interesting relational problems as they try to work together.

Source: The Personality Characteristics of Anglican Ordinands: Feminine Men and Masculine Women? Leslie J Francis, Personality and Individual Differences, volume 12 1991, and LL June 1991.

Oxfordshire

Area (sq km)	Population 1989 Men	Women	Total	Percentage change 1979-89	Percentage under 15	Non-churchgoers 1989
2,609	287,600	290,000	577,600	+8.9%	19%	516,000

Churchgoers 1989 Men	Women	Total	Percentage of population	Percentage change 1979-89	Percentage under 15	Number of churches	Percentage built before 1500	since 1950
27,100	34,500	61,600	10.7%	−0.2%	24%	715	44%	10%

District	Area (sq km)	Population 1989	Percentage change 1979-89 %
S Oxfordshire	687	130,100	−0.9
Cherwell	590	123,300	+16.2
Oxford	36	116,500	+0.3
Vale of White Horse	581	112,000	+10.4
W Oxfordshire	715	95,700	+21.8

Source: Regional Trends 26, HMSO 1991 and English Church Census.

P

The poor and the lost

What happens when you combine two views of the world: the one that looks at the number of Christians or churches in each country, and the one that looks at food production, child mortality, wealth?

MARC International and World Vision have charted these dimensions of worldwide human need, and found that whether you approach the data with a desire to learn where the Gospel needs to be heard, or a desire to find the poorest of the poor, the answer is the same. The poor are the lost and lost are the poor.

Bryant Myers of World Vision International concludes from this that 'first, anyone who is called to share the Good News must do so in a way that makes sense to the poor. Second, any ministry to the poor done by citizens of the Kingdom of God must include the Good News.'

The principle that the Gospel needs to be lived as well as preached is the mission strategy of today, particularly since the majority of 'the poor and the lost' live in Muslim or Marxist countries hostile to the Good News. And of course it is still relevant to the witness of each local church in even the more affluent parts of the world.

Source: Target Earth, Global Mapping International and University of the Nations 1989 and LM 90/1.

Population change

A 1986 forecast by the Office of Population Censuses and Surveys of the age structure of the British population in the period up to 1996, indicated significant changes in the teenage and 20s groups.

While the number of babies is increasing, the number of teenagers and those in their early 20s are showing quite a drastic decline.

What are the implications for the Church? To start with, the number of young people available to join Youth Fellowships has decreased. Coupled with the general tendency of young people to stop attending church, the effect on the churches may be severe. It may be difficult for Christians in their late teens and early 20s to find Christian friends their own age, thus creating an urgent need for ways to help these people to stay walking in the Christian path.

At the other end of the age spectrum, the figures forecast a steep rise in the number of people over 45, many of whom are likely to attend church if past patterns are anything to go by. Christian leaders will therefore need to think through the problem of how to help an ageing population participate and remain active in evangelism.

Source: LM 87/1.

Population in Europe

It doesn't take a statistician to tell you that society is changing fast in all European countries. But such basic figures as the number of births and marriages make clear the extent of the change and its implications. Not just politicians and social scientists, but churches too need to be living in the present and planning for the future. And it is significant to look for spiritual causes behind the numbers.

Births and deaths

The most basic feature is the steep decline in fertility rates: fewer babies, in other words. This means Europe's population is likely to remain static, largely because Europeans are marrying later and having less children, while the world's is exploding. The emancipation of women in Western society is a major influence on the changes, as more take up the option of career rather than family, so remaining single or childless. This is likely to increase as women become less dependent on men and less bound by social sanctions.

The result of a low birth-rate is a change in the age-structure of European countries, increasing the proportion of older people. Longer life-expectancy in Europe adds to this. However, it is forecast that the population will not shrink, as increased immigration will compensate for the falling birth rates.

Marriage and divorce

Demographers expect the Scandinavian countries to be the trendsetters in Europe, with southern European countries around 25 years behind. This is particularly noticeable in the areas of marriage and family building, where the role of the family as the basic cultural institution is changing. From a peak of popularity in the late 1960s when the proportion of adults who were or had been married was at 95%, marriage rates have decreased in all European countries.

Cohabitation, on the other hand, has increased, to the point where in Sweden and Denmark couples are almost as likely to live together as to marry. In the 20 to 24 age group 45% of Danes and 44% of Swedes cohabit. While some of these will marry when they are older, they are less likely to do so than previous generations. The number of single people is also increasing, ranging from 20% to 35% of the population in Northern and Western European countries.

Some say that living together before getting married makes divorce less likely, since people have had a trial period before committing themselves. However, Sweden and Denmark, the countries with the highest rates of cohabitation, are also those with the highest divorce rates. Nearly half of all marriages end in divorce, most occurring in the first five years of marriage.

	Churchgoers as percentage of population	Percentage births outside marriage	Divorce per 1000 existing marriages	Percentage women 20-24 cohabiting
	(1990)	(1988)	(1987)	(1986)
Sweden	4[1]	51	12[1]	44[2]
Denmark	4	45	13	45[2]
United Kingdom	11	26	13	18
Spain	14	10[1]	0	n/a
France	13	28	9[3]	12[4]
West Germany	21[1]	10	9	14[4]
Netherlands	27[1]	10	6	16[4]
Belgium	30[1]	11[1]	8	7[4]
Italy	36[1]	6	2	1[5]
Irish Republic	82[1]	12	0	2[4]

[1] Estimate   [2] 1998   [3] 1986   [4] 1982   [5] 1983

What are the implications for churches? Firstly, there will be needs that small or fragmented families will no longer be able to meet, for example those of the elderly who risk becoming increasingly isolated. There will also be more single people, more single mothers, more divorced people and vastly more children who have grown up without a stable home. There will be more immigrants and perhaps more racism; more elderly people and perhaps the rise of ageism.

Demographers point to the shifts in values which underlie the population changes. Individualism and the value placed on freedom of choice go along with the decline in traditional values which have determined behaviour in the past — specifically, with the decline of the Church's influence. As Christians, do we see this as an inevitable aspect of social change? Or do we think hard about what the Church is called to be and do, and how that applies in the context of today — and tomorrow?

See also: World population.
Source: Based on the Council of Europe's Seminar on Present Demographic Trends and Lifestyles in Europe, September 1990, quoted in LL New Year 1991.

Population per church

The map on the following page shows the number of people per church living in each county. The lower the number, the more churches there are in that county to cater for its population.

So if everyone in Cornwall went to church, each congregation would have a mere 520 people. In the West Midlands, however, each would have to hold 2,100 people.

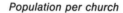

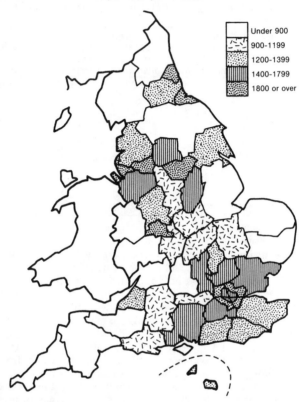

In England there was in 1989 one evangelical church for every 3,640 people. In Canada the same year there was one for every 3,490 people.

Source: ECC and LM 90/2.

Pornography

Oppressor or Liberator?

The Christian response to pornography has always been divided between those pleased that the Church is concerned and those horrified that the subject has been mentioned. When those connected with the Greenbelt Festival first raised the issue a number believed that Christians should never hear anything unwholesome, overlooking the fact that if we ignore everything unpleasant because it might damage our spiritual health, we are in fact consenting to it continuing.

Pornography does not have to be examined for its nature to be understood. But some knowledge of its extent and what is involved is necessary. When we came to write *Dark Glasses,* both Steve Shaw and I were grateful to those feminists who had struggled to understand the nature of pornography and commit their discoveries to paper. They had discovered that, once the nature and appeal of pornography is understood its power and mystery can be removed.

The feminist writers discovered that it is not freedom for people to indulge themselves in whatever sexual behaviour appeals. Nor does pornography remove the threat of sexual aggression by providing a safe channel through which men can diffuse their lust.

The opinion that pornography can have a cleansing effect on those who use it is based on the unbiblical and heretical belief that human nature is split into higher and lower levels of mind and body.

Pornography can never have a purging effect because it is a symptom of the sickness and pain it is purported to cleanse.

I have come this far without an actual definition of pornography. To turn to the feminist writers once more, Laura Lederer in *Take Back the Night,* defines pornography as a 'verbal or pictorial explicit representation of sexual behaviour that has a distinguishing characteristic, the degrading and demeaning portrayal of the role and status of the human female sexuality'.

I would add that it is not just women and their sexuality that is degraded. Pornography degrades and demeans men as well.

Oppression involves the powerful exploiting the weak. In the case of pornography the weak are many. There are those who cannot withstand the physical and financial threats and inducements of pornography makers. Women, young boys and children can be motivated by the need for money, the desire to find a sexual identity, or are exploited from a position of trust.

There are other victims, particularly women and children, who are subjected to sexual and physical abuse by those who have been duped into believing that sexual force is acceptable, even necessary.

Finally, we all suffer from a constant media bombardment which demeans and objectifies people.

As Christians we should be seeking to understand the desire for pornography. We must reject the view that human beings are made up of separate, unrelated compartments. We must work towards a belief that sees salvation, not as a means of escape from the body's power, but as a restoration of all created life.

We should affirm the equality of men and women, reclaiming God's gift of sexuality to be enjoyed as He intended. And let us not forget to bring help and healing to the victims and to involve ourselves in the fight against the power of pornography.

Source: LM 88/3. Article by Sue Plater, Chairman of the Greenbelt Festival.

Women's attitudes

In a survey about women's attitudes to pornography, 80% of the respondents wanted government legislation against it, and 60% wanted restrictions on all pornography. The survey was of over 4,000 readers of *Cosmopolitan* magazine — far from being women with old-fashioned views.

While it's no surprise that almost the whole sample found blue movies and sex phone lines offensive and pornographic, 84% were similarly offended by pin-up calendars and 80% by Page 3 girls. What would happen if they told their husbands or work colleagues what they thought?

If Christians feel strongly enough about the issue to speak out about it, they shouldn't fear being in a minority. Half the population might thank them for it.

Source: Cosmopolitan March 1990, and LM 90/4.

Priorities of Christians

People's physical needs are more important than their spiritual needs, according to 60% of churchgoers and 43% of clergy in England and Wales, reports the Bible Society in a 1989 survey.

In a list of reasons for their interest in mission marked by supporters of one large missionary society, even helping the physical needs of others fell into second place behind the motive of self-fulfilment. Making disciples of all nations came well down the list.

Little surprise then that the 'Christian world' spends 1,300 times as much on itself as on the unevangelised parts of the world. We keep 99% of Christian literature, 99.9% of Christian radio and TV, and even 86% of all missionaries to ourselves. What hope for the church, let alone the world?

Source: Bible Society and Lausanne Statistics Task Force, LM 90/1.

Q

Quote unquote

'One band of locusts may consume in one day what 50,000 people eat in one year.'

Source: LM 86/4.

'In the last 12 months 15 million infants and children died, mostly in the Two Thirds World. That's equivalent to over 100 jumbo jet crashes every day with no survivors.-

Source: LM 87/1.

'For every teenager in the United Kingdom who dies from abusing other drugs, 100 die from alcohol-related causes, mostly in driving accidents.'

Source: LM 87/2.

'While after three pints of beer most people would not drive a car, they are allowed to operate a forklift truck, an overhead crane, or take a corporate decision crucial to a company.'

Source: LM 87/3.

'Many years ago, a woman was at a mission meeting led by the preacher Gipsy Smith. She wrote to him afterwards, "Dear Sir, I feel God is calling me to preach the Gospel. The trouble is I have 12 children. What shall I do?" Gipsy Smith replied, "Dear Madam, I am delighted to hear that God has called you to preach the Gospel. I am even more delighted to hear that He has provided you with a congregation."'

Source: Taken from 'Rolling in the Aisles', by Murray Watts, LM 87/3.

'Today it is estimated that a quarter of all the country's small businesses are owned and run by women.'

Source: Moneycare July 1987, LM 87/4.

'Once a person has developed AIDS, he or she will almost certainly be dead within three years.'

Source: Dr Caroline Collier, The 20th Century Plague, LM 88/2.

'Nearly one in four of all households in the United Kingdom were occupied by one person in 1986, compared to one in 10 in 1951.'

Source: Government Statistical Service, LM 88/3.

'Britons gave the same amount of money to animal welfare as to World Mission in 1987.'

Source: LM 89/2.

'In his or her lifetime, the average Western professional will spend three years in wasteful meetings, four years being interrupted, five years waiting in queues, six years eating and seven years in the bathroom. One year is spent looking for things, eight months spent opening advertising mail and six months waiting at red lights.'

Source: Michael Fortino, 'Time Flies When You're Not Having Fun', LM 89/3.

'To understand God's thoughts, we must study statistics, for these are a measure of His purpose.'

Source: Florence Nightingale and LM 89/4.

'There are 30,000 Christian clergy of all types in West Germany but 90,000 registered witches and fortune tellers.'

Source: Theological News 1989 and LM 90/2.

'I find it bizarre that we are now spending 100 times as much on the legal costs of divorce as we are on pre-marriage and marriage counselling services.

'It is curious because over one third of those who have been divorced say subsequently that they regret it.'

Source: Julian Brazier, MP, LM 90/3.

'Chances of being killed by terrorists:	1 in 420,000
Chances of being killed by homicide in Norway:	1 in 100,000
Chances of being killed in the womb of a British woman:	1 in 5.3
Chances of being killed in the womb of a Romanian woman:	1 in 1.6'

Source: Interpol Trends 1990 & OPCS, LM 90/4.

'Christmas used to be a religious festival years ago, didn't it?'

Source: BBC Radio 5 interviewer to Christmas card publisher October 1990, LM 91/1.

R

Radio religion in Britain

Every week about 11 million people in Britain hear a religious programme on BBC Radio. Almost as many watch a religious programme on BBC Television, and nearly as many as that watch one on ITV. Add on the audiences for religion on independent radio, and even while allowing for quite a degree of duplication, you have an audience of at least 20 million adults. That is probably one of the largest in the world as a percentage of the population. More people listen to the 'Sunday Programme' on Radio 4 than to 'Woman's Hour'.

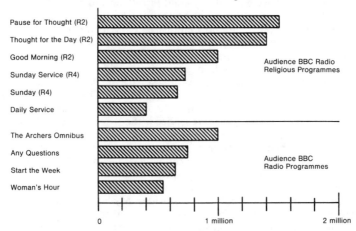

Audiences for various BBC Radio Programmes 1986

Yet this is, we are told, a secular country, where only about a sixth of the population regularly engages in acts of religious worship. How then do we account for these large audiences for religious programmes on radio and television?

One answer, I suspect, is what whereas a generation ago 'nominal' Christians went to church a couple of times a year, now they are people who do not switch off 'Songs of Praise' or 'Thought for the Day'. Some of our radio programmes attract four times more non-churchgoers than churchgoers — 'Good Morning Sunday' for instance. And even the broadcast services have a substantial proportion of listeners who are non-churchgoers, have lapsed from attending, or go infrequently.

A second explanation, well supported by evidence from letters, is that this country is now in a condition of widespread religious ignorance, but not indifference. People (being made in the image of God) have the same spiritual needs and ask the same ultimate questions as those in earlier, more religious times. But having lost contact with the churches, they seek the fulfilment of those needs and the answers to those questions through broadcasting. You don't have to go anywhere, be embarrassed or sign anything to listen to 'The Good Book' or even the 'Daily Service'.

Certainly there is a ready audience for programmes explaining religious belief and experience. Three years ago *Priestland's Progress* attracted a huge audience, 24,000 letters and enough purchases to put the book of the series into the national bestsellers' list for several months. Yet many Christians found it altogether too tentative, speculative and uncommitted. In 1987 Brian Redhead's series on the Bible, *The Good Book,* quadrupled the Radio 4 audience and again evoked an enormous and enthusiastic mailbag, while similar complaints came from the already committed. Radio seems to have created in Gerald Priestland's memorable phrase, a 'great church of the unchurched', and those who have experienced it are aware how widespread and how enthusiastic its 'members' are.

There may be other explanations for this phenomenon of large audiences for religious programmes at a time of relative decline in active church membership. Indeed, in one way it could be simple cause and effect. If you haven't gone to the evening service, for whatever reason, you are at home to watch 'Songs of Praise' or 'Highway'. The 16 million people or so who watch these programmes, however, could absorb the total attendance at the nation's evening service without even noticing it. Indeed, I doubt if 16 million people have ever attended evening services on any one Sunday in the history of Britain.

Most religious broadcasters, and certainly that goes for me, do not wish to increase their audiences at the expense of actual church attendance. I believe nothing can replace the reality of human fellowship in worship which even the worst 'read' service provides. My hope is that the present growth in radio audiences for religion is the precursor of a return, not only to church, but also to widespread commitment to the Christian faith. And I believe it is a realistic hope.

Source: LM 87/2. Article by David Winter, then Head of Religious Programmes, BBC Radio.

Radio worldwide

Vision

The 'World by 2000' commitment made by four international Christian broadcasting organisations aims to make gospel radio available in all 'mega-languages' — those spoken by over one million people — by the year 2000. This will mean that 94% of the world population will have Christian radio broadcasts in their own language.

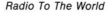

Radio To The World

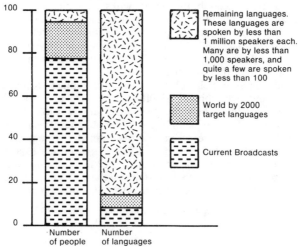

Remaining languages. These languages are spoken by less than 1 million speakers each. Many are by less than 1,000 speakers, and quite a few are spoken by less than 100

World by 2000 target languages

Current Broadcasts

Number of people   Number of languages

Research

There are just over 300 mega-languages in the world today, but of the 200 languages with Christian radio broadcasts, only 130 are mega-languages. This leaves a sizeable task to be achieved in the 1990s, one which is too big for the broadcasters alone.

Strategy

Reaching the target will mean different missions working together and including radio broadcasts as part of their strategy to unreached areas, particularly to groups which are more difficult to reach. It will mean more personnel, both broadcasters and project co-ordinators for the new languages.

Faith

Not least, says the 'World by 2000' research office, 'we must conclude that only by the grace of God will this goal be met, and it is only because of that grace we dare attempt it'.

Source: Ricefields Journal, March 1990, LM 90/4.

Rape

Gerald Howarth, MP, spoke at the National Viewers' and Listeners' Association Convention in April 1987 on the alarming increase in rape.

'During the past 30 years in England and Wales recorded rape cases have increased by 560%, from 480 in 1957 to 2,288 last year. Recorded cases of violence against the person have increased by 1,145%, or 12-fold, from 10,961 to 125,000. No doubt the experts will say the increase in rape cases can be accounted for by more sensitive policing, not only by the availability of the pornographic literature that I have mentioned. I prefer to take the commonsense view that if women are increasingly portrayed as mere sex objects, it should surprise no one if the readers of such magazines are encouraged to treat them in that way.'

A National Opinion Poll in 1987 revealed the public's attitude towards too lenient sentences for sexual offences, particularly rape. Of those questioned, two-thirds believed that rape should carry a minimum sentence of at least ten years; 27% said this should be 20 years against the current minimum of five years. 2% maintained that rape should be punishable by death. This did not vary much according to age or sex, although men were more reluctant to advocate life imprisonment. Perhaps the most interesting point is that 84% felt that the prosecution in such cases should have the right to appeal against over lenient sentences.

Source: National VALA. Political and Social Economic Review, NOP, April 1987, LM 87/4.

Reading

Three-quarters of British adults bought at least one book in 1988, either for themselves or for someone else. And eight out of 10 adults read at least one

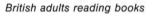
British adults reading books

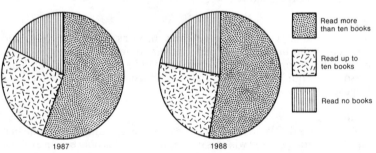

book, according to a MORI poll for the *Sunday Times*. Over half claim to have read more than 10 books a year. However, the survey showed a slight decline in book-buying and reading between 1987 and 1988.

What sort of books are people reading? Let's hope that the Saatchi and Saatchi packaged Bible catches the eye of the book-buyers — and let's encourage Christians to give their book-hungry friends something more wholesome to read than the war stories and horror fiction that seems to be the staple diet of many.

Source: LM 89/3.

Refugees

About 30,000 people were given leave to remain in the UK as refugees during the period 1979-88. Over 20,000 of these were South East Asians accepted for settlement.

In 1988 there were about 5,100 applications for refugee status, a little below the peak in 1985 but still 3,500 more than in 1979. A higher number of these applications was granted than in previous years, reflecting a large number of grants to people from Somalia, Ethiopia, Sudan and Afghanistan.

Source: Home Office Statistical Bulletin Issue 25/89, LM 90/2.

Religiosity

Notional Christianity, as measured by a 'religiosity factor', is declining in Britain. The downward slide is fastest among those aged under 24, the

Percentage of people giving five or more positive responses to the variables used to determine 'religiosity'

	Britain 1968	Britain 1987	N Ireland 1986
	%	%	%
Men	39	26	71
Women	58	45	54
Age: 16-24	36	19	38
25-34	37	28	49
35-44	41	33	
45-54	50	36	} 72
55-64	64	48	
65+	61	52	82
Social Class: AB	53	39	71
C1	49	37	65
C2	47	30	55
DE	51	38	63
All	49	36	63

middle-aged and those in the skilled manual social class. The rate of decline has been the same between men and women.

Statistics published by the Independent Broadcasting Authority indicate the following attitudes:

- Women tend to be more religious than men, except in Northern Ireland where the opposite is the case.
- There is no difference in religiosity between the social classes.
- Older people are more religious than younger.

Is this decline bad news for the church? C S Lewis would have argued that such a downward trend has its good side. When the 'fog' of notional religion lifts, it becomes clear 'what side people are on' and thus makes clearer the issues that confront them.

Variables used to measure 'religiosity'

	Percentage of interviewees giving positive responses (1987)
	%
● They are 'very likely' or 'fairly likely' to think of God when they are happy	50
● They are 'very religious' or 'fairly religious'	47
● They believe that 'God does watch each person'	47
● They are 'certain that there is a God'	42
● Their everyday lives are affected 'a great deal' or 'quite a lot' by their religious beliefs	40
● They are 'very likely' to think of God when they are worried	35
● They are 'certain' that religion helps to maintain the standards and morals of society	32
● They are 'certain' that without belief in God life is meaningless	22
● They are 'certain' that to lead a good life it is necessary to have a religious belief	20

Source: Godwatching Viewers, Religion and Television by Svennig, Haldane, Spier and Gunter, IBA/John Libbey 1988, LM 89/2.

Religious allegiance

Different surveys at different times have sought to measure British 'religious allegiance' and have adopted varying assumptions in the process. The *UK Christian Handbook 1992/93* put the total Christian community at 65% of the population (community being defined here as all those who would say they were Christian), and the total religious community at 73%. This extra 8% relates to the total adherent communities of the non-Trinitarian churches like the Jehovah's Witnesses, Mormons, Church of Scientology, Christadelphians, Christian Scientists and others, as well as the major non-Christian religions like Jews, Islam, Hinduism, Buddhism and Sikhism, and the multitude of new religious movements which have appeared in the last 20 years. This 8% is made up as follows:

UK membership and community 1990

Church/Religion	Adult members	Community (including children)
Church of Scientology	75,000	600,000
Other Non-Trinitarian Churches	383,914	900,000
Jews	108,400	300,000
Hindus	140,000	400,000
Muslims	990,000	1.300,000
Sikhs	390,000	500,000
Other religions	229,630	400,000
Total	2,316,944	4,400,000
As percentage of 1990 adult population	5%	9%

Other studies (like MORI in October 1989) put 1% of the population attending a Jewish, Muslim, Hindu or Buddhist place of worship at least once a quarter. The same study and the British Social Attitudes Report of

Organisation	When conducted	Question	Percentage of GB population indicating allegiance to	
			Christianity	Non-Christian faith
			%	%
MARPLAN 86 Omnibus	'Religion Poll' November 1986 Sample of 1,522	'Were you brought up or are you a member of any non-Christian religion?'	–	2.4
Independent Broadcasting Authority, with Insight Social Research	'Attitudes to Religion' June/July 1987 Sample of 1,496	15 options	79	2.0
British Social Attitudes, Social and Community Planning Research	Fifth Report 1988 Sample of 2,847	'Do you regard yourself as belonging to any particular denomination?' If YES, 'Which?'	63	2.5
MORI	Living in Britain March 1989 Sample of 1,458	'What is your denomination?' Choice of options	89	2.4
Gallup 89	December 1989 Sample of 969	'What is your religious denomination?'	77	–
MORI 91	Easter Poll March 1991 Sample of 1,100	'What is your religious denomination'? Choice of 11 options	85	2.2

1990 by Social and Community Planning Research put weekly church attendance at between 12 and 15% against the more detailed English Church Census figure of 10% and a UK figure of 11%. Declared atheists are relatively few — 4% in an Independent Broadcasting Authority study of 1988 and also in a MORI study of March 1989. The same IBA study indicated 7% of British people have been or have had a 'born again' experience.

Source: As given.

Religious beliefs

Different surveys have sought responses to key elements of religious belief. A poll by Insight Social Research on attitudes to religion June/July 1987 for the Independent Broadcasting Authority found that 74% of population of Great Britain agreed that Jesus Christ is the Son of God and 54% believed in the miracles of the Bible.

In 1986 Gallup undertook the European Value Systems Study in many countries. In Britain the percentages of affirmative answers to the question 'Which, if any, do you believe in?' were:

		Religion				Age-group	
	All	*Roman Catholic*	*Protes-tant*	*Other*	*None*	*18-24*	*65-74*
	%	*%*	*%*	*%*	*%*	*%*	*%*
God	76	94	78	82	28	59	86
Sin	69	84	68	74	52	58	66
A soul	59	81	57	72	24	50	64
Heaven	57	76	58	66	17	46	68
Life after death	45	65	44	58	16	44	46
The devil	30	63	25	46	8	30	32
Hell	27	58	22	40	6	23	24
Re-incarnation	27	35	27	24	14	29	30

Another survey a year later, Britain Twenty Years On, gave rather lower percentages on the whole for what people believed in.

	Overall	*Men*	*Women*
	%	*%*	*%*
God	70	66	75
Sin	51	49	55
A soul	50	44	56
Heaven	48	41	54
Life after death	43	37	49
The devil	31	30	31
Hell	29	28	29
Astrology	22	15	28
Re-incarnation	20	16	23
Transcendental meditation	9	9	9
None of these	14	18	11

See also: Beliefs and Religiosity. Source: As stated.

Religious education

A 1987 Gallup survey among 214 prospective members of parliament asked a number of questions on moral issues. The figures represent affirmative answers and exclude the 'don't knows'.

		Political party		
	All	Conservative	Labour	Alliance
	%	%	%	%
'Are you in favour of church schools in the voluntary sector continuing?'	92	99	83	100
'Are you in favour of compulsory religious education in State Schools?'	90	100	74	90
'Do you think that today's decline in religious beliefs and practices is a very important contributory factor in increasing family breakdown?'	65	84	38	59
'Do you think that today's decline in religious beliefs is a very important contributory factor in the decrease of law and order?'	62	80	38	54

Religious education is not Christian

Most children in British state secondary schools learn little or nothing about Christianity after the age of 14, according to a survey by Culham College Institute.

In the hour of religious education (RE) which has been compulsory since 1944, only a quarter of fourth- and fifth-form pupils are taught mainly or exclusively about Christianity, and the proportion falls to one in 14 by the sixth form.

This survey was carried out shortly before the Education Reform Bill decreed that school RE lessons should reflect Britain's mainly Christian traditions — but many parents say they are happy with the way things are. Nearly 40% of parents interviewed by Public Attitude Surveys thought RE should not be compulsory. And if it was, then they said they would rather their children learnt about different religions.

The issue of RE in schools is a sensitive one. While the education system is basically secular and the occult is in vogue among many school children, we need to be praying that teenagers who are so open to influence get a chance to hear the Christian Gospel presented in a clear and relevant way. And we need to support the Christian teachers, school governors and parents in our congregations, perhaps considering how we could be further involved.

Source: Universe 1987, LM 88/1, 90/1.

Robots

Once robots existed only in the domain of science fiction, but now they are becoming increasingly part of life in manufacturing industry.

Despite the prominence given to the robots used in Japan, it is actually a European country — Sweden — which has the most robots in relation to its industrial workforce, with 20 robots for every 10,000 workers, while Japan has only 12. But the country with the fastest growing proportion of machines to staff is the United Kingdom, as the following table shows:

Robots per 10,000 industrial workers

	1983	Percentage Increase 1980-83
		%
UK	3.4	+6
West Germany	6.3	+5
Italy	3.4	+5
France	4.1	+4
Japan	11.8	+3
Sweden	20.3	+2

Should Christians welcome machines which are helping to reduce boring, repetitive, soul-destroying labour, or resist them because they are taking away the jobs, self-respect and livelihood of people?

Source: Management Today September 1986, LM 87/1.

Rural churches

The village church is a familiar sight in rural Britain, as in other parts of Europe. One imagines it as the focus of an elderly and long-established community, undisturbed for many years.

Yet rural populations are now the fastest-growing in Britain, increasing at 20 times the national average rate. About a quarter of the population now live in rural areas, and the housing developments which continue to mushroom are attracting people of a variety of classes to a greener lifestyle.

Whereas thousands of rural churches had been closing since the 1960s, in 1985 research by Rural Sunrise found that churches of all denominations in country areas had begun to show signs of growth. Nearly 20% of those surveyed in 1985 were growing numerically, compared with around 5% in 1980.

The main reason for this growth was reckoned to be the changing nature of the population, with new people, including young families and long-distance commuters moving into old-established communities. Other factors seen as contributing to growth were the character of the minister and the church's involvement in the community. Overt evangelism was considered to have little effect.

Source: Rural Sunrise 1985, LL February 1990.

S

Schools and Christianity

Christian schools normally take pupils from nominally Christian or unchurched families as well as the children of churchgoers. To what extent does being part of a 'Christian community' at school encourage children to have a positive attitude to Christianity? Or does it put them off it altogether?

This is a question addressed by Leslie Francis and his colleagues in the context of Roman Catholic schools, in England, Wales, Scotland, Australia and most recently the USA. The findings have implications for Christian schools of all kinds.

At the four American schools surveyed, 87% of the pupils were baptised Catholics and 77% came from families where both parents were Catholic — a far higher proportion than usual in the UK. However only half the mothers and two-fifths of the fathers went to mass regularly.

Attitude towards attending the Catholic school

	Practising Catholic	Non-practising Catholic	Non-Catholic
	%	%	%
'My parents made the correct decision by sending me to a Catholic school.'	88	62	75
'Attendance at Catholic school has helped me to understand the real meaning of life.'	53	16	44
'I am happy to be a pupil in my school.'	81	60	74

The survey found that the pupils who had the most positive attitude to attending a Catholic school and towards religious education in the school were the ones who attended mass regularly themselves. Of these, 88% thought their parents were right to send them to a Catholic school, and 69% said religious education lessons had helped them to know Christ more deeply.

Since churchgoing was so important in predicting children's attitudes, the research looked at what influenced their mass attendance. Parental example and practice was found to be the key. If the parents went to mass, the children were much more likely to do the same. But if one or both parents had ceased to attend, the children were less likely to go to mass themselves than children from a home where only one parent was a practising Catholic and the other was not a Catholic. As the researchers state, 'parental disaffection has a stronger negative influence on pupils than a non-Catholic background'.

Attitude towards religious education in the Catholic school

	Practising Catholic	Non-practising Catholic	Non-Catholic
	%	%	%
'Religious education is more important to me than any other subject that I study in my school.'	10	0	12
'Religious education lessons have helped me to know Christ more deeply.'	69	40	64
'Religious education lessons provide me with the principles with which to deal with the important problems of life.'	65	44	60

Likewise, the children of non-practising Catholics who didn't attend mass themselves were the most negative in their attitude to school and religious education (RE) lessons. Only 44% felt RE lessons provided principles to help them with the important issues of life, while 65% of practising Catholics and 60% of non-Catholics felt this was true.

Non-Catholic children were generally more positive about going to a Catholic school, and about RE lessons, than were the non-practising Catholics. Three-quarters thought their parents were right to have sent them there, and 64% had been 'helped to know Christ more deeply' through the religious education at the school.

The researchers conclude that Catholic schools do most good for the children of practising Catholics, but the children of nominal Catholics are most likely to be seriously disaffected. They suggest that 'if Catholic schools are to exercise an effective ministry among Catholic pupils from non-practising backgrounds, they need to consciously abandon the assumption that all pupils can be treated as if they are part of the faith community characterised by practising Catholics'.

See also: Religious education.
Source: The Catholic School as Faith Community – An Empirical Enquiry, by Leslie J Francis and Josephine Egan, Religious Education, Volume 85, Number 4, 1990 pp 588-603, and LL June 1991.

Science versus Christianity

Research in 1990 in Scotland looked at the relationship between school-children's attitude to Christianity and to science. It looked too at the popularity of views influenced by 'scientism' and of the view that Christians have to believe in a seven-day creation. It is thought these may account for the apparent negative correlation between interest in science and positive attitude to Christianity.

The research, among 11 to 15 year olds, confirmed that pupils who are very interested in science have a slightly less positive attitude to Christianity than average. Views consistent with 'scientism' were held by a quarter to two-fifths of those surveyed: for example 25% believed 'science will one day give us complete control over the world' and 44% thought 'scientific theories can always be proved true'. Pupils who held these views were very keen on science lessons and had negative attitudes to Christianity.

About a third of pupils see Christianity as being 'creationist' and this correlates with a slightly more positive attitude to Christianity and slightly less interest in science. Those who attend church weekly have more positive attitudes than average to Christianity, as one would hope, but no less interest in science. They are, however, considerably less likely to agree with the statements characteristic of scientism, and more likely to agree that Christianity necessarily involves belief in a seven-day creation.

The older pupils in the sample were less interested than the younger in both Christianity and science lessons. However, they did not demonstrate a greater understanding of either the nature of science or of Christian belief. The researchers suggest that while churches may replace unquestioning belief in science with unquestioning Christian faith, schools do little to help understanding of either.

Comparison between pupils who believe science will eventually give complete control over the world and those who do not

	Agreement	Rest of sample
	%	%
'I think church services are boring.'	58	45
'Saying my prayers helps me a lot.'	21	30
'I know that God helps me.'	29	41
'More scientists are urgently needed.'	53	35
'Studying science gives me great pleasure.'	56	44

Source: Attitude towards Christianity, Creationism, Scientism and Interest in Science Among 11-15 Year Olds by Leslie J Francis, Harry M Gibson, Peter Fulljames. British Journal of Religious Education, Autumn 1990, Volume 13, No 1, LL December 1990.

Second marriages

The number of children born to mothers in second or later marriages increased by more than half in the 10 years 1977-86 and stood at 42,900 per year in 1986. These accounted for one in 12 of all births within marriage.

The average age of women at childbirth has continued to rise, partly as a result of this. The average age of a woman having a child within marriage was 28.1 in 1986, the highest since 1956.

Source: Population Trends, OPCS 1988, LM 89/1.

Secondary school pupils' attitudes to Christianity

Secondary school pupils in Britain are obliged to sit through morning prayers, but how much good does it do them? Only 29% think God listens.

Research by Leslie Francis over a 12 year period shows 'a consistent, widepsread and large drift further away from the churches among secondary school pupils'. Only 22% of those surveyed in 1986 agreed with the statement 'God is very real to me'; whereas 41% agreed with this in 1974.

Could this be partly a result of the lack of Christian teaching in state secondary schools — despite the fact that religious education (RE) has been compulsory in Britain since 1944? A survey by Culham College Institute showed that in their compulsory RE lessons, only a quarter of fourth and fifth years (age 14-16) learn mainly or exclusively about Christianity. And in the sixth form (16-18 year olds) only one in 14 were taught anything of substance about the faith.

This is the way the parents like it. Three-quarters of parents interviewed by Public Attitude Surveys recently said they would prefer their children to learn about a wide range of religions, if they had to learn about religion at all. But nearly 40% thought religious education should be abolished.

Source: Drift from the Churches: Secondary School Pupils' Attitudes toward Christianity by Leslie Francis, published in the British Journal of Religious Education Volume 11, 1989, pp 76-86, and Culham College Institute and Public Attitude Surveys Research Ltd, LL November 1989.

Secretaries' pay

Britain's secretaries, bus drivers, bank clerks and saleswomen are among the best paid in the world. But cooks and electrical engineers are poorly paid in comparison with those in other European countries.

A study of prices and earnings in 53 cities across the world by the Union Bank of Switzerland shows that secretaries in Britain earn more than primary school teachers, bus drivers, car mechanics, construction workers, toolmakers, cooks and saleswomen.

Secretarial pay and conditions 1989

	Earnings gross	Earnings net	Earnings per hour	Working week	Annual Holiday
	£	£	£	Hours	Days
Zurich	18,600	14,500	7.81	40	20
Geneva	17,000	14,300	7.70	40	20
Luxembourg	13,450	9,900	5.52	40	28
Copenhagen	15,850	9,200	5.33	38	25
Frankfurt	14,900	8,800	4.95	40	30
London	11,700	8,100	4.91	36	23
Brussels	12,400	7,800	4.67	36	20
Amsterdam	11,000	6,500	3.74	40	35
Oslo	11,800	5,300	3.02	38	21
Paris	10,000	5,300	3.02	39	25
Dublin	7,500	5,100	2.98	37	21

From this and from the chart showing the earnings of secretaries across Europe, it is clear that the secretarial support is highly valued in industry. How much do our Christian organisations and churches invest in their much-needed secretaries?

Source: LM 89/2.

Seventh-Day Adventists

A 35 year old member of the Seventh-Day Adventist Church has a life expectancy on average 8.9 years longer than non-Adventists, according to an ongoing research project being carried out in the USA.

The comparison between Adventists and the population of California showed that Adventists live significantly longer than non-Adventists of the same background and marital status. This is attributed largely to their healthy lifestyle, which involves no smoking or alcohol and a vegetarian diet.

This finding acts, it is claimed, as a pointer to what will happen to the average life expectancy of society in general as more and more people follow the current trend for health and fitness.

Life expectancy (additional years) of SDA and California male population 1960-85

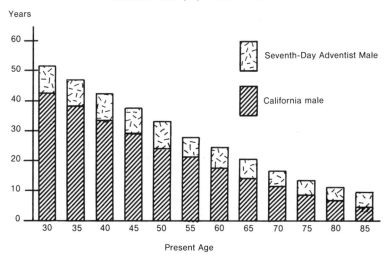

Source: Adventist mortality studies by Seventh-Day Adventist churches in Norway and the Netherlands. A report of the American study appears in Ministry, September 1989, and LL November 1989.

Sex education

In July 1991 the *Independent on Sunday* newspaper commissioned a survey which included asking 760 parents of children aged between 11 and 16 about their sex education. Percentage replies are given below, with 'don't knows' excluded for simplicity.

	Agree strongly	Agree	Neither	Dis-agree	Disagree strongly	Score
	%	%	%	%	%	
'Mothers are bound to play a bigger part than fathers in bringing up their children.'	14	52	8	23	3	+0.5
'It is up to parents, not schools, to teach their children about sex.'	5	40	32	22	1	+0.3
'Parents should tell their children that sex before marriage is wrong.'	6	29	12	49	4	−0.2

The score is calculated by multiplying the 'agree strongly' answers by +2, 'agree' by +1, 'neither' by 0, 'disagree' by −1, and 'disagree strongly' answers by −2; such scores facilitate a comparison between the three questions and their answers.

Parents may tend to feel they should tell their children the physical facts of sex but not about its moral elements. Fathers with sons felt even less inclined than mothers to tell them that sex before marriage was wrong (score −0.3) though were more inclined to tell their daughters (score −0.1)!

One in seven, or 14%, of single parents thought their child was likely to have had sexual intercourse before they were 16, against 4% of other parents (overall 5%, or one child in 20).

Parents were also asked about particular aspects of sex they had discussed with their child(ren).

	Overall	Mother with . . .		Father with . . .	
		Son	Daughter	Son	Daughter
	%	%	%	%	%
Pregnancy	54	55	79	40	35
Contraception	50	54	65	45	31
How to avoid AIDS	49	56	59	46	32
How intercourse takes place	44	50	58	36	29
All of these	33	38	45	24	23
None of these	32	27	14	37	55

The table shows one-third of parents tell nothing, a third everything, and a third somewhere in between. Mothers are much more likely than fathers to have intimate conversations with daughters.

See also: Teenage Sex.
Source: NOP Political, Social and Economic Review No 86, July 1991.

Shropshire

Area (sq km)	Population 1989			Percentage change 1979-89	Percentage under 15	Non-churchgoers 1989
	Men	Women	Total			
3,492	198,500	204,700	403,200	+7.6%	19%	364,200

Churchgoers 1989			Percentage of population	Percentage change 1979-89	Percentage under 15	Number of churches	Percentage built	
Men	Women	Total					before 1500	since 1950
16,000	23,000	39,000	9.7%	−4.0%	22%	565	37%	7%

District	Area (sq km)	Population 1989	Percentage change 1979-89 %
The Wrekin	291	136,000	+10.7
Shrewsbury and Atcham	603	90,800	+4.3
N Shropshire	680	56,600	+13.3
Bridgnorth	634	50,600	+0.3
S Shropshire	1,028	36,000	+6.5
Oswestry	256	33,200	+6.5

Source: Regional Trends 26, HMSO 1991 and English Church Census.

Smoking of cigarettes

On average men smoked 118 cigarettes and women 97 each week in the United Kingdom in 1990.

Three out of every 10 people smoke by the age of 18. Although fewer people smoke than 10 years ago, this decline was not evident among 16 to 19 year olds: in 1980 32% smoked and by 1990 this figure had decreased by only 2%.

The number of smokers between 20 and 60 does not vary considerably by age. Four out of every 10 people in their early 20s smoke as do 35% of those between 25 and 39. People over 60 smoke significantly less.

Approximately a third of men surveyed said they had given up smoking against only one in six of the women. However, about half the women surveyed said either that they never, or only occasionally, smoke a cigarette.

Source: Office of Population Censuses and Surveys: General Household Survey 1990, LM 88/3.

Social attitudes

In 1986 the *British Social Attitudes Survey* found that there is deep support for marriage as an institution, linked with widespread concern that it is treated too frivolously. Some 75% of those questioned agreed that society ought to do more to safeguard marriage. Exactly what should be done wasn't said.

A woman with children under five years old should stay at home while her partner worked, 76% of those questioned told researchers. Equality within marriage was also backed by about a half with 51% saying partners should pool the money, against 33% favouring one partner managing all the money and giving the other their share.

As in previous years the survey found widespread agreement that the government should do more about unemployment and the proportion of the public willing to pay higher taxes to finance better social welfare increased. However, 37% believed that poverty is 'an inevitable part of modern life', a noticeable increase on the 1983 figure.

However, there is another side to all this bouncing optimism. According to the 1988 *Social Trends,* published by the Central Statistical Office, the gap between the rich and poor has yawned wider.

While far more people own their homes, almost 109,000 homeless households were recognised by the local authorities in 1985, compared with 97,000 the year before when 14% of people on local authority waiting lists had been waiting nine or more years.

Source: British Social Attitudes, The 1987 Report, The Times and The Independent, and Social Trends LM 88/4.

Social class

Attitude towards Christianity

Analysis of a study of 10 and 12 year old children attending state-maintained schools in England shows that the apparent lack of relationship between social class and attitude towards Christianity disguises two significant but contradictory patterns of influence.

On the one hand, parents in higher social class occupations attend church more frequently and take children with them. Church attendance tends to promote positive attitudes to Christianity. On the other hand, children from lower social class backgrounds appear to have more conservative social attitudes, which also tend to promote more positive attitudes towards Christianity.

Thus, after controlling for differences in parental church attendance, children from lower social class backgrounds tend to hold more positive attitudes towards Christianity than children from higher social class backgrounds.

Source: The relationship between social class and attitudes towards Christianity among 10 and 12 year old children. Leslie Francis, Paul Pearson and David Lankshear. Personality and individual Differences Vol 11, No 10 1990, pp 1019-27, and LL June 1991.

Scotland

Relatively few studies have examined the impact of Christianity among different socio-economic groups. Peter Sissons in a 1973 report explored the make-up by class in churches of the Borough of Falkirk in Scotland, and found that over the town's churches as a whole, the socio-economic class make-up by parentage was:

		Church of Scotland	Roman Catholic
		%	%
I	Professional	11	0
II	Intermediate	29	20
III N & M	Skilled	52	60
IV	Partly skilled	7	16
V	Unskilled	1	4

Source: The Social Significance of Church Membership in the Borough of Falkirk, Report to Hope Trust and Church Ministry Department, Peter L Sissons, 1973.

Still exists

Social classes no longer exist! Or so says the Office of Population Censuses and Surveys (OPCS).

The OPCS has come under considerable pressure from politicians to stop using the six social classes it has employed since 1911. Formerly the classes were categorised by employment.

However, although statisticians may decide otherwise, people still define themselves by social class and, according to the annual *British Social Attitudes Survey,* traditional British values on marriage, manners and class remain.

Source: British Social Attitudes, The 1987 Report, LM 88/4.

Somerset

Area (sq km)	Population 1989			Percentage change 1979-89	Percentage under 15	Non-churchgoers 1989
	Men	Women	Total			
3,451	223,300	237,600	460,900	+8.8%	18%	410,300

Churchgoers 1989			Percentage of population	Percentage change 1979-89	Percentage under 15	Number of churches	Percentage built	
Men	Women	Total					before 1500	since 1950
20,200	30,400	50,600	11.0%	−11.3%	22%	769	45%	5%

District	Area (sq km)	Population 1989	Percentage change 1979-89
			%
S Somerset	959	142,700	+9.1
Sedgmoor	567	97,400	+10.2
Taunton Deane	458	94,800	+9.3
Mendip	739	94,000	+5.9
W Somerset	728	32,000	+10.9

Source: Regional Trends 26, HMSO 1991 and English Church Census.

South Africa

The 1990 *South African Christian Handbook,* edited by Marjorie Froise, is a comprehensive directory of Christian activity in a country where nearly 60% of the population are church members.

The largest denominations are the Lutheran and Afrikaans Reformed Churches but Roman Catholic, Methodist and Pentecostal churches also have substantial memberships. The handbook shows that while many of the major denominations are losing members or remaining static, the Roman Catholic and Pentecostal Churches are both growing. The fastest-growing group is the International Fellowship of Christian Churches which tripled between 1986 and 1989.

The extensive list of mission and evangelistic organisations shows that more were established in the 1970s than in any other decade. Many theological colleges were also established around the same time; there are now 91 of these, with 4,400 full-time students. This large number amounts to 23% of full-time ministers and evangelists in South African churches. Only about 400 South Africans are in Christian work abroad, over half of these in other African countries.

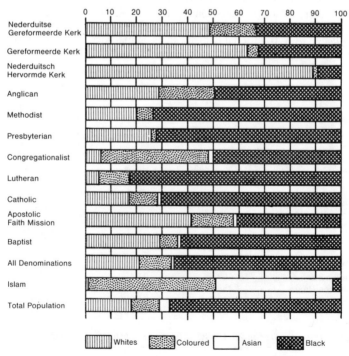

Ethnic composition 1980

The handbook lists church headquarters, mission and evangelistic agencies, training institutions, media, youth work, accommodation and a growing number of service agencies, reflecting the increasing awareness of Christian social responsibility.

Church growth

What needs to happen if every person in a nation is to be reached with the Gospel? Johannes Combrink examines the history and growth of the church in South Africa, looking particularly at the Dutch Reformed Churches and the charismatic churches.

His study provides evidence that churches were most effective when they were actively planting new congregations. Revivals and the availability of trained leaders also heavily influenced fulfilment of the church's evangelistic mandate. The evidence of his research shows the same historical factors to be relevant today.

Based on an overview of the Church in South Africa and detailed case studies of individual congregations, the thesis aims to provide an accurate and up-to-date picture of the South African church in context. As project co-ordinator for the DAWN movement (Discipling A Whole Nation), the author hopes it will be a starting point for strategy on the part of the whole church to disciple Southern Africa.

Source: South African Christian Handbook 1990, edited by Marjorie Froise, published by Christian Info, and Christian Origins and Growth in South Africa: A Dutch Reformed and Charismatic Church Case Study. Thesis for the School of World Mission, by Johannes Jacobus Combrink, 1990, and LL June 1991.

Southampton

The Rev David Jackman gave the following account of two surveys done in his church.

'Ask several different people how many were present at a certain meeting and you will find a considerable variation in the figures. This may not matter greatly until we start to plan for the future on such a basis. We need facts, diligently gathered and accurately presented, if we are to move forward confidently.

'In our local church we have benefited greatly in our planning for growth from two surveys, separated by nearly five years, which have given us a detailed profile of our congregation. The first was carried out in 1982 when the church was experiencing considerable growth, although we didn't really know why. The survey helped us identify the causes and nature of the growth, and provided a firm basis on which to take appropriate action. In our case the survey helped us make the decision to introduce a second Sunday morning service.

'Five years later growth had slowed somewhat, and a second survey showed that this was largely due to a decrease in the number of young adults in the congregation. It seemed the church was not meeting the needs of this particular age group, so we appointed a youth pastor as a member of the church's staff. Since then there has been a noticeable increase in the numbers of young people, especially students, joining our congregations.

'Our experience of recording and analysing church data has made us realise that things don't just happen. We need to plan for advance and growth. Armed with detailed information, we can all be better stewards of the time and resources God gives us. In this way we can begin to discover His direction in getting out the good news of Christ more effectively, across our increasingly needy land.'

Source: Rev David Jackman, Minister, Above Bar Church, Southampton, LM 89/4.

South Yorkshire

Area (sq km)	Population 1989			Percentage change 1979-89	Percentage under 15	Non-churchgoers 1989
	Men	Women	Total			
1,560	634,100	661,100	1,295,200	−2.0%	19%	1,212,800

Churchgoers 1989			Percentage of population	Percentage change 1979-89	Percentage under 15	Number of churches	Percentage built	
Men	Women	Total					before 1500	since 1950
32,300	50,100	82,400	6.4%	−15.9%	25%	703	14%	17%

District	Area (sq km)	Population 1989	Percentage change 1979-89
			%
Sheffield	368	526,600	−4.9
Doncaster	580	293,300	+1.0
Rotherham	283	253,600	+0.5
Barnsley	329	221,700	−2.2

Source: Regional Trends 26, HMSO 1991 and English Church Census.

Spain

The *Spanish Christian Handbook,* published in October 1991, reveals that Spanish church life in the 1980s has been characterised by three main trends:

- Nominal Christianity has declined.
- Roman Catholic mass attendance has declined.
- Protestant churches have experienced growth.

Nominal Christianity

The decline of nominal Christianity is clear — 78% of the population were attached to a church in 1980 compared with 69% 10 years later. Far fewer Spaniards were active church members — 27% in 1980 and 24% in 1990 (using attendance at mass as the equivalent of Protestant membership). Churchmanship declined during the 1980s despite a population increase.

Roman Catholicism

In 1990 the Roman Catholic Church, with 99.1% of the active church members and 94.1% of the churches, had on average 430 people attending mass per church.

While the majority of Spanish people consider themselves Roman Catholics, recent polls have suggested to some that, 'For the Spanish people to be Catholic means to be baptised, to be married and to be buried following the Catholic rites' (Miguel de Unamuno). Opinion polls have revealed that 20% of Spaniards declare themselves to be without faith and around 50% could be said to be non-practising Catholics. The percentage of Roman Catholics in the population varies enormously from diocese to diocese. For example, almost two-thirds of the people in Leon are Catholics, compared with a quarter of those in Sevilla and only 7% of those in Almeria.

Catholics as percentage of total population 1985

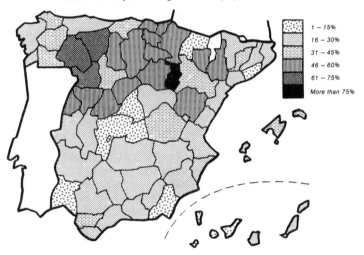

Protestantism

The Protestant church in Spain consists of four main groups — Baptist, Pentecostal, Reformed and 'other' churches. The 'other' church category includes groups such as the Salvation Army, the Seventh-Day Adventists and ethnic churches such as the German Protestant church. Each of the four main groups grew during the 1980s. This was most pronounced in the Pentecostal churches where active membership increased by 147% between 1980 and 1990.

The Protestant churches, which accounted for 5.9% of the churches but only 0.9% of the active church members had far smaller congregations than Catholic churches — 60 on average.

Losses and Gains

The Roman Catholic Church lost almost 761,000 mass attenders during the 1980s, a fall of 7%. In contrast, active church membership in Protestant churches rose by 87% during the decade. The number of Protestant churches increased from 700 in 1980 to an estimated 1,400 in 1990, while the number of Roman Catholic churches remained static.

The number of foreign missionaries in Spain more than doubled during the 1980s: by 1990 there were 1,100 foreign missionaries in the country. Almost a third were based in Andalucia. Rev Stuart Brown, formerly an English missionary in Spain with the Spanish Gospel Mission, wrote in 1991, 'There is a need for more Spanish workers. There is a need for more non-Spaniards to go to Spain, prepared to integrate fully into the Spanish life and culture.'

Source: Compendio Cristiano Espanol: Iglesias y Misiones. Spanish Christian Handbook: Churches and Missions. Edited by Mary Lawson, MARC Europe, London, 1991, and LL September 1991.

Statistical Sources

Reviews of UK Statistical Sources, Volume XX: Religion

The Royal Statistical Society published detailed sources by topic of many of the statistics published in this country in the 1970s and 1980s. Volumes were produced on health, housing, land and road use, energy, construction, rail and sea use, crime, weather and water. The twentieth and penultimate to be issued is on religion.

Although the title is Religion, only 110 of the book's 621 pages refer to religions other than Christianity, reflecting the paucity of published statistical data on other religions. Half of these 110 pages refer to Jewish statistical publications as the Board of Deputies releases pertinent data.

The first part of the book deals with recurring Christian data and was compiled by Lynda Barley, former research officer with the Bible Society. After a chapter on definitions, she divides her work into two main categories, trinitarian and non-trinitarian. Within the trinitarian group the statistical sources on the whole church community come under examination. Subjects included here are membership, attendance, clergy, training and missionaries. Church buildings, schools and places of higher education are covered in another chapter as are the issues of finance, rites of passage, religious agencies, broadcasting and publishing. The same topics are covered for the non-trinitarians although the actual published data for these is much less.

The second section, on topical and 'one-off' statistical studies, was compiled by Dr Clive Field, a librarian at Manchester University who is to be commended for the incredible search through the religious data of the last 50 years, noting questions on every religious topic. These are now collected together, allowing the enquirer to search for a subject by country, denomination, belief and religious practice, among others. A whole chapter is devoted to church attendance. Attitudes to sexual and marriage issues, politics, church changes and evangelism are also covered. This is a thorough and comprehensive selection, not of statistics themselves, but of their sources.

This is a volume giving a complete look at the quantitative aspects of today's church, its people and its leaders and their opinions. It still remains for someone to convert all these source references into layman's terms. A similar need exists for a qualitative study of contemporary church life in Britain.

As the volume was compiled up to the end of 1982, more recent publications are not included. However, it is a unique publication which is unlikely to be repeated as project funding has now ceased. It is an essential addition to any serious library covering Christianity. There is no other source volume like it and it is therefore highly recommended.

Source: Published by Pergamon Press, £57.50, LM 89/1.

Staffordshire

Area (sq km)	Population 1989			Percentage change 1979-89	Percentage under 15	Non-churchgoers 1989
	Men	Women	Total			
2,716	513,800	525,200	1,039,000	+2.7%	19%	939,700

Churchgoers 1989			Percentage of population	Percentage change 1979-89	Percentage under 15	Number of churches	Percentage built	
Men	Women	Total					before 1500	since 1950
37,700	61,600	99,300	9.6%	−0.9%	23%	777	19%	13%

District	Area (sq km)	Population 1989	Percentage change 1979-89
			%
Stoke-on-Trent	93	247,100	−2.6
Stafford	599	119,100	+2.0
Newcastle-under-Lyme	211	118,200	−2.5
S Staffordshire	409	109,100	+15.2
Staffordshire Moorlands	576	97,800	+2.5
E Staffordshire	388	96,900	+0.8
Lichfield	330	93,000	+5.7
Cannock Chase	79	88,800	+5.4
Tamworth	31	69,000	+7.3

Source: Regional Trends 26, HMSO 1991 and English Church Census.

Students

Ambitions

A survey of student opinions in Britain in the summer of 1988 showed that

73% of students in higher education consider themselves 'caring' and 71% as 'responsible'.

However, the survey, carried out by Gallup for the *Daily Telegraph,* shows that these self-attributes do not seem to be reflected in students' attitudes to jobs.

In the list of important aspects of a job, usefulness to society and responsibility come a long way down, and the least respected jobs are teaching, followed by social services.

The aspect students said they were most looking for in a job was to 'feel they can achieve something' (75%) followed by 'an opportunity to use initiative'. The emphasis appears to be on the importance of self-fulfilment and good rewards — something which advertisers aiming at graduates are obviously aware of.

The first choice of career is industry for 18%, and 10% would ideally like to set up their own business. The popularity of these attitudes and aspirations reflect the climate of the 'enterprise culture'.

How does this affect the Church? Not surprisingly, 'the ministry/ priesthood' was the chosen career of only 1% of those interviewed. This fits in with the downward trend in the number of clergy — down by one every two days — and the decreasing numbers of British missionary personnel.

Should the local church be trying harder to encourage Christian young people to seek God's calling on their lives, being prepared to give them the essential support they will need if this means going against the trend of their generation?

Source: LM 89/1.

Image of Christianity

Students in the UK do not see Christianity as Good News, at least not for their own personal development. A survey of students at Newcastle's university and polytechnic found that non-Christian students saw Christians of their own age as more boring, less fashionable and worse-off in most respects than themselves.

Their image of a Christian was definitely not something to which the students aspired. In almost every dimension of character and lifestyle, the students interviewed saw Christians as further away from their ideal than they considered themselves to be. They thought Christians on the whole were more inhibited, less part of a crowd, less happy and so on.

It would be significant to see to what extent these negative perceptions put students off getting involved with Christianity. And it is important to try and do something about them if it will help give the message of the Gospel a fair hearing in the student world.

'Christians are . . .
>Less free
>More unfashionable
>More isolated

	More emotional	Less realistic
	Less sexually fulfilled	Less involved in the "real world"
	More boring	Less happy
	Psychologically weaker	Less friendly . . .
	Following fewer interests	than me.'

Newcastle student.

Source: Negative Attitudes to Christianity, by J S Bloice-Smith, LM 90/3.

Religious attitudes

Valuable insight into the religious attitudes and practices of students comes from research by Dr John Mulholland over 24 years among students at Sheffield University.

	1961	1972	1985
	%	%	%
Some religious upbringing	94	88	51
Holder of religious belief	73	53	38
Say private prayers	65	42	30
Say private prayers daily	31	16	9
Attend church	46	25	15
Attend church four times per month	23	12	8
Active church member	38	16	9
Member of student religious group	15	9	6

From the figures it is clear that religious belief among students, at least in Sheffield, has declined considerably since 1961. The proportion with such belief has virtually halved and those with religious upbringing has also halved. Increasingly, nominal Christian parents are producing agnostic children.

Nevertheless, despite the radical drop in proportions of students who do adhere to some religious practice, approximately one in three still say private prayers. Almost one in seven attends church at some time, and just over half of these attend weekly. The survey reveals there are many more student churchgoers than actual church members.

Secularisation, the research also shows, increases faster among men than women. How can the Church stem this tide of nominalism? For ministers with prospective students in the congregation, it is essential to urge them to join a Christian Union or other Christian group, not only for fellowship but to share their faith among their peers.

Additionally, new students with some church background may initially attend a fellowship on first coming to university, college or polytechnic. The autumn term is an ideal opportunity for local churches to arrange welcome meetings for students, to open up homes, to break out of the normal routine of insular youth fellowships and to evangelise these young people. After all, tomorrow's leaders are probably studying today.

Source: LM 87/1.

Successful churches

What makes a successful church? Recent research in the USA found that churches which attracted growing numbers of highly committed people had several things in common. You might like to see how the church you are involved with compares.

People . . .

    . . . came before programmes. Members weren't required to fit into available slots in the church structure.

    . . . could all articulate the church's vision — not just the leaders.

    . . . took prayer seriously. A prayer ministry was seen as very important, not just something for those who couldn't do anything else.

    . . . were keen to grow in their faith.

    . . . were proud of the church and brought along friends and neighbours.

Programmes . . .

    . . . were flexible. Structures of programmes which were no longer valid could be dropped, and new ones developed to fit new ministries.

    . . . made youth work a priority.

    . . . concentrated on doing a few things well. Aiming for excellence in what the church was called to do was more important than doing a bit of everything.

Source: Successful Churches. What they have in common, Barna Research Group 1990, and MARC Monograph No 33, and LM 21/1.

Suffolk

Area (sq km)	Population 1989			Percentage change 1979-89	Percentage under 15	Non-churchgoers 1989
	Men	Women	Total			
3,797	314,500	326,500	641,000	+8.9%	20%	554,800

Churchgoers 1989			Percentage of population	Percentage change 1979-89	Percentage under 15	Number of churches	Percentage built	
Men	Women	Total					before 1500	since 1950
36,200	50,000	86,200	13.4%	−11.4%	26%	895	51%	9%

District	Area (sq km)	Population 1989	Percentage change 1979-89
			%
Ipswich	40	113,600	−7.0
Suffolk Coastal	889	112,800	+21.4
Waveney	370	107,100	+8.8
St Edmundsbury	658	91,800	+6.8
Mid Suffolk	871	78,100	+13.2
Babergh	595	78,000	+6.8
Forest Heath	374	59,600	+16.6

Source: Regional Trends 26, HMSO 1991 and English Church Census.

Suicide

The countries with the greatest proportion of suicides and self-inflicted injuries are Hungary and the Soviet Union. In 1980, 45 out of every 100,000 people in these countries killed themselves.

In Europe Switzerland has the highest suicide rate at 25 per 100,000 of the population each year. In West Germany the figures stand at 21, in Sweden 19 and in France 17. The Japanese statistic is 18. In the United Kingdom the story is slightly better, with only nine for every 100,000 people.

How do we combat the tendency to suicide? Should Christian teaching, witness and evangelism point more clearly to the intrinsic worth of the individual to a loving, personal God?

Source: Private Opinions — Public Polls 1986, LM 87/1.

Sunday

Sunday is seen as a 'family day' by 92% of mothers surveyed by the Harris Research Centre: 'a day when you give time and attention to those around you'. Both playing with the children and spending time with their husband or partner are important features of Sunday, which is seen by 69% as 'a breath of fresh air in the week'.

What's more, three out of five mothers believe Sunday is the only day the family eat together — and they don't want to lose it!

Source: Keep Sunday Special Campaign, LM 89/3.

Surrey

Area	Population 1989			Percentage change	Percentage under	Non-churchgoers
(sq km)	Men	Women	Total	1979-89	15	1989
1,680	485,600	514,400	1,000,000	−1.9%	18%	889,300

Churchgoers 1989			Percentage of population	Percentage change 1979-89	Percentage under 15	Number of churches	Percentage built	
Men	Women	Total					before 1500	since 1950
47,600	63,100	110,700	11.1%	−6.7%	24%	669	18%	20%

District	Area (sq km)	Population 1989	Percentage change 1979-89	Total Church-goers 1989	Percentage of 1989 population
			%		%
Guildford	271	122,900	−2.0	15,800	13.1
Reigate & Banstead	129	114,900	−2.2	11,300	9.8
Waverley	345	109,500	−3.0	15,200	13.7
Elmbridge	97	107,300	−5.7	14,100	12.5
Woking	64	85,700	+5.8	11,300	13.3
Spelthorne	56	85,500	−9.9	6,500	7.4
Surrey Heath	97	83,600	+9.7	5,700	7.3
Mole Valley	259	76,200	−2.0	7,900	10.2
Tandridge	250	75,500	−4.0	8,800	11.7
Runnymede	78	70,500	−4.6	6,900	9.8
Epsom and Ewell	34	68,400	−1.7	7,200	10.9

Source: Regional Trends 26, HMSO 1991 and English Church Census.

Switzerland

A visit to Geneva gives the impression that Christianity is an important part of Swiss life and John Calvin a national hero. The *Christian Handbook* for the French-speaking part of Switzerland shows that a tourist's impression can be misleading. However it shows that the trends in church life in Switzerland have much in common with other Western European countries.

Components of Christian community in French-speaking area

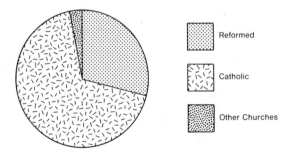

Reformed

Catholic

Other Churches

Nominalism

Many people have some Christian connection, but most are not church members, and notional Christianity is on the decline. About 84% of the French-speaking Swiss are attached to a church, a decline from 95% in 1980. Only 24% are church members.

Catholic church decline

The Catholic church, which has 66% of church members, is declining slowly, the loss of manpower being a major problem — although less so than in France and the Netherlands. The church will have lost 5,000 members between 1980 and 1995, while the Protestant churches will have gained a similar number.

Pentecostal church growth

Church growth is slow in the Reformed churches, to which 63% of Protestant church members belong, but rapid in some of the Pentecostal groups, which are active in planting new congregations. From 2,000 members in 1980 the Pentecostal churches have grown at a rate of 5% a year to 3,500 in 1990, and are estimated to reach to 4,200 by 1995.

More churches for ethnic groups

New churches have also begun to cater for different ethnic groups in Switzerland, of which there are many. For example, the high number of Romanian immigrants in recent years has meant a huge growth in the Romanian Orthodox churches.

As in other parts of Western Europe, the church faces the challenge of presenting a living alternative to the secular culture which is eroding all but the most vital Christianity.

Changes in French-speaking Swiss churches

Source: Le Christianisme en Suisse Romande/Christian Handbook for French-Speaking Switzerland, MARC Europe, 1990, and LL June 1990 and LM 90/3.

T

Teenagers

Reading

Rosemary Stones, editorial director of children's books at HarperCollins formulates three categories of teenagers for book publishing:

10, 11, 12 year olds	Aspirant teens.
13, 14 year olds	Glad-to-be-teens.
15 and above year olds	Don't patronise me, I'm a person.

Books written specifically for teenagers are mostly read by the aspirant teens, seeking role models. The genuine teenager either reads hardly any books or feasts on gentle fiction such as fantasy, romance, science fiction or is reading adult books.

Source: Article by Mary Hoffman in The Bookseller, 11 October 1991, p 1047.

Population

Between 1987 and 1995 the number of 16 to 19 year olds in the United Kingdom will decline by 25%, a fact of consequence to churches as well as to businesses.

Past surveys have shown that many young people are converted in their late teens and a number of these end up in full-time Christian work. If there are fewer young people in this age-group, maybe there will be a smaller number becoming Christians and so possibly less potential leaders.

At a time when there is a downward drift in church membership, a decline in the number of full-time workers or even potential youthworkers would cause problems.

Strategic thinking to overcome this must begin now, with thinking on how to reach the often neglected teenage groups.

In West Germany, where the same problem has existed for longer, official state church figures show a six-fold increase in the number of women ministers in the 20 years.

See also: Young Britain.
Source: Labour Market Quarterly Report, July 1988, LM 89/1.

Pregnancy

A survey in December 1990 revealed a dramatic change in the sexual habits of teenagers in the UK. Half the girls surveyed and a third of the boys said they had had sex before they reached 16, the legal age of consent. In the mid-1960s the proportion was just one in 50 girls and one in 17 boys.

This has inevitably resulted in an increase in unwanted pregnancies. The number of teenager pregnancies in 1985 was 119,000, 84% of them outside marriage. In 1988, 76% of all illegitimate births were to teenage mothers, compared with 22% in 1964. Pregnant teenagers in the UK would rather have an abortion or an illegitimate child than marry their child's father, said the Department of Health in a 1988 report. Of all teenage pregnancies in the years 1969-71, 13% ended in abortion. In the years 1984-85, this had increased to 34%, or 20,000 babies.

Teenage girls who become pregnant are far less likely either to be married at the time, or to have 'shotgun weddings' than was the case in the late 1960s, as marriage is less of a social obligation. Just 15% of the girls are married, and 11% get married, compared with 21% in 1975, leaving 41% of teenage mothers to bring up their children alone.

Outcome of conceptions by girls under 20 in England & Wales

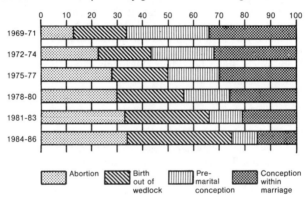

This number of teenage pregnancies is a cause for concern. The question is also raised as to what happened to sex education in schools. The 1988 Education Act increased the number of school governors, and one aspect of the legislation requires these to examine afresh the sex education given in schools. Should churches press Christian school governors to urge a more complete sex education, which includes a social or moral framework?

A Christian context remains the responsibility of the family and the church, but what of the large numbers of children who will not get any clear guidelines from either? A society which does not teach young people the value of life cannot expect them to live accordingly and will inevitably suffer the consequences.

Source: Family Policy Studies Centre, reported in the Daily Telegraph, LM 89/2, LM 91/3.

Sexual activity

Josh McDowell and David Day have studied one of those areas less frequently discussed by Christian researchers — teenage sexuality. Their book *Why Wait?* contains a thorough investigation of all aspects of the subject, written to assist Christian parents in helping their children to resist one of the most obvious social trends in American life. The average American girl these days will first experience sex at 14 years old, the average boy at 13. Not surprisingly, there are well over a million teenage pregnancies per year.

Particularly disturbing is the importance of the parents' influence on the way the children will behave: for example girls from fatherless homes are 60% more likely to have premarital sex than those with both parents at home.

After analysing the problem, authors suggest practical solutions, one of the simplest being that parents spend more time with their families. One study in the USA of church parents and their teenage children found that the majority of teenagers spend less than 30 minutes a day with their father. Over 40% spend less than 30 minutes with their mother.

No surprise that 46% of fathers in this study admitted they worry 'quite a bit' or 'very much' about how their child feels about them.

See also: Sex Education.
Source: Why Wait? Josh McDowell and Dick Day, Here's Life Publishers 1987, and LL February 1990.

Spending power

When it comes to achieving happiness, British teenagers prefer money to love and friendship. They value money and possessions as signs of personal worth and social value.

This is the result of a survey into young people's attitudes by McCann Erickson reported in *The Times* in 1987. Based on a sample of 985 people divided into two age categories, 15-19 and 20-25, the results suggested that the 'over-riding discovery was the feeling that money was the doorway to modern life and that to consume is to have worth'.

Young people are also becoming financially active. The survey showed that 43% of teenagers aged 15 to 19 had a bank account, 28% a building society account and 8% a credit card.

According to Christine Bestell, a director of McCann Erickson, the effects of consumerism will have long term effects on teenagers. 'Economic security will be necessary to satisfy the consumer hopes of the young, and they will carry that as emotional baggage for the rest of their lives,' she told LandMARC.

Given that these attitudes must rub off on Christian teenagers how can the Church show them the proper biblical priorities for life? Do they see biblical standards reflected in their own Christian communities, or is the economic spirit of the 1980s influencing the Church?

Source: LM 88/2.

Independence

The *Independent on Sunday* newspaper commissioned NOP to study parents with younger teenage children in 1991. One question asked what they would allow their children to do. Answers varied by age as the table below indicates (percentages add to more than 100% as multiple answers were given).

Percentage who would allow son/daughter to	under 16 years old	under 18 years old
	%	%
Hold a party at home while parents were out	8	32
Stay out at an all night party without supervision	3	29
Smoke cigarettes	4	14
Drink alcohol regularly	2	14
Have a girl/boy friend in his/her room overnight	5	11
None of these	81	35

The dramatic change in control by parents between 16 and 18 years is clearly seen by these figures. Teenagers are allowed to act far more independently in these years — equivalent to being in the sixth form at school. How does your church teenage programmes reflect this relaxation of control?

Source: NOP Political, Social and Economic Review No 86, July 1991.

Teenage values in the USA

Half the 13 to 19 year olds in the USA go to church in a typical week, compared with 8% in England. And 29% of American teenagers would call themselves 'born-again' Christians.

This rises to 33% of the 18 year olds surveyed in a 1991 report from the Barna Research Group, compared with 34% of American adults, supporting other research showing around two-thirds of Christians are converted before they reach their 20s. However, the survey found that 25% of the sample were converted even before they reached their teens, again far more than the UK's 17%.

The report gives details on leisure and church activities, beliefs, worries, values and attitudes of American teenagers. It provides a wealth of insights for churches and others concerned with reaching teenagers, some encouraging, some disturbing.·

A lack of commitment: only 38% of Christian teenagers considered the Bible, churchgoing or Jesus to be 'very important'.

The importance of parents: 54% of Christian teenagers said they were converted because of the influence of their parents, 23% said it was through the church.

Peer group pressure: while 33% of teenagers think churchgoing is important themselves, only 13% think their friends see it as important.

The importance of music: it is more important than religion to teenagers, but despite the variety of contemporary Christian music available in the USA, most teenagers have never heard of Christian artists.

The critical issue: 'Having a goal or purpose in life' is important for 93% of the teenagers surveyed. Over a third of them, and almost half the 18 year olds, see it as their biggest concern.

Source: Today's Teenagers, A Generation in Transition, Barna Research Group 1991, and LL June 1991.

Television

Children's viewing
Children in Britain spend more time watching television than playing, taking part in sports or reading, according to the autumn 1987 edition of *Omnibus.* Among 10 to 14 year olds it was the most frequently mentioned pastime.

Computer games are also very popular, though enthusiasm declines with age. Although 58% of eight to 10 year olds said this was their favourite activity, the percentage fell to 28 in the 15 to 19 age group.

So, what are the 15 to 19 year olds doing with their time if television and computer games do not appeal? Of course Saturday jobs and weekday and weekend sporting activities take up quite a lot of time for some teenagers.

Is there an activity gap the church could be harnessing, encouraging older teenagers to become involved by making programmes for them contemporary and attractive?

Source: LM 88/2.

Influence
A 1988 survey shows that 82% of Britons watch an average of four hours television every day. Only 62% of them can tear themselves away to eat their dinner!

An NOP survey for the *Mail on Sunday* asked people how they thought television affected both their lives and society as a whole. Replies showed that 53% considered that television could influence people's behaviour in only minor ways, the figure being higher among the 18 to 24 age-group.

Most people didn't consider that they had changed their attitudes to groups such as homosexuals as a result of watching programmes like 'East Enders'. Neither had it changed attitudes towards racial groups. However, 36% of respondents claimed to have changed their opinion of an issue after watching a documentary on the subject.

This gives great power to the producers of TV programmes. And although many people do not consider television to have a great influence on them, this may be an indication of the power of TV to influence people without them realising it.

Whereas when reading a newspaper report or listening to the radio, we are aware that we are getting someone else's opinion, watching an event on TV gives the illusion of actually being there.

As far as its effect on society goes, the majority of respondents did not consider television a major influence. A fifth thought it had some effect on the increasing violence and 17% on the increasing number of sexual attacks.

Source: NOP Political, Social and Economic Review No 71, LM 89/1.

Religious

It is assumed that it is churchgoers who are most likely to watch religious programmes on television. Nearly half the people surveyed by the Independent Broadcasting Authority in 1987 thought so, whereas only 15% thought people who never went to church would be likely to watch.

However, the viewing figures prove otherwise. The regular, networked religious programmes in the UK are watched by a majority of viewers, 62%, at least occasionally. And although about a third of viewers switch them off, another third switch on their sets specially to watch religious programmes. Yet church attenders make up only around 11% of the UK population.

The audience for religious programming is very similar to that for the current affairs programmes, often broadcast at peak time on weekdays. By this standard, religious broadcasting could be fairly said to be of mainstream interest, comparing favourably with the much-publicised breakfast TV, which 60% of viewers never watch.

This is certainly good news for those wanting to see Christianity given a higher profile on television, and indicating that a large proportion of those outside the church aren't averse to Christianity if it comes through their normal channels. This is an opportunity not to be wasted.

Percentage of audiences for religious TV programmes, February 1988

	All aged 4 and over	All adults	Gender		Age-group					65 and over
			Men	Women	16-24	25-34	35-44	45-54	55-64	
Saw at least one religious TV programme	57	62	56	66	33	45	50	65	78	87

Source: Godwatching Viewers, Religion and Television by Svennig, Haldane, Spier and Gunter, IBA John Libbey 1988, LM 89/3.

Worldwide ownership

	Radio sets (excluding wired receivers) (millions)					Televisions (millions)				Video cassette recorders (millions)
	1955	1965	1975	1985	1990	1965	1975	1985	1990	1990
Europe	86	176	279	462	568	74	190	293	353	71
Middle East Including North Africa	2	12	29	58	74	1	6	19	36	10
Africa South Africa	1	3	5	10	12	0	1	3	4	1
Rest (excluding North Africa)	0	5	18	43	59	0	1	8	14	2
South Asia/Far East China	1	6	35	120	290	0	1	56	150	2
Japan	12	27	87	100	120	18	42	70	75	25
India	1	5	24	50	75	0	0	2	30	3
Other countries	2	13	50	111	127	1	9	31	61	11
North America USA	111	230	380	500	560	68	110	175	185	65
Canada	5	14	23	32	42	5	9	14	16	6
Caribbean	0	1	4	6	6	0	1	2	2	1
Latin America	13	29	63	133	164	7	23	55	84	10
Australasia and Oceania	3	8	13	25	27	3	5	9	10	4
World total	237	529	1,010	1,650	2,124	177	398	737	1,020	211
% increase per year	–	8	7	5	5	–	8	6	7	–

Source: World Radio and Television Receivers, International Broadcasting and Audience Research, BBC, June 1991.

European ownership 1990 (% of households)

	Households (millions)	Television %	Video %	Teletext %	Cable %	Direct-to-house satellite reception equipment %	Radios per 100 population
Austria	2.8	99	42	15	20	4	118
Luxembourg	0.14	98	59	9	71	*	81
Belgium	3.9	98	46	17	86	*	78
Spain	11.0	98	45	5	*	1	60
USSR	97.5	98	2	n/a	*	*	41
Sweden	3.9	97	68	39	38	3	164
UK	22.1	97	67	32	2	7	144
Netherlands	5.8	97	49	32	81	3	94
Italy	19.1	97	25	15	*	*	97
France	21.1	96	47	19	2	*	109
Germany	32.8	96	47	14	31	3	96

(continued on page 189)

European Ownership 1990 (% of households) (cont. from page 188)

	House-holds (millions)	Tele-vision	Video	Teletext	Cable	Direct-to-house satellite reception equipment	Radios per 100 popula-tion
		%	%	%	%	%	
Denmark	2.3	96	43	30	36	2	136
Norway	1.9	95	57	37	26	4	83
Ireland	1.03	95	53	6	35	2	60
Finland	1.9	95	52	26	35	*	76
Switzerland	2.5	94	51	25	65	*	80
Greece	3.2	94	38	n/a	*	*	59
Portugal	3.1	94	31	n/a	n/a	1	41
Turkey	9.7	93	33	*	*	2	18
Poland	12.0	83	12	*	*	1	52
Czechoslovakia	5.9	81	14	8	3	1	61
Yugoslavia	6.2	79	10	*	4	1	47
Bulgaria	2.95	76	5	n/a	*	*	56
Hungary	4.0	75	11	5.5	10	1	81
Romania	7.4	53	6	n/a	*	*	38

* less than 0.5%   n/a = not applicable

Source: CIT Research 1991, published in Independent Television Commission magazine, Spectrum Autumn 1991; International Broadcasting and Audience Research, BBC June 1991.

Tenure

Housing costs are always a key item in any domestic budget. The following table shows how the proportions of different types of accommodation changed over 20 years, with a dramatic increase in mortgages and owner-occupied property, and a decline in rented housing, particularly in the private sector.

Household tenure Great Britain

	1971	1975	1981	1985	1990
	%	%	%	%	%
Owner occupied, owned outright	22	22	23	24	25
Owner occupied, with mortgage	27	28	31	37	41
Rented from local authority or New Town	31	33	34	28	24
Rented from housing association or co-operative	1	1	2	2	2
Rented with job or business	5	3	2	2	2
Rented privately, unfurnished	11	10	6	5	4
Rented privately, furnished	3	3	2	2	2
Sample size (= 100%)	11,936	11,970	11,939	9,933	9,578

Source: OPCS General Household Survey Monitor 1991.

Theological training colleges

The priority of theological colleges in the United Kingdom is not the training of leaders for the church of the future, but the spiritual development of the student. Unlike training for most other professions, that of Christian leaders tends to concentrate on the theoretical rather than the practical aspects of the job.

Rev Ian Bunting's report *The Places to Train* sets out to investigate why colleges turn out the kind of people they do. A survey among all the theological colleges in the UK asked them to identify the way they saw the role of the Church and of the minister. From the responses it is clear that different places are training their students for different jobs.

Models of Ministry

The order of circles, from left to right, shows the average rank given to each model overall. The area of the inner circle indicates the percentage of institutions which identified at all with the model, against an outer circle of 100%. The solid black shading relates to the number of times the model was ranked first or second on the scale of importance.

	Preacher	Master	Practical Theologian	Priest
Average rank of model	2.4	3.1	3.1	3.2
% identifying at all with model	87%	86%	55%	43%

	Builder	Manager	Therapist
Average rank of model	3.4	4.1	4.1
% identifying at all with model	81%	79%	76%

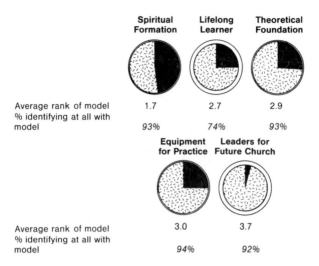

	Spiritual Formation	Lifelong Learner	Theoretical Foundation
Average rank of model	1.7	2.7	2.9
% identifying at all with model	93%	74%	93%

	Equipment for Practice	Leaders for Future Church
Average rank of model	3.0	3.7
% identifying at all with model	94%	92%

Anglican colleges see the minister primarily as a 'knowledgeable teacher of the faith' and 'practical theologian', someone who is always learning, and passing on that knowledge to his congregation. The minister as 'priest' is a model given priority by the higher Anglican colleges and courses, as well as the Catholic colleges surveyed, but is recognised by only 8% of the other denominational colleges. This is in line with the view held by many of the Anglican institutions of the church as 'sacrament'.

The most highly-rated function of the minister was that of 'preacher', generally more emphasised by those who did not see the minister as 'priest'. Those who related strongly to this gave still more weight to the role of the church as 'herald' of the gospel to the world, this difference perhaps reflecting their recognition that preaching is not the only way of communicating the gospel.

All the non-denominational and inter-denominational training centres, which included missionary training colleges and the courses run by some of the 'house' church groupings, identified the Christian leader's role as one of 'church-builder' and 'missionary', as did 93% of the denominational colleges.

Consistently unpopular was the model of the minister as a manager, despite the fact that much of the responsibility which falls on church leaders is the leading, motivating and organising of people and events. However, as the author concludes, many colleges, particularly the Anglican ones on whose behalf the survey was undertaken, still train their students to be communicators of the faith and not leaders capable of animating the life of a local church.

Source: The Places to Train, Rev Ian Bunting, MARC Europe 1990, LM 90/2 and LL February 1990.

Time

How do we use our time?

The British spend on average a third of each week asleep, 56 hours for men, 58 for women. For those in full time employment, men work an average of 45 hours a week, women 41. Domestic work such as cooking, cleaning and personal care ('essential activities' in the table below) occupies 33 hours a week for men and 45 for women, reflecting the continuing unequal division of domestic labour between the sexes.

So how do we use our time? Those in part-time work spend more time on essential activities rather than leisure; 49 hours per week for men, 61 for women. Part-time workers sleep for much the same time as full-time employees, but do manage to have a few spare hours per week; the survey showed four hours for both men and women. Interestingly, they have more free time during the week, but less at weekends.

Housewives spend 46% of their time on essential activities, an average of 77 hours. They have only a third more leisure time a week than women in full-time work. Averaged out over a week, each woman has at least three and a half hours a day for leisure and each man five hours. 'No time for God or for the Church' seems a claim which is hard to substantiate in the face of this evidence.

Hours per Week

	Full-time employees		Part-time employees		House-wives	Retired people
	Male	*Female*	*Male*	*Female*		
Employment	45	41	24	22	–	–
Essential activities	33	45	49	61	77	50
Sleep	56	58	57	57	59	60
Leisure	34	24	38	28	32	58
Leisure as % waking time	30%	22%	34%	25%	29%	54%

See also: Women's work.
Source: Gallup Survey of Britain, Gordon Heald and R J Wybrow 1986, LM 88/2.

Tourists

Nearly half the world's entire expenditure by tourists is spent in Western Europe. 1985 figures released by the Commission of the European Communities show that 47% of total travel and tourism receipts come to Europe, and 44% of total travel expenditure.

Italy has the highest proportion of this total, 11% of the world's travel receipts, followed by France and Spain with 8% each. Next come West Germany and the United Kingdom with 6% each. The remaining seven EC countries account for the final 8%.

This represents a considerable proportion of tourist traffic and thus opportunities to reach people with the Gospel. Europe has a considerable Christian heritage. How might churches and Christian organisations encourage more people to see the cathedrals, churches and other places of interest? Could more people be encouraged to visit churches by having special services where tourists are catered for and made especially welcome? Visitors to churches will often have a prime interest in the history or architecture of the buildings; they should also be encouraged to acquire a positive image of contemporary Christianity, and to have the challenge of the Gospel presented in an appropriate way.

Source: LM 87/2.

Trust giving to religious causes

Over £135 million was given to various causes by the 200 largest grant-making trusts in Britain in 1987.

Only 0.75% of these were given to projects in the category of religion. This includes churches, missions and organisations working in evangelism or church-planting, although not the various Christian charities which are active in other fields.

The average grant given to religious causes is one of the smallest. Are we not asking for enough money for large projects, or do we not have the vision to make plans on a large scale for fear of not having the money to fund them?

Source: LM 89/2.

Turkey

Of the eight million or so Muslims in Western Europe, nearly two million live in Germany, of which 1.5 million are from Turkey. Perhaps the church should focus much more attention on the generation who have grown up in Europe — 100,000 or so in the 15 to 20 age-group in Germany's Turkish population. These are likely to be nominal Muslims and much more open than their parents.

Although many Europeans do not give a warm welcome to the immigrant populations in their cities, Christians ought to be among those who do reach out to them in friendship — and with the Good News.

Source: World Christian News, March 1990, LM 90/2.

Tyne and Wear

'The graveyard of evangelists' was the description of Sunderland which met Billy Graham on his 1984 Mission England tour. It is true that in recent years mission has not been a priority and Tyne and Wear churches have suffered as a result. Unable to maintain levels of income and atten-dance many church buildings have been converted to other uses or demo-lished. The area has also suffered its share of economic depression. The 1981 national census showed, on average, 17% of men between 16 and 64

Area (sq km)	Population 1989			Percentage change 1979-89	Percentage under 15	Non-churchgoers 1989
	Men	Women	Total			
540	546,600	581,500	1,128,100	−2.9%	26%	1,035,700

Churchgoers 1989			Percentage of population	Percentage change 1979-89	Percentage under 15	Number of churches	Percentage built	
Men	Women	Total					before 1500	since 1950
35,100	57,300	92,400	8.2%	−13.8%	20%	626	6%	23%

District	Area (sq km)	Population 1989	Percentage change 1979-89
			%
Sunderland	138	296,200	−0.5
Newcastle upon Tyne	112	277,600	−2.9
Gateshead	142	205,800	−4.4
North Tyneside	84	192,700	−3.7
South Tyneside	64	155,800	−4.7

Proportion of church members in Tyne and Wear

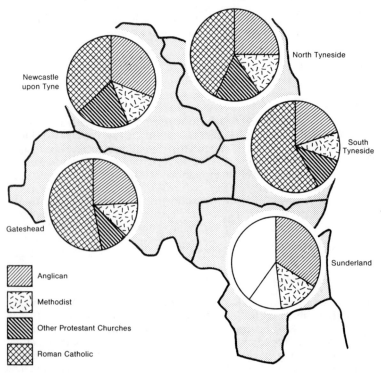

Newcastle upon Tyne

North Tyneside

South Tyneside

Gateshead

Sunderland

Anglican

Methodist

Other Protestant Churches

Roman Catholic

unemployed, and 6% of households with three or more dependent children. In South Tyneside 56% of households are council owned and the figure does not drop below 42% in any of the five Tyne and Wear districts.

Growth and attendance

Against this background a more positive picture of churches bursting with new life is now emerging. Anglican membership is growing at 2% per year, Catholic membership at 1%. The smaller denominations are increasing by 7%. 20% of churchgoers are under 15, against 19% of the population. Nowhere do more men attend church than women, though the numbers are quite close: in Sunderland 49% of churchgoers are men, 51% women, and the greatest difference is only 4%, in Newcastle. 17% of the adult population belonged to a church in 1989, but only 8% attended.

Church attendance is not the same as membership. In an earlier, detailed study, *Prospects for the Eighties,* church attendance in Tyne and Wear was almost half membership. Some denominations had a higher proportion: 85% of Methodists attended at least once a month, as did 75% of Anglicans and those in smaller denominations. Only 36% of Catholics went to church regularly. These proportions had not changed greatly, ten years later.

New organisations

Tyne and Wear boasts 39 Christian youth organisations, 34 Christian social service and welfare bodies and 27 overseas agencies, plus Christian bookshops, evangelistic agencies and education and training organisations. Over 250 Christian or church-based organisations work in the area. Half are registered charities and half started between 1960 and 1985. Of these, 60% are inter-denominational; Christians in the area show a genuine commitment to working together.

Christian caring

This commitment manifests itself in the level of Christian caring in this area. Christians offer all kinds of services to all the community in Tyne and Wear: to other Christians, to those of alternative religions, or none. Organisations like the Calix Society in Newcastle provide spiritual help and counsel to alcoholics; the Tyneside Evangelism Fellowship based in Gateshead supplies tools for Sunday School and outreach workers, and there are many more.

There is vitality about Christianity in Tyne and Wear, with many praying that, by the end of the century, the Church will have grown three or four times. Christians there hope to achieve this, not for any pride in Church growth, but the glory of God in a region in need of the Gospel of Jesus Christ and the power of His Holy Spirit.

Source: Regional Trends 26, HMSO 1991 and English Church Census and The Tyne and Wear Christian Directory, edited by David Longley, MARC Europe, 1987, and LM 87/2.

U

Unemployment

Unemployment may hit individuals and families suddenly in times of recession, business failures, or changing consumer behavioural patterns. They can radically affect church people and bring feelings of uncertainty, unwantedness, apathy, financial stringency and general animosity. The percentage of unemployed in church congregations may be lower than the community at large (this is an unresearched assumption) but even so, a sense of the numbers unemployed in a particular region give a feeling for the prevalence of the problem and allow church leaders to consider appropriate responses.

Unemployment figures can change very quickly. Those given below relate to January 1991 and show general regional differences. These differences are likely to remain even if the overall figures subsequently change.

United Kingdom unemployment 1991

	Number	Percentage of work-force	Percentage unemployed for over 12 months
		%	%
North	136,000	10	30
Yorkshire & Humberside	185,000	8	28
North-West	261,000	8	32
East Midlands	119,000	6	24
West Midlands	177,000	7	28
East Anglia	49,000	5	18
South-East (North)	104,000	5	15
Greater London	257,000	6	25
South-East (South)	126,000	6	16
South-West	133,000	6	18
England	1,547,000	7	25
Wales	102,000	8	24
Scotland	213,000	9	32
N Ireland	98,000	14	50
United Kingdom	1,960,000	7	27

Average unemployment 1971-90
(as percentage of workforce/population)

	%		%		%		%
1971	2.6	1976	4.2	1981	8.1	1986	11.1
1972	2.9	1977	4.4	1982	9.5	1987	10.0
1973	2.0	1978	4.3	1983	10.5	1988	8.1
1974	2.0	1979	4.0	1984	10.7	1989	6.3
1975	3.1	1980	5.1	1985	10.9	1990	5.8

Average unemployment rate 1970-2015

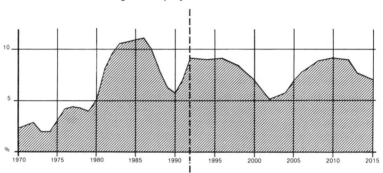

Unemployment forecasts 1992-2015
(as percentage of workforce/population)

	%		%		%
1992	9.2	2000	7.0	2008	8.9
1994	9.0	2002	5.1	2010	9.2
1995	9.1	2004	5.8	2012	9.0
1996	9.2	2005	7.0	2014	7.7
1998	8.4	2006	7.8	2015	7.1

Source: Regional Trends 26 HMSO 1991, Department of Employment. 1992-2015 dates forecast by Henley Centre and quoted in Management October 1991.

Urbanisation

More and more people are living in cities. In 1880 only 5% of the world's population lived in a city — by 1990 it was 43%. But the pace of urbanisation varies by continent, as the following table shows.

World urban population 1965-2015

	1965	%	1990	%	2015	%
Eastern and Western Europe	405m	61	559m	71	658m	78
North America	154m	72	205m	74	245m	77
Latin America	134m	53	324m	72	555m	82
Africa	66m	21	223m	35	666m	51
Asia and Oceania	437m	24	950m	31	2,064m	46
Total	1,196m	37	2,261m	43	4,188m	55
Total world population	3,251m		5,250m		7,636m	

Source: Cities, Population Crisis Committee, New York 1990.

USA, Churches in

American church statistics are amazing, particularly from a European point of view. There are over 350,000 churches in the USA. About 40% of Americans are regular churchgoers, and over 30% would call themselves 'born-again' Christians. With an annual 1989 income of around $50,000m, American churches are wealthier than many of the world's nations.

But while the influence of the church may be very wide, it does not necessarily go deep. Although 58% of the population say they believe in the authority of the Bible, only 12% read it each day, and most Americans cannot identify the names of the first four books in the New Testament. And while 80% say they are 'Christians', only 19% can accurately define what that means.

The church may well be in danger of complacency, warns the report from the Barna Research Group, *The Church Today.* Church attendance has been decreasing in the past decade, as has its perceived influence in society. It is the Mormons, Buddhists, Muslims and New Age sects which are growing rapidly.

George Barna's 1990 book has the odd title *The Frog in the Kettle.* It likens the church, unresponsive to the changing world around it, to a frog in a kettle of water which is being slowly heated. Unaware of the danger, the frog boils to death. In an attempt to help the church avoid the same fate, Barna's book looks at present trends and describes American society in the 21st century. For example, in the area of values:

Quality, he says, will be valued more than quantity, and people will have no time for organisations which appear second rate. Successful churches will aim for excellence in ministry.

Time will be at a premium, of more value than money. Churches will have to be sensitive to this.

Commitment to a tradition or denomination is going out of fashion. Individualism will be respected and people will expect to be able to choose the church or activity which best meets their current needs.

Integrity will need to be proved, but will be highly valued. Churches with a vision which they are pursuing with a passion will be attractive, as will a Christianity which is seen to be not just another religious option, but a way of life.

Barna uses the facts and figures to highlight the needs Americans will experience as they struggle to make sense of a new environment, and suggests ways churches can step in to help. It is a challenge to anticipate tomorrow's world and help shape it, rather than being a passive victim.

Source: The Frog in the Kettle: What Christians need to know about life in the year 2000 by George Barna, Regal Books 1990, and The Church Today: Insightful Statistics and commentary, Barna Research Group 1990, quoted in LL December 1990.

USA television

Most people who watch TV to relax would be better off reading a book instead. A recent survey in the USA found that sitting in front of a television set did not help people unwind. In fact, the longer they stayed there, the more drowsy, bored, sad and lonely they became.

The survey, carried out over a 13 year period, monitored the moods of 1,200 people aged between 10 and 82. Although watching TV takes less effort than reading, or even eating, people were found to feel more relaxed after reading a book than after watching TV.

More Americans have television sets than have refrigerators or indoor plumbing, and the average American spends two hours a day, half their leisure time, in front of the box. Say the researchers, 'TV ranks with the family, the school and the church as one of contemporary culture's prime forces of socialisation'.

Can Christians afford to ignore it?

Source: 'Television and Quality of Life: How viewing shapes everyday experience', reported in the Daily Telegraph, May 1990, LM 90/3.

USA, Young consumers

American children will see an incredible 25,000 television commercials by the time they are seniors in high school, claim US consumer advocates.

The result? American children consume $75,000m dollars worth of goods every year, nearly 2% of the US economy. The products children demand include super hero toys, bed sheets and clothing imprinted with cartoon heroes, tape decks, computer games and synthesisers.

Source: World Christian News, December 1990, quoted in LM 91/3.

V

Violence

Is there too much violence on television? According to the Independent Broadcasting Authority (IBA), opinions vary.

Traditionally, programme researchers assess the violence in any programme by the number of incidents they feel are acceptable. These methods, however, do not take into account the viewers' perception of violence. There is a case for saying that those who watch and measure violence become blunted to its impact, dulling their perception for what is, or is not, acceptable.

Opinions about violence on television 1987

	Agree	Disagree	Neither
	%	%	%
'TV programmes containing violence should be broadcast at night.'	80	8	12
'There are too many programmes containing violence on TV.'	60	19	21

The producers of these programmes are not the only ones to blame. Although there is fairly widespread agreement that television broadcasts too much violence, most participants in the IBA survey believed that parents should take greater care over what their children watch.

Younger viewers in particular were felt to be at risk, as their age did not equip them to discriminate between fact and fiction, something which might develop ill-conceived ideas about violence.

Despite these concerns, the IBA found that parents watch crime drama series with their children and few believe that these have a harmful effect, especially programmes like 'The "A" Team' and 'Minder'.

Family viewing of selected television series

Did you watch this programme with your children?	'Hill Street Blues'	'Miami Vice'	'The Equalizer'	'Knight Rider'	'Minder'	'The "A" Team'
Base sizes	703	476	832	196	527	582
Yes (%)	8	14	15	32	16	40
No (%)	43	35	41	16	36	16
No children (%)	49	51	44	52	48	44

However, respondents were concerned about children watching crime drama series on their own. Most felt that the programmes were suitable for family viewing, although nearly all the subject series were outside designated family viewing time. 'The "A" Team' was the only exception.

But what of news coverage? Violence as a matter of fact? Respondents surveyed in England and Northern Ireland agreed that too much attention was given to the province in television broadcasts, though it was felt that two documentary series about the troubles had a positive effect.

So when is violence on the TV screen acceptable? Is it ever acceptable as news, documentary or as an integral part of a story line? Do Christians respond as they ought? Or is the temptation to watch TV violence in any form, verbal, emotional or physical, one which Christians find hard to overcome?

TV viewing by time of day

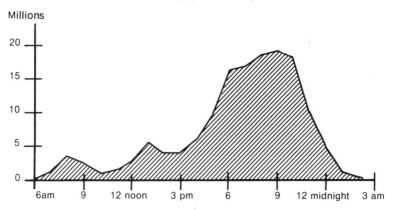

The Jesuit Centre for the Study of Communication and Culture has collected many findings on television and violence from around the world. From Japanese studies it is clear that babies and toddlers watch television if it is on, and imitate actions they see. This leads to kindergarten teachers complaining that language and behaviour deteriorates, with older toddlers imitating kick-boxing, gun fights and so on.

Research in Northern Ireland with secondary school children found that this was linked to personality types. Those with more aggressive tendencies, who enjoyed watching violence, were those who were more likely to be reinforced in their tendency to behave aggressively.

See also: Television.

Source: Violence on Television: What the Viewers Think by Barrie Gunter and Mallory Wober, January 1988, IBA and John Libbey and Co, LM 88/3. Communication and Culture, and LL December 1990.

W

Warwickshire

Area (sq km)	Population 1989			Percentage change 1979-89	Percentage under 15	Non-churchgoers 1989
	Men	Women	Total			
1,981	238,400	244,700	483,100	+1.8%	18%	424,700

Churchgoers 1989			Percentage of population	Percentage change 1979-89	Percentage under 15	Number of churches	Percentage built	
Men	Women	Total					before 1500	since 1950
24,500	33,900	58,400	12.1%	−18.6%	29%	457	40%	11%

District	Area (sq km)	Population 1989	Percentage change 1979-89
			%
Nuneaton and Bedworth	79	116,700	+3.1
Warwick	283	115,200	+0.1
Stratford-on-Avon	977	105,800	+6.4
Rugby	356	85,900	−2.2
N Warwickshire	286	59,500	−1.1

Source: Regional Trends 26, HMSO 1991 and English Church Census.

Wealth

The love of money may be the root of all evil, but today's lifestyle suggests that the creation of wealth and the concept of capitalism is an acceptable ambition.

Church concern for the poor has been with us for 2,000 years and it remains a central part of the Christian faith. But, as Norman Stone writes in *The Times,* 'If concern for the poor has been a central part of Christianity, so is Christianity's involvement with capitalism — or whatever you want to call it.'

He suggests that today's churchmen should pause to ask themselves why the West (with the aid of the medieval church) produced the first sustained political and economic growth in the history of the world.

So, how does this economic greed manifest itself? Towards the end of 1987 National Opinion Polls (NOP) carried out a survey among the top 5% of income earners throughout Europe and the USA.

NOP based their research on UK incomes of £25,000+ per annum, £30,000+ in France and the equivalent of £45,000+ in the USA to allow for currency fluctuations and different standards of living. A total of 450 people were interviewed in each country.

The UK had the highest income per household, with 12% of all households surveyed having four income-earning adults. The USA came next with 10%, but this seems to be unusual for Europe as a whole. No other country had above 4%.

Despite a high level of earnings in the UK, only 8% of those in high income brackets own more than one home. In the rest of Europe, these figures are rather higher.

In Switzerland 36% of those included in the survey were multi-owners, in Spain 38%, Italy 41% and Scandinavia 42%. In fact, Scandinavia scored highest on all counts. 90% of affluent people own and occupy their own homes, in Switzerland only 10% do so.

Not surprisingly that other trapping of wealth, car ownership, was common throughout all the countries surveyed. In most countries, fewer than 2% of these high earners have no car.

In the UK 55% of households have two cars and 28% have three. Italy is similar to the UK with 29% of households owning three, and in the USA the figure leaps to a staggering 44%.

Source: National Opinion Polls Political, Social and Economic Review No 69, March 1988, and LM 88/4.

West Midlands

Area (sq km)	Population 1989			Percentage change 1979-89	Percentage under 15	Non-churchgoers 1989
	Men	Women	Total			
899	1,293,000	1,322,400	2,615,400	−2.6%	20%	2,342,800

Churchgoers 1989			Percentage of population	Percentage change 1979-89	Percentage under 15	Number of churches	Percentage built	
Men	Women	Total					before 1500	since 1950
111,800	160,800	272,600	10.4%	−7.4%	23%	1,246	5%	27%

District	Area (sq km)	Population 1989	Percentage change 1979-89
			%
Birmingham	263	992,500	−3.5
Dudley	98	305,400	+1.9
Coventry	97	304,100	−6.0
Sandwell	86	295,500	−5.7
Walsall	106	263,600	−1.9
Wolverhampton	69	249,900	−3.2
Solihull	180	204,400	+4.0

Source: Regional Trends 26, HMSO 1991 and English Church Census.

West Sussex

Area (sq km)	Population 1989			Percentage change 1979-89	Percentage under 15	Non-churchgoers 1989
	Men	Women	Total			
1,990	335,300	369,600	704,900	+7.7%	17%	629,000

Churchgoers 1989			Percentage of population	Percentage change 1979-89	Percentage under 15	Number of churches	Percentage built	
Men	Women	Total					before 1500	since 1950
33,400	42,500	75,900	10.8%	+2.0%	25%	554	34%	20%

District	Area (sq km)	Population 1989	Percentage change 1979-89
			%
Arun	221	130,800	+13.0
Mid Sussex	338	119,700	−1.5
Horsham	533	108,600	+5.7
Chichester	787	105,900	+9.0
Worthing	33	98,700	+8.4
Crawley	36	84,500	+20.5
Adur	42	56,700	−4.0

Source: Regional Trends 26, HMSO 1991 and English Church Census.

West Yorkshire

Area (sq km)	Population 1989			Percentage change 1979-89	Percentage under 15	Non-churchgoers 1989
	Men	Women	Total			
2,039	1,007,000	1,059,600	2,066,600	0.0%	20%	1,860,600

Churchgoers 1989			Percentage of population	Percentage change 1979-89	Percentage under 15	Number of churches	Percentage built	
Men	Women	Total					before 1500	since 1950
82,400	123,600	206,000	10.0%	−15.9%	24%	1,290	6%	14%

District	Area (sq km)	Population 1989	Percentage change 1979-89	Total Church-goers 1989	Percentage of 1989 population
			%		%
Leeds	562	711,700	−1.1	77,400	10.9
Bradford	370	467,700	+0.8	47,800	10.2
Kirklees	410	375,600	−0.5	36,400	9.7
Wakefield	333	314,200	−0.0	22,500	7.2
Calderdale	364	197,400	+3.0	21,900	11.1

See also: Kirklees.
Source: Regional Trends 26 HMSO 1991 and English Church Census.

Wiltshire

Area (sq km)	Population 1989			Percentage change 1979-89	Percentage under 15	Non-churchgoers 1989
	Men	Women	Total			
3,480	273,700	284,700	558,400	+8.4%	19%	499,700

Churchgoers 1989			Percentage of population	Percentage change 1979-89	Percentage under 15	Number of churches	Percentage built	
Men	Women	Total					before 1500	since 1950
25,200	33,500	58,700	10.5%	−9.1%	23%	631	40%	12%

District	Area (sq km)	Population 1989	Percentage change 1979-89
			%
Thamesdown	230	170,200	+15.6
N Wiltshire	770	113,700	+10.6
W Wiltshire	517	106,100	+7.3
Salisbury	1,005	100,700	−2.2
Kennet	958	67,700	+3.9

Source: Regional Trends 26, HMSO 1991 and English Church Census.

Witches

The Occult Census of 1989 reported 'a conservative estimated population of 250,000 witches/pagans throughout the UK and many more hundreds of thousands of people with a serious interest in astrology, alternative healing techniques and psychic powers'. The author of *Dawning of the Pagan Moon,* David Burnett, considers this figure to be inflated and believes a figure of 100,000 would be more reasonable.

A thousand practising occultists completed the 1989 Occult Census. They showed that they 'by and large have a higher level of education ability and socio-economic grouping than the norm', but it is not known how representative are these thousand respondents. 70% were aged between 20 and 40. When had they become interested in occultism?

> 67% before the age of 18
> 22% aged 18-25
> 6% aged 26-35
> 5% aged over 35

62% were men, 38% women, 50% were single, 37% married, 13% 'considered themselves neither single nor married'.

Source: The Occult Census: Statistical Analysis and Results, The Sorcerer's Apprentice Press, Leeds 1989, quoted in Dawning of the Pagan Moon, David Burnett, MARC, Eastbourne 1991.

Women clergy

The 1992/93 Edition of the *UK Christian Handbook* gives details of the clergy by gender for the first time. What percentage of ministers are female? The *Handbook* gives the following percentages:

	1985	1990
	%	%
Salvation Army	60	60
Afro-Caribbean Churches	38	39
United Reformed Church	10	16
Methodist	6	9
Anglican	4	5
Presbyterian	2	5
Other Free Churches	3	3
Baptist	2	3
Pentecostal	2	2
Independent	1	1
Roman Catholic	0	0
Orthodox	0	0
Overall	7	8

Rather more clergy in England are female (9%) than in Wales (6%), Scotland (7%), or Northern Ireland (3%). 8% of clergy in America's Protestant churches are female, but it is to be hoped that a problem they experience — sexual harassment — doesn't repeat itself in the UK. Their United Methodist Church found 77% of its female ministers had reported incidents of sexual harassment, 41% from church colleagues or other clergy. The United Church of Christ in Cleveland found 45% of their 138 female colleagues harassed on church premises. 'Unsolicited jokes with sexual content' were the most frequently cited form of harassment, but leers, pressure for dates, and actual assault were mentioned. Three-quarters of the women took no formal action.

Source: UKCH 1992/93, and Daily Telegraph article 6th April 1991.

Women's work

The winter 1986 issue of *Survey*, published by the Market Research Society, gave details of a poll by Mass-Observation (UK) Ltd on how married women spend their time. This was a repeat of a series of studies just after the Second World War.

The two most significant decreases are the preparation of meals and housework. Ready-prepared foods and the increasing tendency to eat out has contributed to the former, while housework has been helped through the greater number and variety of labour-saving devices on the market.

Four items have increased considerably: Leisure time at home (mostly watching TV), paid work, personal toilet and outside activities. These figures illustrate the tension many married women experience in working more while still running the home and doing other activities.

Some of these activities will be church-based, but even with an increase in church and leisure to offset working pressures, today's woman is still

Average time spent per week by women

	Hours per week		
	1951	*1986*	*% Change*
			%
Shopping	7	6	*−14*
Laundry	6	5	*−17*
Caring for children	9	9	*0*
Personal toilet	4	7	*+75*
Meal preparation	29	20	*−31*
Housework	17	8	*−47*
Knitting and mending	4	2	*−50*
Leisure in the home	18	25	*+39*
At work	4	12	*+200*
Other outside activities	8	14	*+75*
In bed	62	60	*−2*

Bases: 732 person days in 1986, 700 in 1951.

under considerable strain. How can this be alleviated by the Church? Should women's meetings be rescheduled for the evening so that more can participate? Could the programme include items on stress and coping with pressure? Would some women appreciate a study on the effective use of time, something usually geared towards men in business?

See also: Household Tasks, and Time
Source: LM 87/2.

World Mission periodicals

AD 2000 and Beyond
AD 2000 Movement, 1580 Puerto Vallarta Drive, San Jose, CA 95120 USA. Published four times a year; free on request; contributions welcome.

Evangelical Missions Quarterly
A joint project of EFMA and IFMA, published by EMIS, PO Box 794, Wheaton, IL 60186, USA. $14.95 (Air mail $25.95) per year for four issues.

Evangelical Review of Theology
Articles and book reviews, original and selected from publications worldwide for an international readership. Published for the World Evangelical Fellowship Theological Commission by The Paternoster Press, Paternoster House, 3 Mount Radford Crescent, Exeter, Devon EX2 4JW. £10.50 per year for four issues.

Facts Magazine
Articles, features and lots of news from missions around the world. A ministry of EMA, available from 9 Anwyll Close, Caerleon, Gwent NP6 1TJ. £4 (£4.50 overseas) per year for three issues.

International Bulletin of Missionary Research
PO Box 821, Farmingdale, New York 11737-0821, USA. $18 per year for
four issues.

Missiology
The journal of the American Society of Missiology, 616 Walnut Avenue,
Scottdale, PA 15683-1999, USA. $15 per year for four issues.

Transformation
An international dialogue on evangelical social ethics. The Paternoster
Press, Paternoster House, 3 Mount Radford Crescent, Exeter, Devon EX2
4JW. £8 per year for four issues.

World Christian
An independent magazine for Christians who want their whole lives to
count for the world that doesn't know Jesus. PO Box 40010, Pasadena, CA
91114, USA. $10 (air mail $15) per year for 10 issues.

World Christian News
An easy-to-scan resource of facts, statistics and other concise information
for Christians with — or wanting — a world perspective published by Youth
With A Mission, Prins Hendrikkade 50, 1012 AC Amsterdam, The
Netherlands. Df25; £8; $16 for five issues.

World Evangelization
Information, inspiration and motivation for world evangelism published
occasionally by Lausanne Committee for World Evangelization, 184a,
Cumnor Hill, Oxford OX2 9PJ; free on request, gifts welcome.

World Pulse
News and analysis of events that affect the world and the world of
missions. PO Box 794, Wheaton, IL 60189, USA. $24.95 (add $20 for air
mail) per year for 24 issues.

Source: LL December 1990.

World population

The world population is projected to almost triple by the 22nd century
before it stabilises if preventative action is not taken in the 1990s reports
the Population Crisis Committee.

Until recently most experts assumed that world population, estimated at
5,300 million people in 1990, would stop growing at about 10,000 million.
However, this assumed more rapid declines in birthrate than occurred. At
current birth and death rates world population will double between 1990
and 2030 to 10,600 million.

The 1990 report on Progress Towards Population Stabilization recommends that increased family planning, along with efforts to improve women's status and expand opportunities for the very poor are all needed to achieve this. And it suggests that the major part of the funding for this will need to come from the industrialised countries of the west.

See also: Global Data.
Source: 1990 Report on Progress Towards Population Stabilization, Population Crisis Committee, LL June 1990.

Y

Young people

Social attitudes

The traditional generation gap between 'rebellious youth' and their conservative parents has gone, according to a 1987 survey by the market research company Mintel.

Half the 1,138 young people interviewed said they would like to be seen as 'sensible and responsible'. Although their favourite star, chosen by 20%, was 'cool and streetwise' Eddie Murphy, the qualities which make him famous came bottom of the league of desirable attributes for today's youth.

Young people are also marrying later and having fewer children. In 1981 four out of every 10 women between 20 and 24 and a quarter of the men in the same age group were married. In 1987 just three out of 10 women and 15% of men in that age group were married.

The reason? More women following careers and increasing numbers of couples living together before marrying and starting a family. However, family life continues to be important. 70% of those questioned placed priority on their home life.

Perhaps the church needs to move in the direction of young people by concentrating more on the thought-provoking aspects of the gospel and Christian life which could appeal to the intelligence (as well as the emotions) of the young in the late 1980s.

Source: Mintel Market Research and Daily Mail, LM 88/3.

Numbers and life-stages

Carrick James Market Research interviewed 731 16 to 24 year olds in December 1989 and January 1990 in some detail. This is a synopsis of some of the published results.

Population 15-24 projected to 2000

	15-19	20-24
1981	4,740,000	4,280,000
1985	4,540,000	4,750,000
1990	3,900,000	4,550,000
1995	3,410,000	3,900,000
2000	3,620,000	3,420,000

Numbers in both age categories are declining in the early 1990s and will continue to do so for those aged 20 to 24 in the late 1990s, though the 15 to

19 group will begin to increase again. 13% of the population are between 15 and 24 but this is not a homogenous group. Consider the following:

- 16-21s studying and living at parental home have some money but not much time.
- 16-21s working and living at home have lots of money and some time, especially at weekends.
- 16-21s jobless living at home have not much money, but lots of time.

and, on another dimension:

- 18-24s single living at parents' home.
- 18-24s single living away from parents' home.
- 18-24s living with partner with no children.
- 18-24s living with partner with children.

Finances and activities
Average weekly income, at 1988 prices, goes up from £12 at the age of 15, to £26 at 16, £42 at 17, £58 at 18-19, and £77 for 20-24s. 16-21 year olds with jobs receive almost three times as much as students (£67 to £26). Among those who have left home, those with children get less than those without. Extrapolating those figures means the 1988 direct spending power of 15 to 24 year olds is £27,000 million.

Of working 16 to 24s, 79% had a bank account, 55% a building society account and 31% a credit card, though despite this there was a fairly widespread mistrust of banks.

Given this income and lack of home commitments, large sums of money are spent on entertainment and self-adornment. Top spending categories for young adults (excluding fares and rent) were:

Alcoholic drinks in pubs	Records and tapes
Clothes	Cigarettes
Eating out	Make-up and cosmetics
Soft drinks and 'other things' in pubs	Watching or playing sport
Take-away food	Magazines

Leisure
33% of working 16 to 24 year olds spend a substantial amount of their social life in the pub, with 44% visiting a pub or club on Saturday for an average of four hours. The average weekly spending on drink in a pub by this age group is £14. Pub-going is especially popular among working 18 to 21s living with their parents.

For many young men drinking and getting drunk is an important social ritual with 21% agreeing strongly with the statement 'If I go out drinking, I like to feel the effect by the end of the evening'. 60% of both sexes feel alcohol is a dangerous drug, and 88% said they would never drink and drive.

Other activities which peak in teens or early 20s include playing and watching sport, going to discos, going to the cinema (among 16 and 17 year olds and 18 to 24s living with parents, frequency is three times the overall average), watching hired video films, and listening to records/tapes, especially up to the age of 19.

85% of the sample claimed to have had at least one sexual partner in the previous 12 months, and of these 11% claimed to have had at least two.

Values

81% claimed their family was the most important thing in their lives, with 74% wanting to get married and have children when they are older.

94% believe that you've got to work hard to get ahead in life. Although 57% said no political party took an interest in issues affecting young people, 27% would vote Conservative, 33% Labour, 13% Green, leaving 27% voting for others or 'didn't know'. 67% said environmental issues are the most important political issues of the future.

The seven sub-groups

Seven different sub-groups of working 16 to 24 year olds were identified, based on 40 attitude statements.

Life's a party (18%)
Seek enjoyment
Lager drinkers
Support poll tax
Little ambition
40% smoke
Low social responsibility
Conservative voters
Fashion conscious — like to
   look good and feel good
Racist and anti-gay
London and South-East
Little moral concern
Highest disposable income but still
   think you should borrow now
   and pay later

Outsiders (16%)
Idealist
Self-sufficient
Sexual and racial equality
Low income
Working class origins
Very keen on Green
Alienated by politicians
Low education level
50% smoke
Clothes from market stalls
Unconcerned about a healthy diet
Distrust police, banks
42% live for their holiday

Greying youths (16%)
Old-fashioned and middle-aged
   views
Cash oriented
Work oriented
Not entrepreneurial
47% Labour voters
Very keen on marriage
Not Green
Not sporty
Highly educated
Worry about pensions and
   personal safety
Support the police

Safety seekers (16%)
Middle of the road views
Not sporty
Nervous of using Channel Tunnel
   and flying
38% Labour voters
Non-smoking
Not work orientated
Mildly Green

Authoritarian (13%)
Two-thirds women
Anti-smoking
Anti-gay
Gin and tonic drinkers
Pro-police
SDP supporters
Pro-work and marriage
Fashion conscious
Mortgage holders
Racist
Support poll tax
Good education
London and South
Support identity cards for
    young pub-goers

New moralists (13%)
Austere, cautious and clean-living
Anti-smoking
Hard working
ABC1 Social backgrounds
25% Green voters
Keep fit
Anti-drinking
Egalitarian
Vegetarian
44% are 18-20
Body Shop regulars
Want to be self-employed
    eventually

Young moderates (8%)
Low income
Family orientated
42% smoke
Predominantly Labour voters
Pensions are important
Buy clothes from catalogues
Like cola and hot chocolate

While the interests and activities of young people are very dependent on age, where they live, whether they are working and so on, it's clear that some things are certain to be important to them. Sex, for example, and families, drinking, money. Do these subjects ever get talked about in churches?

Source: Carrick James article in Survey, Autumn 1990, Market Research Society.

Churchgoing
Of the half a million drop in the churchgoing population between 1979 and 1989, 87% were under 30. What might explain this trend — and what might change it?

Part of the reason is a decline in the child population. Children under 15 made up 21% of the population in 1979 and 19% 10 years later, while the proportion of churchgoers who are under 15 years old decreased just 1% from 26% in 1979 to 25% in 1989.

This means that although the same percentage of England's children go to church now as did 10 years ago — about 14% — there was a 5% drop in the number of child attenders or 194,000 fewer children.

However, churches lost more boys than girls, which is not explained by population trends. Other research has shown that boys tend to be less interested in church or school RE lessons. It is suggested in *'Christian' England* that this may be because Sunday school and primary school teachers are often women, and boys do not find suitable role models.

Churchgoers by age-group and denomination

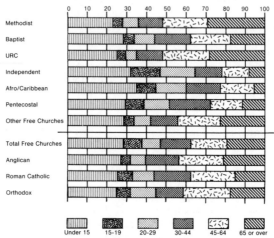

Churches lost 155,000 older teenagers, those in the 15 to 19 age-group, between 1979 and 1989. This is far more than the decline of this age-group in the population; 13% of teenagers went to church in 1979, and only 9% in 1989.

The greatest losses were in Anglican and Roman Catholic churches — although the latter has always had a high proportion of mass attenders in this age-group. Only in the Independent churches did the numbers of 15 to 19 year olds increase.

A government survey, *Young People in the 80s,* found that the main reasons teenagers gave for going to church were 'meeting friends', 'an opportunity to participate' and 'doing something useful'. Perhaps they are attracted to the churches which have a more participative style of worship, often led by groups of young musicians?

The numbers of both men and women between 20 and 29 increased at Methodist, Pentecostal, Independent and Orthodox churches. Other research suggests that unchurched couples often start going to church when they have children of their own, wanting some kind of religious education for them.

However, people in their twenties are still the least likely age-group to go to church. 94% didn't attend regularly in 1989, compared with 91% 10 years earlier.

Source ECC and LM 91/2.

Employment
What do teenagers get up to these days? We need to know if our youth
work aims to be relevant to those both inside and outside the church.

The number of 16 and 17 year olds in employment dropped drastically
between 1975 and 1988. Only 22% of 16 year olds were working in 1988
compared with 60% in 1975. Although more stayed on at school or college,
around 30% chose not to, with youth training schemes and unemployment
being the other options. These trends continued into 1990, when 53% of 16
year olds stayed on at school or college, and a further 22% attended youth
training schemes. (There were 1% fewer teenagers in 1988 than in 1975.)

Following changes in unemployment benefit regulations in 1988,
employment statistics for 16 year olds ceased to be collected, but only 39%
of 17 year olds were at work, contrasting with 72% in 1975.

By the age of 18, however, the majority, 70%, were at work. Four times as
many 18 year olds were unemployed in 1988 as in 1975, and the percentage
still in education was up by half. By 1990, the growth in full-time education
for 18 year olds was continuing with 21% remaining at school or college,
nearly double the percentage for 1975.

Educational and economic activity of 16 year olds in England

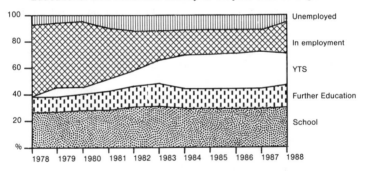

Educational and economic activity of 18 year olds in England

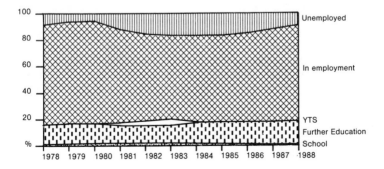

When the 'normal' occupation of teenagers is in a state of change, the pressure on them is increased by the lack of a clear route to follow, coupled with the expectations of older people whose experience can be very different.

What steps should we in the church take to understand and to meet the needs and interests of the young people who are largely on the streets rather than in the churches?

Source: LM 89/6, Statistical Bulletin 13/91.

Standards and preoccupations

In July 1987 John King of the *Church of England Newspaper* reported responses of nearly 1,500 third and fourth formers in Abingdon to a questionnaire. *Young People in Abingdon* is published as a Culham occasional paper at £2.

'Imagine if you can that I am a representative 14 year old boy. The views of people like me rarely get an airing in this paper and I guess that you older people (by which I mean people who have broken the 35 barrier) often have fanciful ideas about me and my generation. Well, here goes.

Right, I spend at least one evening a week hanging about on the streets and I go to a disco at least once a week. If I break the law, it is likely to be when I go under-age drinking. (There's a lot of it about, you know.) I don't see anything wrong in that at all — and I take the same line on cycling after dark without lights. I get depressed from time to time — partly because there are not enough facilities in my town and I don't know what to do with my free time. If I am honest, I have to say that I don't find it easy to chat up the girls. My biggest worry, though, is exams — and another worry is the possibility of being attacked by pupils from other schools.

Suicide

I don't want to be dramatic, but I have seriously considered putting an end to it all. It's not easy to turn to people for advice; I'm more likely to go to my mother than to my father.

As far as my beliefs are concerned, I am convinced of the existence of ghosts and I think God probably exists. I mostly take my horoscope seriously but I can't accept that Jesus rose from the dead. At the same time, I must say that when I have children of my own I shall want to have them baptised. No, I don't go to church — though when I was younger I used to go to Sunday School.

Some of my mates go to church but they're not allowed to have any say in what goes on. They tell me it's not the fault of the vicar (he's quite a decent guy): the problem lies in the hands of the older members of the congregation.

Boring

I read a newspaper most days of the week, but I'm better at delivering them than reading them.

I want to get on in the world and I reckon most unemployed people could have a job if they really wanted to. I'll probably vote Conservative when I'm 18.

Purpose
You're right: I don't have any great sense of purpose in life. If I get a job, perhaps that will follow. Otherwise it will be YTS.'

Source: LM 87/4.

Materialism
Young people in 1990s Britain are going to be a generation of spoilt brats, according to 1990 research report.

The goals of the young generation — which is richer than ever before — will be to have more money and luxury goods. This is good news for the advertising agencies on whose behalf the research was carried out.

Although many are saying that the youth of the 1990s will return to the 'peace, love and caring' values of the 1960s in reaction to 1980s materialism, the conclusion of the researchers is that this is unlikely. They point out that the young people of today are the children of the 1960s generation, and 'no youth culture was ever based on the values of its parents'.

If this proves to be the case, Christian young people will find it harder to hold on to Christian priorities. And those who do will find themselves with an outlook completely alien to that of their contemporaries.

Parents and the adults in their churches are going to need to understand the pressures on young people. And they need to encourage them to think Christianly about their culture and the extent to which it influences them.

As parents try to work this through, it might make them re-think the extent to which they themselves conform to the less blatantly materialistic but still less-than-Biblical values of their own generation.

Source: Spoilt Brats by Gold Greeniess Trott Advertising, reported in the Daily Telegraph 1990, and LM 90/2.

Attitudes to Church
Most secondary school pupils in Britain are obliged to sit through morning prayers, but how much good does it do them? Only 29% think God listens.

Research into their attitudes towards Christianity by Leslie Francis over a twelve year period showed 'a consistent, widespread and large drift further away from the churches'. Only 22% of those surveyed in 1986 agreed with the statement 'God is very real to me', whereas 41% of pupils did so in 1974.

The most common attitude was 'Church services are boring', held by 56%, and 49% 'find it boring to listen to the Bible'.

The number of pupils who 'find it hard to believe in God' rose steadily over the 12 years of the study to 50% in 1986. In an increasingly secular society, what can we do to make God real to young people?

Changing attitudes to Christianity of Secondary school pupils 1974-86

Attitude item	1974 % agree	1978 % agree	1982 % agree	1986 % agree
God is very real to me	41	33	26	22
I believe that God listens to prayers	47	37	33	29
I know that God helps me	42	34	27	25
I think that church services are boring	39	49	53	56
I find it boring listening to the Bible	33	34	40	49
I find it hard to believe in God	36	40	43	50

Source: Drift from the Churches: Secondary School Pupils' Attitudes toward Christianity by Leslie Francis, British Journal of Religious Education, Vol 11, No 2, quoted in LM 89/3.

INDEX

MARC Europe

The vision of MARC Europe is that strategic thinking may become commonplace amongst Christian leaders in Europe by the close of the century. Strategic thinking is partly dependent on an adequate knowledge of our position and the trends around us in society, in our country, and in the world.

MARC Europe has an **information service** which anyone is welcome to approach with requests, either by letter at the address below, or by telephone. The service will help you with factual information about the Christian church, churchgoing, church growth and related subjects particularly in the United Kingdom or other European countries.

MARC Europe **publishes** a variety of other resource books, some of which are described on the following pages. They are available through any Christian bookshop, or, in case of difficulty, direct from us. If you should order direct please add 15% to cover the costs of postage and packing. Nearly 40 research reports have been published as MARC Monographs, on topics from church nominalism to future trends across Europe.

MARC Europe regularly produces **LandMARC,** a free quarterly bulletin, full of snippets of which this book is composed. It seeks to provide facts and figures to inform and challenge Christian leaders.

MARC Europe also **researches** information directly. Sometimes Christian organisations or churches commission a specific piece of work. If you want to move into uncharted waters, ask MARC to provide you with a map! We also initiate research felt to be of major importance, like the English Church Census.

MARC Europe also provides **training** for Christian leaders on many management and leadership subjects. We also run seminars on how to undertake research yourself, and how to interpret numeric information. Please ask for details.

MARC Europe is here to help you in any way we can, so that your ministry can be more effective and run more efficiently.

MARC Europe
Vision Building
4 Footscray Road
Eltham
London SE9 2TZ
081-294 1989

CHRISTIAN HANDBOOKS

Austrian Christian Handbook

Data by Heinz Gerhardt and Robert Schlarb

Comprehensive information on churches, Christian media, theological colleges and mission organisations in Austria. Text in German and English.

72 pages   **£7.95**

Irish Christian Handbook

Data compiled by Peter Brierley

Facts and figures about Northern Ireland and the Republic of Ireland churches and church life. Contains comprehensive listing of over 500 parachurch organisations in both countries.

"A ready source of reference for all who wish to know what ... facilities are available — and where."   (Archbishop Robin Eames)

"A veritable treasure-trove of statistics ... an essential resource." (Bishop Brendan Comiskey)

132 pages   **£9.99**

Norwegian Christian Handbook

Data by Dagfinn Solheim and Rev Ingunn Folkestad

The missionary strength of the Norwegian churches is detailed, along with membership statistics for over 50 church groups, with historical trends in the Lutheran Church. Illustrated with over 40 diagrams and written in Norwegian and English.

64 pages   **£4.95**

Spanish Christian Handbook

Data by Gabino Fernandez Campos

Presents data on church and Christian missions throughout Spain, with a supplementary section on the Roman Catholic Church. In Spanish and English.

68 pages   **£7.95**

UK Christian Handbook 1992/93 Edition

Edited by Peter Brierley and David Longley

A one-volume reference library of the world of British Christianity. Gives ready access to the addresses and telephone numbers of 5,000 Christian organisations, plus the latest statistics on church membership, with tables showing denominational trends and other church related matters.

This is a must for every Christian leader. Since the previous edition it contains 700 more entries, 20% new telephone numbers and 15% new addresses.

"A third arm."   (Ruth Maguire, Agape)

"I just live with the 'UKCH'. I couldn't do without it."
(Val Symonds, Christian Resources Exhibition)

Accommodation — 690 entries in seven groups from hostels to retreat houses and conference centres.

Books — 850 entries in five groups giving Christian bookshops by county, publishers and other producers.

Churches — 740 entries in eight groups giving local and national addresses.

Evangelism — 280 entries in three groups: urban mission, evangelistic agencies and independent evangelists.

Media — 520 entries in 10 groups giving quick access to the many channels of communication and services available for the Christian message.

Overseas — 380 entries in six groups, focusing specially on missionary societies and support organisations.

Services — 940 entries under 24 headings, opening up the richness of organisations active in the Christian scene, from reconciliation groups to financial services.

Training — 350 entries in eight groups covering schools and colleges and agencies extending teaching to all ages and levels.

"Indispensable."   (Social Economic Consultant)

"Invaluable."   (Missions Communications Officer)

"A must."   (Parish Administrator)

850 pages   **£21.99 paperback**   **£25.99 hardback**

English Church Census

On 15th October 1989, 70% of the 38,600 churches in England completed a form giving information on numbers in their church that Sunday. This was a major exercise, and the results cover each and every tradition of the Christian Church in England — every denomination, every form of churchmanship, every type of environment in which churches are located.

Many significant trends are identified, providing the reader with a reliable basis for making strategic decisions.

'Without any question the survey is the most thorough and comprehensive ever done of English churchgoing. . . . I believe it gives us crucial data for strategic planning as we seek to find ways of meeting the spiritual needs of our fellow countrymen.'

(Archbishop George Carey)

"Christian" England

The Report of the Census showing what it reveals. Gives an overview of the results, where people go to church, churchgoers by age and gender, growth and decline, the age of churches, giving to the Third World, and implications for the future.

The 'carefully collected and analysed statistics make this book essential reading for anyone concerned in the re-evangelisation of England'.

(Roger Forster)

266 pages   **£5**

Who goes to Church? Where are they growing?

The 48 full colour maps in *"Christian" England* separately produced to aid class work in looking at the strengths and trends of English church attendance.

12 pages   **£0.99**

Prospects for the Nineties

The full statistical tables of the English Church Census. Gives national totals for every denomination and churchmanship, and four pages of tables on churchgoing for every county in England, with commentaries for every region.

412 pages   **£15**

Each region in the country is also available in a separate booklet giving the same statistical tables as in *Prospects*. While stocks last these are available at £1 each.